# Life-Trends

# Life-Trends

## YOUR FUTURE FOR THE NEXT 30 YEARS

**JERRY GERBER, JANET WOLFF,
WALTER KLORES & GENE BROWN**

FOREWORD BY JANE BRYANT QUINN

AVON BOOKS ◆ NEW YORK

AVON BOOKS
A division of
The Hearst Corporation
105 Madison Avenue
New York, New York 10016

Published by arrangement with Macmillan Publishing Company
Library of Congress Catalog Card Number: 89-8233
ISBN: 0-380-71345-4

The Macmillan edition contains the following Library of Congress Cataloging in Publication Data:

Lifetrends: the future of baby boomers and other aging Americans/by Jerry Gerber...[et al.].

  p.    cm.
   "A Stonesong Press book."
   Bibliography: p.
   Includes index.
1. Old age—United States.  2. Baby boom generation—United States.
3. Age groups—United States.  4. Aging—Social aspects—United States.
5. Life cycle, Human—Social aspects.  6. Intergenerational relations—
United States.  I. Gerber, Jerry.
HQ1064.U5L553   1989
305.26'0973—dc20      89-8233   CIP

First Avon Books Trade Printing: March 1991

TO LYN

TO EDITH, JIM, AND EMILY

# Contents

# Acknowledgments

We would like to thank the following people for their assistance: Phyllis Andrews, George Baker, Ph.D., Estelle Brown, Dianne Davis, Yvonne Dodd, Renna Draynel, Nancy Dubin, Joseph Eastlack, Ph.D., Pat Edwards, Bill Eldridge, Kaethe Fine, Jacqueline Halpern, Milton Hans, Ken Keller, E. Susan Kellogg, Christina Lindstrom, Joe McGlone, Jean Phillips, Louise Rader, Barbara Raines, Margaret Rose, Al Rosenstein, Ph.D., Kato Roth, Robert Roth, Harilyn Rousso, Judy Schwartz, Ellen Sills-Levy, Stan Swenson, Jerry Williams, Lieselotte Winters, and Debra Wollens.

We would also like to thank the following organizations for supplying research material and other assistance: American Association of Retired Persons, American Geriatric Education Society, American Health Care Association, Elderhostel, the Gray Panthers, the International Center for Integrative Studies, National Association for Home Care, National Council on the Aging, the New School for Social Research, Self-Help for the Elderly (San Francisco), Support Source, United States Department of Health and Human Services, United States Senate Special Committee on Aging.

Dawn Sangrey's wonderful editorial skills improved every page of our manuscript. Her comments, both pointed and generous, were a pleasure to receive, even when they made us reconsider matters of style or substance. Harilyn Rousso was a pillar of strength throughout every moment of this project, whether giving us the benefit of her critical intelligence or just keeping the fires burning. Pam Hoenig, our editor at Macmillan, paid us the ultimate compliment: she settled for only our best. Bill Rosen, also of Macmillan, contributed valuable suggestions at every stage of this endeavor.

Finally, this book would not exist without the vision and support of Paul Fargis of The Stonesong Press.

# Foreword

by JANE BRYANT QUINN

As we approach the millennium, it increasingly appears that, for Americans, demography may be destiny. The size of the baby-boom and baby-bust generations looms large as a factor that will determine what life will be like for us at the beginning of the twenty-first century.

In my area of expertise, money, there are early storm warnings up for the baby boomers. They have probably been more concerned with the savvy management of their personal finances than any other generation in history. But when it comes to old-age insurance, they've dug themselves into a hole. Private pensions, CDs, IRAs, and mutual funds are all important. But for most Americans the bedrock of a secure old age begins with the Social Security program, including its Medicare component. Yet, that system looks as if it's headed for trouble by the time the boomers need it. Surpluses should be building up to pay for the boomers when they retire. But we are effectively spending those surpluses today—so where is the money going to come from?

In a larger sense, the problem isn't a lack of money. You don't put money into Social Security to make it work; you put children into it, so *they* can work and contribute to it in their parents' old age. The boomers simply haven't had enough children to do the job.

This could create problems between aging baby boomers and the children they did have. In theory, Americans born since the late 1960s should expect to prosper. Theirs is a generation smaller than the one that preceded it. They would normally expect to inherit a large economy with fewer people sharing in its output. While baby boomers had to get on line for everything, postboomers should benefit from decreased competition for jobs, housing, and all the other basics of life. Yet instead of being in a position to draw from the American economic machine, it now looks as if much could be asked of the children of the baby bust. Who else is going to pay into Social Security in the twenty-first century so that the huge generation of aging boomers may take from it?

It's ironic. Today's middle-aged (and soon-to-be-middle-aged) Americans have shown a reluctance to tax themselves for government services. Yet in two or three decades they figure to be asking for some substantial tax sacrifices from their adult children and other working Americans. Can they reasonably expect their offspring's generation to keep digging deeper into their pockets to fund their parents' old age— for continued automatic pensions for almost everyone and even better medical insurance than we have now? Hardly. At some point, the boomers' tax-weary children are going to say "enough." The result: there could be big changes coming in the relationship between older people, the government, and the young.

I'm not saying that the doomsters are right in predicting a war between the generations. But we could be seeing some troubling tensions before the dust settles. Where are we likely to come out of it? The probable scenario is a shift in expectations about what you do for yourself when you get older and what you count on other people to do for you. The constant increase in government benefits for older people that the parents of the baby boomers have experienced will have to end. Without such changes, Social Security could go down the tubes.

Who needs an old-age pension, catastrophic medical insurance, and help in paying for a nursing home? More important, who *doesn't* need it, who can afford to pay for it themselves? That's the question we agreed not to ask when we created Social Security in the 1930s and ruled out a means test for collecting benefits. The "entitlement" phenomenon started there: Everyone is entitled to be helped, no matter what income or assets they have. Only a fool would look such a gift horse in the mouth.

The parents of the baby boomers have been the lucky generation—and they've been no fools. They're the ones who bought a house for thirty thousand dollars in 1950 and have lived to see its value increase by as much as tenfold. Between the prosperity of the postwar years and the acceptance of pensions as a normal job benefit, many of today's elderly have managed to stash away comfortable nest eggs for their later years. A contributing factor to their well-being is the peace of mind that comes from a guaranteed Social Security check and medical insurance, whether or not they really need it. They paid a lot less into the Social Security system than people do today, and they have benefited from handsome payoffs.

This generation is already transferring part of their wealth to their children, allowing them to begin claiming their inheritance far sooner than previous generations could get a taste of theirs. By helping their kids start businesses and make a down payment on a house, many of these elders have insulated their offspring from the income slippage that middle-class Americans felt in the 1980s. But tomorrow's adults—the baby-bust generation, who will make up the tax base that's supposed to provide for the future old—may not be so fortunate.

The partial tax on Social Security benefits—already a few years old—offers a clue to the resolution of the impending crisis. Everyone will stay on the rolls to maintain the program's political support. But benefits won't be worth as much to people who don't really need them. That implies a means test by another name. Those who can afford it will buy supplemental insurance for such potential needs as nursing-home care, while the government picks up the tab for all others. It's the only fair way of seeing to it that our limited resources ensure a decent old age for all Americans. It's the only way to distribute benefits without imposing a ruinous tax.

The other basic change we should anticipate involves greater investment in the economy to make it more productive. We must create more wealth if we're to pay for programs like Social Security and Medicare. This especially means an enormous investment in human capital, in education and training. The government may have a role to play here, but more will be shouldered by private businesses. It will be in their self-interest to do so, because of the coming shortage of workers.

One way this will come into play is through private efforts to upgrade the skills of the socially and economically disadvantaged young, so that they can fill twenty-first-century job openings. The high schools and colleges also have a big part to play, in working with the business community to provide tomorrow's work force with all of the technical skills the computer age requires. This kind of cooperative effort will be good for these institutions, the people they help—and, indeed, for all of us.

Immigration will also be a source of new workers—and of new taxpayers. But before we look abroad we should more fully draw on the still unrealized potential of American working women. And that means more day care. Again, business will lead the way. Day care as an employee benefit is *the* issue for working women, and the only way to sustain a sizable full-time work force.

The ramifications of the aging of the baby-boom generation go far beyond the challenges it poses to Social Security. *Lifetrends,* a comprehensive and realistic look around the corner of the year 2000, reports on how this phenomenon will change everyone's life—from family relationships to careers to what it will be like to go shopping. All things considered, we will be living in interesting times.

# Life-Trends

# 1

# Generations

"How old would you be if you didn't know how old you was?"
SATCHEL PAIGE, baseball pitcher

During the 1990s, the number of Americans in the 35–50 age bracket will grow four times as fast as the number of those in any other. Most of these new middle-aged will be baby boomers, the first of whom will turn 50 in 1996. They are members of the celebrated generation born between 1946 and 1964, whose youth had such a profound impact on our society.

These days baby boomers find intimations of their aging whenever they open a newspaper or watch the evening news. Jerry Rubin, the 1960s culture hero who said, "We ain't never gonna grow up. We're gonna be adolescents *forever,*" and "Don't trust anyone over 30," is now a stockbroker to yuppies. When *he* turned 50 the media took note. Bob Dylan, the boomers' troubadour, recently joined with George Harrison of the Beatles, Roy Orbison, and several other aging rockers to tour as the Traveling Wilburys. But no sooner did they produce one album than Roy Orbison died of a heart attack. Meanwhile, Joey Dee, of "Peppermint Twist" fame, now heads a fund-raising organization whose goal is to establish a retirement home in Florida for old rock and roll stars.

The 1960s ended a mere two decades ago. Two decades from now, in the year 2011, the first baby boomers will be turning 65. By 2020, almost all of the most influential segment of their generation—those people born in the first decade of the baby boom, who created the 1960s youth culture—will have reached that landmark birthday.

What will old age mean for them and for American society? In the following pages we will offer a detailed look at the most likely scenarios. This book is an informed speculation about the lifestyle of baby-boomer elders and the way they will continue to change America at the beginning of the twenty-first century. But it is also something more.

"In our time we shall have to rethink everything about what it means to be old in America," wrote Landon Y. Jones in 1980 in his book *Great Expectations: America and the Baby Boom Generation.* "The baby boomers will change what has heretofore been the principal stereotype of elderly—namely, that they are poor, uneducated, and unemployed." Jones was right about the rethinking and correct in suggesting the central role that the generation born between 1946 and 1964 will play in the transformation of the later years. But his stereotype of old age is already off the mark.

While the baby boomers will change the very nature of old age, they will not be starting from scratch. Their parents have already begun to explore and settle this new stage of life. Theirs is the first older generation to arrive at their later years with a majority still relatively healthy, active, and affluent. They are the New Elders, who have aged in a time when becoming old is so different from what people their age experienced in the past that they have been forced to undertake the reinvention of old age. This book is their story too.

## THE GRAYING OF AMERICA

In 1982, when NBC News reporter Susan Peterson tried to get her boss to give her the old-age beat, his reaction was: "Are you crazy? You're committing media suicide. You'll never get on the air." In the mid-1980s, *The Los Angeles Times* switched Bob Rosenblatt from writing about the economy to covering the activities of elders. His father, retired and living in Fort Lauderdale, thought his son had been demoted.

Most of us have only recently become aware that something important is changing among people in the later years of life. And yet the aging of America has a long history.

"This aging of the population is not a new process but one that has gone on for more than a century. What is new is the greater speed in recent years and the extent of the changes which have resulted. . . ." No, this is not from the latest issue of *Time* or *Newsweek*. It appears in a report on recent social trends in the United States put together by some of the most prominent social scientists in the country at the request of the president—Herbert Hoover—in 1929.

Until 1950, the American population grew progressively older for 130 years. The median age of the population—the age at which half of all inhabitants are older, half younger—rose in every decade, starting in 1820, the first year for which we have reliable United States statistics, when it was 16.7. It finally peaked at 30 in 1950, and then the statistical weight of the first group of the seventy-five million baby boomers threw it into reverse for two decades. Had it not been for the baby boom, Americans might have turned their attention to their elders sooner than they have.

After bottoming out at 28 in 1970, the median age has resumed its upward trend. It is now at 33, and the United States Bureau of the Census projects that it will reach 36 in the year 2000, temporarily plateau at 39 in 2010 and 2020, climb to 41 in 2030, and level off at 42 by the middle of the next century.

Only twenty years after being obsessed with the young, Americans have now become preoccupied with aging. The number of Americans over 65 has more than doubled since 1950. As recently as 1965, the over-65 population of the United States stood at eighteen million; today, their numbers approach thirty million. There are now more people in the United States over the age of 65 than there are people of all ages in Canada. Finally, for the first time in our history, American elders outnumber American teenagers.

By the year 2000, the Census Bureau projects, we should have almost thirty-five million people over 65; they will number over thirty-nine million in 2010 and about fifty-one million in 2020. Only about 4 percent of the population in 1900, elders now represent more than 12 percent of all Americans and should make up close to 17 or 18 percent of the population by the year 2020.

## REWRITING THE LIFE SCRIPT

An agequake is coming that will shake America as much as the youth culture of the 1960s did. Not only are there more older people, but they are different. This change is part of a wider social trend: A person's chronological age no longer necessarily determines behavior and lifestyle. The images associated with specific years in the human life cycle are no longer so clear. The country is not just aging; the landscape of age is changing.

"All across adulthood, age has become a poor predictor of the timing of life events, just as it is a poor predictor of health, work status, family status, interests, preoccupations and needs," say social scientists Bernice L. Neugarten and Dail A. Neugarten. This phenomenon suggests the need to interpret more loosely the view of life expounded in developmental psychology, in which adults are supposed to grow through several well-defined life stages. We are confronting what the Neugartens call "the fluid life cycle."

In fact, many of us are no longer even certain to which age group we are referring when we speak of "the young," "the middle-aged," or "the old." An opinion survey given to a middle-class, middle-aged population sample two decades ago found people certain of the relationships between specific ages and life stages. For instance, they overwhelmingly agreed that a young man was somewhere between ages 18 and 22. But in a recent follow-up the subjects expanded that bracket to 18–40.

With one stage of life blending into another, it has become less clear who a person should "be" at any given time in life. When today's older people were young, a mother in her thirties with several children might have identified with the term *matron*. It implied a kind of sedate maturity, a lifestyle that was somewhat retired, dignified, quiet. But that word and the lifestyle it describes are hardly appealing to a mother in her thirties today. She is likely to have more in common with a career woman in her early twenties than with the matron of yesterday.

Baby boomers approaching 40 now are not in the same life situations that their parents experienced at this age. The current 40-year-olds stayed in school longer, started work later, married and had children later, have based their families on two incomes—have, in fact, led lives that bear little resemblance to those lived by the previous generation. Being 40 today doesn't mean what it did in, say, 1963. Thus the boomers cannot assume that they will soon be ready for a "mid-life" crisis, if in fact there ever was such a thing.

The script for each stage of human development keeps getting revised. One result is that the stage directions and lines bequeathed to each generation by its predecessors often seem to be from another play, and each generation has to improvise. The process of aging has become different for each successive generation.

## NEW LIFE STAGES

The formation of a new life stage where one did not previously exist is not in itself revolutionary, although the pace of such innovation has picked up in the whirligig of twentieth-century social change. Previously, however, these new stages occurred in the earlier years of life.

For example, childhood as we know it is less than two hundred years old. A decline in infant mortality made it more likely that a child would survive his or her early years, permitting parents to become more emotionally attached to each of their children. The greater value placed on children eventually led to restrictions on child labor and laws to prevent cruelty to children, as well as to the sentimentalizing of childhood. Compulsory schooling finally specified the years in which children were to undergo a period of training for the real world.

Adolescence, a stage between childhood and adulthood, is a twentieth-century creation. In 1900, only about 13 percent of 14- to 17-year-olds were in school. That number rose to 50 percent by 1930, 73 percent by 1950, and 95 percent by 1965. Enter the teenager.

Young adulthood is more recent still. Living alone or with a lover before marriage as a social norm for people in their twenties, for example, begins with the baby boomers. Of those Americans marrying for the first time between 1965 and 1974, 11 percent had lived with a lover, but 44 percent of those entering their first marriages between 1980 and 1984 had done so.

## OLD AGE TODAY

The new old age—a life stage still in the process of formation—is first of all the product of modern medicine. Primarily by allowing more people to survive childhood—and more women to survive childbirth—improved medical care has enabled a significant number of people to reach old age. Life expectancy at birth in the United States was 47.3 years for both sexes in 1900. By 1950 it had reached 68.2 years and by 1985 had climbed to 74.7 years. What's more, a person surviving to old age now is likely to remain alive much longer. The number of years one who had reached age 65 could expect to live increased modestly from 11.9 years in 1900 to 13.9 years by 1950; by 1985 it had risen to 16.8 years.

Women now tend to outlive men. Their life expectancy at birth is 78.2 years, while a man can expect to live 71.2 years. This, too, is a recent phenomenon. Now "we take for granted this uneven sex ratio in the last stage of life," notes historian Michel Dahlin. "But in the 19th century men slightly outnumbered women in old age. It was not until 1940 that women became the majority of the aged population."

More people living longer is only part of the story. Medical breakthroughs, from high-blood-pressure medications to heart bypass surgery, have changed the quality as well as the number of the later years. Now older people are as likely to play tennis as checkers. "Our society is getting older but the old are getting younger," says Robert B. Maxwell, vice-president of the American Association of Retired Persons. "The 70-year-old today is more like a person of 50 twenty years ago."

Older people are also more likely to travel now than to sit in a rocking chair. That's because so many of them can afford it. The current generation of elders 55 to 75 is the first to benefit from Social Security indexed to the cost of living (from 1970 to 1983 benefits rose 273 percent while inflation went up 138 percent), private investments, and widespread pensions. Many of them attended college for free under the GI Bill and took advantage of Federal Housing Administration loans to buy houses at prices their children will probably never know.

The median net worth of people in this age group is just over sixty thousand dollars—almost double the average for all Americans. Although they constitute only about 12 percent of the population, more than 25 percent of the federal budget goes for their needs. Poverty is far from a dead issue for elders—it is concentrated among older women living alone—but the poverty rate among elders has dropped from 28.5 percent in 1965 to 12.2 percent now.

They also benefit from special senior-citizen discounts on many of the goods and services they buy. At Omni and Marriott hotels, for example, New Elders receive discounts on regular room rates of as much as 50 percent. Northwest Airlines has even offered them percentage discounts equal to their age. In the first month of the program it had to provide free tickets to twelve passengers who had passed their hundredth birthday!

## GENERATIONS

Every day we hear about hardy elders who are rewriting the book on the later years—getting college degrees, launching new romances, traveling, running in marathons. If most people their age never lived this way before, what influences how the New Elders choose to live now? And how can we tell what today's 30- and 40-year-olds will be like when they reach their later years in two or three decades?

The key to understanding both the present and future of old age in America is in the idea of generations. "In an epoch of change, each person is dominated by his birth date," wrote demographer Norman Ryder in an essay on generations and social change published in 1965, just when the "generation gap" between young and old was beginning to become evident.

When the experience of one generation differs greatly from that of the preceding generation, social change becomes the norm. Much common sense about life can't be passed on because it no longer contains accurate information and useful advice. Succeeding generations must modify institutions and values to deal with the world as they find it.

People of different generations thus age differently, as sociologist and Associate Director of Behavioral Sciences at NIA/NIH Matilda White Riley has noted. One cannot assume that because people of one generation experienced a part of their life in a certain way, their children will duplicate their experience. Young people in America in the 1960s found that the gap between their experience of adolescence and their parents' was so great that they had to develop their own approach to living—the youth culture.

As they were for youth of the 1960s, the conditions that now characterize old age are so different from those confronted by previous generations who got this far in life that few of the old rules of conduct apply. It is as if we are watching a play in which all the actors are improvising.

## THE PLAYERS IN THE DRAMA

The players in the generational drama of old age can be roughly differentiated by their ages:

*The Old Guard.*

Born between the turn of the century and the mid-teens and now past their 75th birthdays.

*The New Elders.*

Born from the mid-teens to the mid-1930s and now at least 55.

*The Eisenhower Generation.*

Born between 1935 and 1945 and now aged 45 to 55.

*The Baby Boomers.*

Born between 1946 and 1964 and now aged 26 to 44; the Early Boomers, born in the first ten years or so of the baby boom, have often experienced life differently from the Late Boomers who followed them.

*The Reagan Generation.*

Born after 1965.

These are not rigid categories. As we've pointed out, in our time and in the foreseeable future, a person's life experience will be the final determinant of values and conduct. Our observations will concern averages and trends. There is also a good deal of crossing over at the borders of these generations. Many younger members of the Eisenhower Generation, for example, have lived their lives and experienced an adulthood similar to that of the Early Boomers.

Nor are these age groups equal in the impact they have had and will have on old age in America. The New Elders have drawn the attention of the media for good reason. They are the first generation to experience old age as healthy, active, and relatively affluent elders. But not everything they have done as elders has been groundbreaking. In fact, as we will point out, the newness of this life stage has often led to their simply continuing to live as they did in middle age for as long as they can.

Their children, the baby boomers, will be the true revolutionary generation of elders. Their numbers will figuratively color America gray. As elders they will have unparalleled political and social clout. They will put old age on the map.

In the supporting cast, the Old Guard loom large. They took the first steps of change in the 1960s and 1970s. It was people now in their eighties, for example, who first populated the planned retirement communities of Florida, California, and Arizona. Nor have they all withdrawn from active life. Many of them have the attitude of the woman who, tired of hearing how "remarkable" she was to be active and involved at her age, complained, "Hell, I am just an 84-year-old version of my 20-year-old self—I was always remarkable." But although many of her generation have combined longevity with the fruits of America's postwar affluence, they have generally lived a quiet lifestyle as elders. They are the generation who bore the brunt of the Depression, an experience that left them careful and cautious. They are survivors!

Not every generation changes its times, even when many of its members are influential. The Eisenhower Generation, for example, *as a generation* has been fated to play a supporting role. They supplied many culture heroes and role models for the baby boomers—Elvis Presley, Bob Dylan, Abbie Hoffman, Gloria Steinem, and numerous entrepreneurs, for example. They have often been the point men and women, blazing trails for their younger brothers and sisters. But *as a group* they have not been the trendsetters that those just behind them chronologically have been. Nor have they had enough consciousness of themselves as a separate generation to make their imprint on history. They were teenagers during the Eisenhower era, a time that was relatively free of political and social upheaval. When the social revolution of the 1960s came, most members of this generation were already on the career ladder or raising families, with too firm a stake in the establishment to take part in the youth culture. Now in middle age, they approach their later years in the shadow of the New Elders, and are not likely to alter old age significantly.

The Reagan Generation, the "baby bust," take their identity as much from what they are not as from what they are. They are not the baby boomers—although the line separating them from the Late Boomers is often a thin one—and compared with that cohort their numbers are small. They are politically conservative and not socially innovative. Career-oriented, they are a quiet generation who will go through life being noticed for their contrast to the generation before. Each age bracket they reach will seem relatively depopulated after the Late Boomers have aged out of it, for example. The present shortage of teenage help in the fast-food industry is a dramatic case in point, but this phenomenon will manifest itself in all areas of our culture, even in popular culture.

In 1988 major league baseball suddenly suffered from a diminished crop of good rookies. Since players usually make it to the big leagues in their early twenties this shortage may well have marked the coming of age of the Reagan Generation, the baby bust that began in the mid-1960s. The rookie crop will fluctuate somewhat from year to year because talent is randomly distributed, but it's likely that the general trend will be toward slimmer pickings in the coming years because the pool of potential ballplayers has decreased sharply, while the number of job openings remains the same.

The role of the Reagan Generation in the developing drama of old age lies in their potential to play the spoiler. Will they feel an obligation to contribute a substantial part of their income to entitlement programs for the increasing number of elders in our society? Or will they refuse?

## THE NEW ELDERS

Joseph A. King, a retired college teacher who wrote a guest column in *Newsweek* in 1986, saw himself and his wife as not "an insignificant segment of that class of people deceptively and plaintively labeled 'senior citizens.' " King said he was, rather,

a recently retired person and, though not yet 65, I already receive substantial discounts at restaurants and theaters. In a few years I will get a double exemption on my income tax and a 90 percent discount on our public-transit system. My income from pension and investment is several times above the poverty level and growing. My mortgage payment is $128 per month on a 30-year note at 6 percent with 10 years to go. My four children have completed college. My disposable income far exceeds what it was when my wife, Betty, and I were raising them. The government, the capitalist establishment and the Good Lord have been magnificent to us.

What his generation—those currently 55 to 75 years old—brings to old age is expansiveness. People in this group were lucky to have been too young to feel the worst of the Depression and yet old enough to have had their prime earning years coincide with the height of their country's postwar economic abundance. Some of them proved themselves on the battlefields in World War II and are still honored for it. They married young, became parents, settled suburbia on low-interest loans, and grew into middle age in child-centered homes. By the time they grew old, entitlement programs such as Medicare that financially buttress the later years were firmly in place.

From 1980 to 1985, the median income of only one age group rose by more than 1.2 percent—those over 65, who cheated inflation with an increase in income of 15.7 percent. More important than income is the size of their total financial assets. While they make up only 20 percent of United States households, they possess 40 percent of the nation's wealth.

The impact of the New Elders can be seen in the changes over the past decade of the title of the magazine that started off as *Retirement Living.* First it became *50 Plus.* Then, in 1988, *Reader's Digest* bought it and, confirming the New Elders' economic clout and active lifestyle, renamed it *New Choices.*

Only months before the transformation of *50 Plus, Modern Maturity,* the publication of the American Association of Retired Persons, whose advertising rate of $170,000 a page reflects its large and relatively affluent audience, finally pushed aside *Readers' Digest* and *TV Guide* to take the number-one spot in magazine circulation. *Modern Maturity*'s "Laughing Matter" department offers some insight into its readers' lifestyle. "Almost 500 years ago Columbus set out for the East Indies and wound up in the Caribbean," begins one joke. "Today when you set out for the East Indies you *get* to the East Indies. It's your *luggage* that winds up in the Caribbean."

The emergence of a large group of elders with money to spend has already forced American business to rethink marketing "common sense." Having concentrated for so long on the youth market, American corporations, as we shall see, are just now arriving at a new wisdom about how to reach consumers of all ages.

The New Elders are not only better off economically than the generation that most recently populated this age bracket, they are also more educated. From 1970 to 1986, the percentage of high-school graduates in the over-65 bracket increased from 28 percent to 49 percent. This in turn has made late-life education an important activity among many New Elders, engendering the Elderhostel and other programs devoted to lifelong learning.

What's more, the New Elders are assertive. They are the generation that fought World War II. "Don't tell me the nation doesn't owe me something in my old age," a 68-year-old Los Angeles native declared when somebody questioned the amount of tax money devoted to the needs of his cohort. They stand up for their rights, particularly through their most important lobbying organization, the American Association of Retired Persons. Legislators who would like to cut Social Security fear the wrath of "that eight-hundred-pound gorilla," as they call the AARP.

Having sacrificed for their children, many New Elders now want to do a little living of their own. This has called into question old assumptions about the relationship between older people and their adult children and grandchildren. Lucille Isenberg, a housewife, mother, and recent widow, tells of how her uncle tried to console her following her husband's death. "Now you'll live for your grandchildren," he said. "Like hell I will," she replied. "Now I'm going to live for me."

## BABY-BOOMER BAGGAGE

The New Elders have shaped their old age using the life experiences of their generation and adapting to the social and economic conditions that have prevailed as they have aged. Their children, the boomers, will re-create the later years to reflect the values and style of living *they* will bring to this stage of their lives, again combined with the society they find there.

The New Elders were the first American generation smaller than the one that preceded it, while the baby boom's most essential characteristic is its huge size. Between 1946 and 1964, Americans temporarily wrenched the birth rate off its steadily declining path and thrust it upward. The baby boom was a demographic digression not likely to be repeated in our lifetime. Held back first by the Great Depression and then by World War II, married couples suddenly found themselves free to build families in the midst of unparalleled prosperity. For one generation, as historian Paul Carter put it, the population of the United States "was expanding at a rate comparable to India's."

The surge in births that made America temporarily younger was in vivid contrast to the drop-off in procreation that preceded it. Births hit a low of 2,300,000 in 1933 and did not increase substantially until the beginning of World War II. When the troops came home in 1945, Americans shifted their attention from war plants and battlefields to nurseries and playgrounds. They had more than 3,400,000 babies in 1946, an increase of 20 percent from the previous year, and the boom was under way. Births peaked at over 4,300,000 in 1957 and stayed above 4,000,000 a year through 1964. Thereafter the rate gradually rolled off until the beginning of the 1970s, when it dropped into the 3,100,000-per-year range.

Members of this unique generation have held the public spotlight at each stage of their lives, a constant reminder of just how special society considers them to be. As children they heard stories about how the schools and colleges were overcrowded because of them (enrollment in United States schools increased *52 percent* between 1950 and 1960); as adolescents they found many of their elders emulating what they wore and dancing to their music; and as adults, their enormous buying power would determine what was "in" for the whole culture. *Time* magazine, in the 1960s, would even make them its "Man of the Year."

True, they were the generation that had to wait in line. But businesses tried to accommodate them, smoothing their way to secure their lucrative patronage. In the process, the little social innovations that companies were forced to develop slowly changed the tone of daily life for everyone. Just when boomers were getting old enough to have their own checking accounts and travel on their own, for example, banks and airlines, in the late 1960s, began replacing multiple lines of customers with single lines that funneled all customers more efficiently to counters, a practice that is still widespread.

The baby boomers are a generation for whom communal behavior comes as second nature. It began with their suburban upbringing. In 1950 there were 776 Little Leagues; ten years later they numbered 5,700. "The baby boomers were trained in groups," observed Landon Y. Jones. "They looked not within themselves or even to their parents for guidance but to their peer group."

The parents of the baby boom, the New Elders, were child-oriented. Sacrificing for the kids, saving for their college education, indeed, the migration to suburbia, were "for the kids," who always came first. But those children, as parents themselves, have had a more complicated list of priorities, in which *their* children have had to share a place with their parents' careers, among other concerns.

The baby boomers, too, are having many babies now, but that's because there are so many women of childbearing age. They are having smaller families than the ones in which they grew up, and they are having them at a later age. The approximately 3.5 million children now born each year in the United States are produced by many more parents than those who gave birth to the 4 million–plus children who were born each year in the baby boom. The United States fertility rate—the average number of babies that women have in their child-bearing years—reached a high of 3.68 in 1957. It was 3.17 in 1964, the final year of the baby boom, and then dropped sharply—the baby bust—to 1.74 in 1976. It has hovered in the 1.8–1.9 range in recent years.

Boomer women are the first generation to have almost complete control over the size of their families. Compared with their mothers, they have freer access to birth control information and improved contraceptive techniques—the birth control pill came into widespread use in the early 1960s. They also can take advantage of legalized abortion.

The New Elder mothers of the baby boomers anticipated careers as housewives and mothers. Indeed, their young adulthood encompassed a marriage boom as much as a baby boom. In 1940, 15 percent of women over 30 were unmarried; by 1960 only 7 percent of women in this age bracket had not married. The men who fathered the generation born in the years 1946 to 1964 expected to go to work for a company, moving slowly up through the ranks, eventually retiring after decades of service. Their children, sons and daughters both, know that company loyalty will play little or no role in their careers, and that if they want to raise a family they will have to manage it within the context of two working parents. Given divorce rates much higher than their parents experienced, today's 20-, 30-, and 40-year-olds also know that marriage to the same person is not necessarily for life.

The baby boomers face an uncertain economic future, one about which experts disagree. They "are more likely to make a little money than a lot," according to demographer Cheryl Russell. Their real wages have not kept pace with what their parents made at similar ages, *The Wall Street Journal* reports. Harvard economist Benjamin M. Friedman foresees the boomers aging during a period of steady decline for the American economy, and "by the time the members of the next generation are old enough to begin asking who was responsible for their diminished circumstances they will not even know what they have lost."

On the other hand, the Conference Board, a widely respected nonprofit corporate think tank, counters gloomy assessments of babyboomer financial prospects with a reminder: "Never have so many been destined to inherit so much." Their families function on two incomes. Nor should all baby boomers necessarily be lumped together when discussing their economic future. Many Early Boomers bought houses before real estate prices started climbing, and they are sitting on a considerable amount of equity. It's their younger brothers and sisters who are more likely to have a relatively low net worth. "The ones who are not moving into home ownership are not going to accumulate wealth," says George Masnick of the Harvard Joint Center for Housing Studies. "They are just not getting started."

## 2020 FORESIGHT

Given the characteristics of their generation and the political, social, and economic changes America is likely to undergo in the next thirty years, what will the baby boomers' old age be like? This is what the social landscape figures to look like three decades down the road:

• In *a new matriarchy* made up mostly of Early Boomers, many women will head families, some of them complex, structured by divorces involving themselves, grandparents, parents, and grandchildren. Large numbers of independent elder women living alone will join with others to form new kinds of families made up of unrelated people.

• *Early retirement will prove to be a unique event,* passing from the scene by the year 2010. People will change jobs more often after 45 than they did in their twenties. Elder boomers, working part-time, will alter the very tone of office life; because of their influence, for example, meditation breaks will replace coffee breaks.

• The baby boomers' later years will mark *a return to community* and new uses for the millions of three-bedroom houses that will clog suburbia, white elephants in a time of smaller families.

• *The Social Security system will be rescued* and boomers will collect benefits, but at a price: Full benefits will not start until age 70, a means test will determine benefit levels, and the cap on income subject to the payroll tax will be lifted, making this payment part of the general income tax. To save Medicare from bankruptcy, some costly medical procedures, such as bypass surgery, will be curtailed. Money will be funneled away from heroic measures and into preventive medicine; funding for nursing homes will be minimized, expenditures on home care substantially increased.

• *Intergenerational coalitions rather than an age war* are in the offing. Equal access for people with disabilities will become a major focus of cross-generational activism.

• Cancer will become a chronic rather than an acute illness. Elder baby boomers will engage in mental- as well as physical-agility workouts at health clubs. Doctors will lose much of their authority (and income) as other health professionals take over some of their duties, and *patients will take more responsibility for treating themselves.*

• By the year 2008, we may see *the first woman president of the United States.*

• Based on the experiences of the new older woman, *books on the developmental psychology of adults will be rewritten* to stress the importance of friendship in emotional growth and well-being.

• Boomer consumer dollars will still hold sway. By the time boomers are old enough to need them, virtually every product sold in America will be engineered with their comfort in mind—from clothing with Velcro fasteners instead of zippers to cars with swivel seats to ease getting in and out. But *senior citizen discounts will end.*

• A renewed sense of group cohesiveness, freedom from full-time work pressures so they can follow where their instincts might lead, and discontentment over not quite living the adult life they thought they would, will produce *an elderculture reflecting some of the spirit of the 1960s youth culture.*

## LOOKING TOWARD 2020

Nineteen forty-six marked the beginning of the baby boom and the publication of the first edition of Dr. Benjamin Spock's *Baby and Child Care.* In that same year the American Psychological Association set up a new Division on Maturity and Old Age and the first issue of *The Journal of Gerontology* appeared. Gerontology was then emerging from the backwaters of biomedical research.

These two trends could hardly have been farther apart: the first swell of what would become a demographic tidal wave making America think young, and the emergence of a new profession concerned with the oldest members of society. And yet in no more than three decades they will converge and change almost every aspect of American life. How that is likely to happen follows.

# 2

# Unfamiliar Families

INTERVIEWER: "Did you do anything when you were younger to take care of yourself in your old age?"

OLD MAN: "Yes, I had children."

In 1987, Robert Adams, secretary of the Smithsonian Institution, asked readers of *Smithsonian* to suggest the "significant trends" of the present that ought to be reflected in the collections of the National Museum of American History. The evolving American family was one of the trends most often mentioned. Adams speculated that the following settings and artifacts would be among those that would have to be represented to do justice to this subject: "efficiency apartments, singles bars, day-care centers, convenience stores, catalog shopping, frozen foods, dishwashers, microwave ovens."

Such a display would also chronicle much of the life of today's adult baby boomers. To represent their childhood adequately we might add the playroom of a three-bedroom suburban house, a nineteen-inch black-and-white television, an overcrowded classroom, Little League uniforms, and a family bowling center. And what of their future? What would be needed to depict their family lifestyle as elders? The exhibit might include a personals ad written by an older single woman looking for partners in an affinity group that could grow into an informal family, a handbook of resources for assisting an even older parent, family-tree personal-computer software to enable children to understand their relationship to stepgrandparents, and a business card in which the name of the business ends with "& Granddaughter."

The members of the generation that began in 1946 will establish more varied and in many ways closer ties between themselves and their adult children and grandchildren than the ones between themselves and their parents, the New Elder generation. And many of these relationships will be colored by a phenomenon with which the New Elders have only recently had to cope: the increasing prevalence of stepfamilies.

Boomer women, having come to their later years with a consciousness entirely different from that of their New Elder mothers, will constitute a new matriarchy. They will face a new adulthood in which care of elder parents becomes a major task, and will master it by forming new social networks and coping through the use of some of the same kinds of service businesses that have enabled them to handle both parenthood and careers.

We will also see a predominantly female older generation create entirely new kinds of families. Many of them divorced, widowed, or single, they will develop their own support systems to compensate for the scarcity of younger relatives, a product of the population bust that followed the post–World War II boom. Out of necessity, these socially inventive adults will alter the very meaning of the word *family* for their own time and for the future.

In all of these roles they will reshape the family in the light of their generational experiences and lifestyles. But they will not reinvent old age in a vacuum, for their parents are already laying the groundwork.

## ELDERS WITHOUT PRECEDENT

If gerontology is a relatively new field of study, family gerontology is newer still. Scholarly books and articles on the subject did not appear in any great numbers until the early 1980s. Only now is that information beginning to filter into more general publications. In the mass media, until recently, the relationship between old and young in families was portrayed as dismal, with the old passive and dependent on their young, or not depicted at all.

In 1937, for example, Paramount Pictures released *Make Way for Tomorrow*, a film *The New York Times* recently called "Hollywood's finest drama of old age." Following the appearance on the screen of the biblical injunction "Honor Thy Father and Thy Mother," the film tells of a couple in their seventies, split up by economic circumstances, each living with the family of one of their children. Their offspring barely tolerate their dependent parents' presence and can find no useful role for them in their families. In a telling vignette, an elderly friend of the father's says bitterly of *his* children, "They leave me alone. They don't need me and I don't need them."

*Make Way for Tomorrow* ends with a separation at a train station—probably final—the father going to live with a daughter in California because his health requires a milder climate, his wife about to enter an old-age home in New York. The film was a critical success but a box-office failure to the degree that the *Times* noted in 1952, "It virtually stands as legislation against any further frank inspection of old age."

Real older people were missing from television's idealized picture of cozy domesticity in the fifties, sixties, and seventies. Active life seemed to end with middle age on the tube. Older people were depicted as cute, comical, or pathetic, and they were almost always incidental. They were played by "character" actors. People over 60 had no serious place in anyone's life including, presumably, their own.

But what happens to the relationships between young and old in the family if a generation of older adults have enough assets to be financially independent of their children, as is true of many of today's New Elders? What if parents become a significant source of funds for mortgage payments and college tuition for their children and grandchildren?

In 1946, when the first of the baby boomers were born, 30 to 40 percent of elderly parents received more than half their income from their children. But a 1987 Harris poll showed that figure to have declined to fewer than 1 percent. The New Elders' prime earning years coincided with robust economic growth, substantial union pensions, a burgeoning stock market, and big increases in the value of the single-family houses that they bought years ago. Some wags are already referring to this older generation as woofs—well-off older folks—a designation that may give *yuppie* a run for its money.

This increasing level of economic well-being is even shared by older people who live alone, traditionally the least well-off among the old. A recent Harris poll of such people, commissioned by the Commonwealth Fund Commission on Elderly People Living Alone, surveyed twenty-five hundred individuals. The president of Louis Harris and Associates, Humphrey Taylor, remarked, "It is striking to see how many still act as providers of assistance for their families rather than as recipients: 21 percent . . . give regular financial aid to family members or friends while only five percent get regular help. This goes against the common image of the elderly as an economic drain on their children's resources."

## Nesting and Renesting

New Elders have confronted later years in which they have relationships with their adult children that might have been hard to believe only a few decades ago. Some of them have also had to cope with caring for their own parents while they themselves have already become grandparents. As grandparents they have discovered that little they learned when they were young prepared them for the modern version of this role. Without a map they have been asked to pioneer the new land of old age.

Gunhild O. Hagestad, a specialist in human development at Northwestern University, summed up current family uneasiness when she wrote, "Adults in the family now confront each other in relationships for which there is no historical precedence and minimal cultural guidance, while they individually find themselves in life stages that also have few culturally shared expectations attached to them."

For example, the existence of the "empty nest" stage of family life is more recent than many people realize. In 1900, a 22-year-old woman who married would, on the average, become a widow at 60 and die herself at age 64. Since it's likely that she would have had many children throughout her reproductive years, there is a good chance that her last child would still have been living at home at the time of her death.

Longer life spans gradually increased the chances of a couple sharing years alone after raising their children, but then the Depression kept many adult children at home. In World War II it was not uncommon for a young wife to move in with her husband's parents while her mate was in the service. So it wasn't until the parents of the baby-boomer generation that couples were left alone after their children set up housekeeping for themselves.

Despite much worrying by social scientists over how Americans would cope with this new stage in the life cycle, most seemed to do just fine. In fact, many relish their new freedom—perhaps in reaction to all the sacrificing they did when their children were young. One Ohio woman wrote that she and her husband "had never had it so good. WE can make plans to fit OUR schedules, WE can plan meals (or eat out) as WE please, WE can impulsively stop on the way home from work, WE can go away for the weekend. . . . It's wonderful."

But many New Elders now have to deal with the refilled nest as well. "Thirty years ago it was considered shameful not to stay home until you got married," observed one parent, reflecting on the confusing turn of events that has made many Late Boomer and Reagan Generation young adults dependent on their New Elder parents. "Then it became wrong not to be independent—you were supposed to leave home and get your own place. Now things have changed again."

Some of today's parents feel they will never see the end of their parenting period. In 1986, a former employee of the United States Information Service, in a guest column in *U.S. News & World Report,* called attention to New Elders who found themselves with parental responsibilities they had not anticipated:

My wife and I are 66 and supposedly retired, but we haven't weaned all of our children yet.

We are among a growing number of Americans 55 and older who provide homes for 10.3 million offspring. That is 13% of all children living with parents, according to Census Bureau figures. It is also a significant increase from 1970 when the comparable statistics were 8.4 million and 10%, respectively.

It's not just the unmarried kids who are staying around or coming home again. In 1980, according to the United States census, almost five hundred thousand divorced men and women in their twenties and three hundred thousand married couples lived with their parents. As one young married man recently put it: "It [living with Mom and Dad] seemed the only way we would ever be able to buy anything." The 1990 census is almost certain to produce even higher numbers.

What would the producers of *Make Way for Tomorrow* make of this? *Prevention*, a prominent magazine concerned with health, nutrition, and the good life, and widely read by people over 60, posed this question to its readers: "Your daughter asks to borrow $5000 toward a downpayment on her first house. Your son asks you for a loan so he can pay off his credit cards. As you say 'yes' to both, a small inner voice is nagging: These kids are grown up now. Should you really be doing this?"

Even young adults who do not return to their parents' homes may remain financially dependent on them. Constantly appreciating real-estate values and high mortgage rates have made New Elders family bankers to their adult children. Buying a house has become the arena in which the new economic relationship between generations is often tested. While home ownership is becoming difficult for young adults to achieve, particularly Late Boomers, most of their parents own their own homes—about 21.5 million Americans over 65, or 75 percent of this age group. In 1949, the parents of the baby boomers could pay their mortgages with 14 percent of their gross income; in 1970 those payments still only took 18 percent of the homeowner's earnings. By comparison, the baby boomers have to part with an average 29 percent of their increasingly harder-to-earn paychecks in order to keep a roof over their heads. One 30-year-old woman who makes a salary in the low thirties in the advertising industry put it in a nutshell: "My $225 car payment is more than my parents' mortgage payment."

Lawyer Stephan Pollan, an expert on home buying, says: "Some of the most delicate negotiations I conduct are not between buyer and seller, but between children and their parents. Some kids are scared to ask to borrow from their parents, and some parents are worried about never getting paid back."

## A Job New Elders Never Anticipated

By the mid-1980s, observers noted that a few of the retirees moving to the retirement community of Sun City in Arizona were bringing their parents along to live with them. Ethel Shanas, a prominent gerontologist, commented in 1987 that she was often hearing remarks such as these: "I want to enjoy my grandchildren; I never expected that when I was a grandparent I'd have to look after my parents."

The over-85 age bracket is the fastest-growing one in our population. Now numbering about 3.3 million, 1.3 percent of the population, it will increase to at least 7 million and 2.4 percent of the population by the year 2020. It is no longer uncommon to find adults in their sixties caring for elderly parents. This responsibility is even more familiar among the Eisenhower Generation, now in their mid-forties to mid-fifties. By the time those now in their thirties and early forties reach their fifties, sixties, and early seventies, their lifestyle could be significantly affected by the long life span of their parents.

What have the pioneers of this new life stage found? As a college teacher who spoke from personal experience put it: "Being a middle-aged child is difficult." A University of Michigan School of Nursing study showed that those caring for the aged suffered from depression three times as often as the older people they cared for. At its worst, this pressure can bring people close to the breaking point. "I can't stand it another day," a 51-year-old woman who took in an elderly parent and was now near the end of her rope blurted out to gerontologist Jane Porcino. "My children are finding excuses for staying overnight with friends. My husband is threatening to leave me. My mother sleeps all day and wanders around the house at night. This just can't go on. Our family is falling apart." A daughter who took in her mother-in-law described how this new task interfered with her "own mid-life crisis." She "had been considering new career directions and opportunities, but now everything has screeched to a halt."

Women usually play the key role in this family drama. "They find it easier to cross age and generation boundaries than men do," according to sociologist Gunhild O. Hagestad. They are the multigenerational caregivers, looking after the young, the old, and the very old in the family, sometimes simultaneously. This is why Eisenhower-era women are often called the "sandwich" generation.

Eisenhower Generation and New Elder women burdened with this responsibility have been coping as best they can. Family wisdom on the subject is lacking, since the phenomenon has never occurred before on such a large scale, and institutional support is just beginning to appear. It is the Early Boomer women who as elders will develop the resources and create the traditions that will make it possible to deal with this phase of life without being swamped. We will consider this more closely later in the chapter.

## New Elder Grandparents

As a result of their increased affluence, today's grandparents are already a greater economic force in their children's families than they were just a generation ago. Duquesne University in Pittsburgh discovered this when it set up a plan that permitted alumni a discount for the prepayment of tuition for children who were still in diapers. More than 10 percent of those who took advantage of the plan were grandparents.

But some contemporary grandparents are opting for distance instead of closeness, choosing to attend to their own busy lives and let their children raise their grandchildren. They are forsaking anything resembling the traditional role of grandparent. Psychiatrist Arthur Kornhaber has deplored this phenomenon in a series of books and articles, contending that modern grandparenthood has left us with a generation of "grandorphans." He has led a movement, embodied in his Foundation for Grandparenting, for the return of the active, dedicated grandparent.

But when an article about his ideas, titled "Let's Put the PARENT Back in Grandparent," appeared in *50 Plus*, it engendered some stiff opposition. One grandparent wondered if Kornhaber "would be so glib about 'grandorphans' if he had gone through [his adult child's] divorce, single parenting, coping with learning-disabled children, drug and/or alcohol abuse, or unemployment in *his* family."

Sociologists Andrew Cherlin and Frank F. Furstenberg, Jr., also quarrel with Kornhaber's analysis. Interviews that they conducted showed strong ties between New Elders and their grandchildren, although the researchers acknowledged that "noninterference" with the way that New Elders' adult children are raising their kids is the rule. They concluded that "being a grandparent is still deeply meaningful. But grandparents, like most other Americans, increasingly find meaning in their lives through personal fulfillment."

For New Elders who choose to act the part of the grandparent, the question is: What is the part? In our present culture, grandparents have one unofficial role: nonjudgmental older "pal." A grandmother's response to a 1985 magazine survey defines this contemporary role: "They [grandchildren] need an unbiased adult to talk to, just to be with at times—someone who has no rules to impose, no formalities to enforce, someone just to have fun with."

While this can be an important role, it is the only one available to New Elders, except when their adult children experience the fractured family. When that happens, wider possibilities present themselves. We can already see the beginning of a new intergenerational assertiveness in the recent moves by grandparents to secure visitation rights to their grandchildren when their children divorce. In many states grandparents now have legal standing to ask for such rights. And some are doing a lot more than visiting. Sociologists Furstenberg and Cherlin discovered in their sample of 500 grandparents that many, out of economic necessity, served temporarily as surrogate parents to their grandchildren after their children were divorced.

The increase in divorce can complicate grandparenthood. As columnist Ann Landers put it: "There is no chart in heaven showing which pew is to be occupied by grandparents and which by stepgrandparents." Older people have been forced to develop new types of relationships when their children's marriages split up. And they are coming up with some interesting ones.

In a divorce, paternal grandparents, especially grandmothers, are more likely to stay close to former daughters-in-law than are maternal grandparents to keep ties to their former sons-in-law. The husband's parents, after all, have an incentive to stay close to their grandchildren's mother, who usually has custody of the kids, while maternal grandparents get a free ride. Colleen L. Johnson and Barbara M. Barer, specialists in gerontology and medical anthropology, studied grandparenting after divorce and found Byzantine complexity and wonderful intricacy. Consider this cluster of new relationships:

> The paternal grandmother and the paternal grandfather's new wife babysit for the grandchildren and both help financially with occasional gifts of money. Through their contacts with their grandchildren and their former daughter-in-law, the grandparents are also acquainted with their former daughter-in-law's new husband's former spouse and their children through their linkage with their grandchildren. Because the children of divorce and remarriage live within a few blocks of each other, the grandchildren and their stepsiblings are in frequent contact.

## THE FAMILY IN OUR FUTURE

What happens to the relationships between young and old in the family if family elders come to their later years well educated (almost one-fourth of them college graduates), numerous enough for their age cohort to make up one-fifth of the population, their female members having had careers outside the home, conscious of their historical importance and uniqueness as a generation, veterans of many variations on the traditional nuclear family, and having already had the active New Elders as role models and precedent-setters, as will be true of the baby boomers?

In the multigeneration family in the decade 2010–20, the New Elder parents of the baby boomers will range in age from their seventies to their nineties. The Early Boomers will be moving into their sixties and all the Late Boomers will be well into middle age. Adult children of the baby boomers will range in age from about their late teens to their mid- to late forties. And the generation of 1946 to 1964 will have grandchildren ranging in age up to 25.

In the photograph of a family gathering in 2015, there will be a lot of gray heads, with more people over 55 in the shot than children under 18. Demographers would describe this family as "top-heavy." It's nothing like the photograph of the extended family that might have been taken, say, in 1971, at a sit-down family dinner. In that picture there are kids all over the place—and the communal meal stands out in the photograph as much as the representation of age groups. Between flexible school schedules, flextime at work, and the institution of grazing that baby boomers originated in the eighties and never quite gave up, the family dinner has survived only on nostalgic greeting cards.

The occasion of the gathering in 2015 is a formal family reunion. Geographical mobility in our society and the evolving role of the family made family reunions a particularly American phenomenon, starting in the nineteenth century with gatherings at family burial plots on Memorial Day, according to folklorist Roger D. Abrahams. But by the second decade of the twenty-first century, geographical dispersion, smaller families, and divorce and remarriage will cause aging baby boomers to convene these meetings regularly as a matter of family survival.

As the baby boomers come into their late fifties, sixties, and seventies in the next century, they will continue to have a strong interest in maintaining family ties. Motivated by the sustaining myth of the nurturing family of the 1950s, they are likely to cherish family connections, particularly in difficult times.

According to Gunhild O. Hagestad, they "may go down in history as having had the ideal childhood, growing up in a sea of tranquility between disruptions due to mortality and disruptions due to divorce." Compare their experience with that of their parents, about half of whom, born around the time of World War I, experienced the death of a sibling or parent by the time they reached the age of 15.

Baby boomers were raised in a world of Little League games, backyard barbecues, and high school proms. It was a life lived for and around children, who had everything, from tap dancing lessons to orthodontic work to the best colleges. The families of their formative years provided a stable, relatively benign environment. They learned about life in the glow of antibiotics, Dr. Spock, and couples living together "until death do us part." Toughlove and divorce came later.

Television celebrated the child-centered post–World War II nuclear family in which they grew up, fixing it as the domestic ideal, a norm that has persisted. We saw something in "Ozzie and Harriet," "Father Knows Best," and "Leave It to Beaver" that many of us still find hard to let go, something familiar and comforting.

Many boomers will divorce as adults, but their remarriage rate is also high. Their vision of domestic happiness has such a powerful tug that they will keep trying to reproduce the idealized family conditions of their youth.

Arranging these family reunions is likely to be a major industry in the future, particularly beneficial to midwestern cities like Chicago, which will be favored for their central location. Reunions will become an important part of the travel business, involving airlines, hotel catering, and photographers. Desktop publishing software specifically designed for producing family bulletins to update geographically separated relatives periodically on the latest news will constitute one replacement for the annual Christmas letter to far-flung kin. Another will be the videotape mailed from household to household, each part of the family recording its own portion of this quiltlike family chronicle. Conference calls on video telephones will also be a frequent occurrence, especially on "Family Day," which aging baby boomers will probably make a national holiday by the year 2010.

### Matriarchal Burdens

Because of the longer life spans of their aging parents, baby boomers will spend more time fulfilling a greater variety of overlapping family roles—child, spouse, parent, grandparent—than any other generation in our history. Their lower fertility rate will result in their passing fewer years than previous generations as parents of dependent children but more years as the children of older parents. Some of these 60-year-olds will supervise the care of their very old and possibly frail parents at the same time they are developing relationships with their grandchildren. In their late sixties, close to one-third of boomer women will still have a living parent.

Increasingly, adulthood will come to be seen as much as a period in which one interacts with aging parents and grandchildren as it will as a time for raising the next generation. Eventually this changing emphasis in roles will filter into the upbringing of children, probably beginning with the boomers' grandchildren. Children are socialized now to expect the role of parent to occupy a major phase of their lives. In the future they will be taught values that support other roles, namely those of interacting with and caring for elder grandparents and parents. For example, it's likely that by the year 2000 children will be playing with dolls that represent older people as well as "the mommy and the daddy."

Gerontologist Elaine Brody sees the caretaking function remaining a woman's issue for the foreseeable future. And that could be especially problematic for older boomer women. She says that New Elder women

> may have to quit their jobs to take care of their mothers, but they weren't socialized to have "careers" to begin with. The conflicts may be a lot worse for women who are younger now. There's also the question of the criss-crossing loyalties that might be caused by divorce. And there's the question of what it's going to mean now that more and more women are having their children later; a lot of them will be dealing with young children and old parents at the same time.

Careers have been part of the ethic of self-fulfillment, a cardinal value for the generation that came of age in the 1960s and 1970s. As the baby-boomer women age, they are likely to feel the same kinds of conflict over elder-parent care that they now do managing the tensions between career and family. Meshing their responsibilities to their aging parents with the fabric of an active social and work life will increase the role strain of elder baby-boomer women enormously, and they will look for help.

One place they will find it is at work, where fringe benefits, as we note in a later chapter, will focus more and more on providing assistance to adult children with older parents. But benefits will not provide the whole answer, and to fill in the gap between what is needed and what the government and employers provide, baby-boomer women and men are likely to turn to the many service businesses that will be started to take care of their parental-care needs. The day-care, after-school centers, tutoring services, and summer camps that now assist them in child rearing will serve as the precedent for this sort of out-of-home caregiving.

For example, in the future, when aging parents live far away, their adult children will hire a local agency to visit and periodically call on them to make sure nothing is wrong. The boomers will receive written reports on their parents' condition, if appropriate, and the agency will arrange for any health or other services that are needed. There is at least one business in Florida that already fulfills this need, a harbinger of things to come.

Adult children are also likely to make large-scale use of "care managers," professionals who will lighten the burden of looking after elderly parents who live nearby. These consultants will help adult children to negotiate the intricacies of the Social Security and Medicare bureaucracies and to secure other necessary private services for their parents. Since the mid-1980s, the number of such companies has grown from one hundred to six hundred one- to two-person operations—barely a skeleton outline of a future burgeoning industry.

As the Early Boomers move now into middle age and begin to confront the problems of taking responsibility for aging parents, elder support service centers are starting to take shape. These institutions will help adult children who spend a good deal of time with their possibly frail parents, perhaps even living next door or with them. Senior Service Corporation, only a few years old, is one of the first chains of adult day-care centers for older people who do not need substantial medical attention. Maurice Thompson, its chief executive officer, has already reaped the rewards of his involvement with SmokEnders and Evelyn Wood Reading Dynamics—he's a man who knows where the action is. He predicts that these daytime centers for the fourth or fifth generation of the families of the future will ultimately constitute a multibillion-dollar service field.

As true products of their generation, baby-boom elders with older parents will also resort to their own collective solutions to the problem of how to shoulder the burden of parent care while also living their own lives. Within ten years we can expect to see the appearance of baby-boomer women's eldercare collectives, with a group like the National Organization for Women (NOW) coordinating this activity through a national federation of these organizations. The organizations will trade information and pool their resources to hire services at group rates for their parents.

The industry of self-help publications and counseling services already responding to these problems will mushroom in the future to become a major part of our culture. We could even reach a point where one book will break through and become the "Dr. Spock" for caring for very old parents. That's likely to happen by the year 2000.

Newsletters, the vanguard of a future flood of similar publications devoted to the subject, have already appeared. A prospectus for a new newsletter called *The Later Years* recently promised to advise middle-aged children on:

- What to do about the reversal of parent/child roles
- How to side-step guilt while doing the right thing for everyone
- What to do when parents come to stay

and to address such specific questions and complaints as:

- My mom still treats me like a child. How can I change this?
- My dad is 80, but he insists he's still boss—in my own house!
- My dad says we are after his money. What does this really mean?

By providing themselves with adequate support for the task of care-taking, baby-boomer elders may find that their relationship with their aged parents brings them a sense of reward and fulfillment that transcends the specific burdens it involves. The upshot could be a greater sense of family intimacy in their parents' final years.

## The Age of Family Therapy

A besieged adult daughter of the Eisenhower Generation, now in her mid-fifties and under the gun from coping with a frail and fading elderly mother, was ready to throw in the towel. "You get in a rage against nature," she seethed. "I am permanently angry at the whole damn situation. But we're never angry at Mom, who's an angel. My husband's been a prince." If Mom's an "angel" and the husband is a "prince," who could possibly be blamed (or be the object of self-blame) when things go wrong? You guessed it.

Baby-boomer women, having grown up in the therapeutic age, will never settle for such martyrdom. Family therapy, already a growth field in the helping professions, will experience explosive growth in the next decade as more and more families get at least a taste of these new complications. Only a handful of hospital mental-health units now deal with family problems in which there are elders involved—New York City's Beth Israel Hospital in conjunction with the Ackerman Institute of Family Therapy is one of them. But by the middle of the first decade of the twenty-first century family therapy will be one of the prime growth fields among the helping professions.

Therapy sessions could enrich the later years of both aging baby boomers and their New Elder parents and lead to an unprecedented closeness between them. Often these days when an adult loses a parent one can hear deep regret that family conflicts remained unresolved right to the end. But with parents living longer and a greater frankness between adult generations and a willingness to work on problems, older people, both parents and children, are likely to feel a greater completeness and inner peace. This is likely to be especially true of elderly baby boomers and *their* adult children in the years after 2020 when all generations of adults will have matured in the therapeutic era.

### At the Head of the Table

Exercising multigenerational responsibilities will make the baby boomers—particularly women—the fulcrum on which many extended families will balance. As the mediators between—and sometimes caretakers of—several generations, they will find themselves at the center of family relationships, the people other family members will naturally look to for leadership.

While multigenerational responsibilities have already begun to fall on New Elder women, they come to this role with a different viewpoint. Most of them were always primarily caretakers—wives and mothers. They derived their identity from these roles. But elder baby-boomer women will be winding up careers as well as parenthood. Many of them will have steered their way through the new roles and responsibilities produced by the multifamilies of divorce and the difficult role of single motherhood. They will be veterans of just about every family role one could devise for those approaching their later years, the new family professionals.

A 1977 Metropolitan Life Insurance Company study predicted that because women have longer life spans than men, 20 percent of mothers then in their early twenties who were giving birth to sons would outlive them. These peculiarities of the mortality statistics for the families of some baby-boomer women will make them not only the matriarchs who embody family traditions, but also those who actively carry on the line and even occasionally outlive a younger member of it.

Much closer mother-daughter ties between elder baby boomers and their adult children may further strengthen the matriarchal tone of the family, as Gunhild O. Hagestad suggests:

> Young-old mothers in the 21st Century may have more shared experiences with their daughters than has been the case for older women at the end of this century. In the future, mothers and daughters will typically look back at involvements in education, work, and family. Many of them will also share some of the life changes associated with aging. A greater fund of shared life experiences may make the female axis even more central as the dominating force in the maintenance of intergenerational cohesion and continuity.

Men are less likely to head extended families. First, they tend not to live as long as women and will thus have less time to establish themselves in this role. Just as important, a typical aging man is more likely than a woman to still be married in old age, and thus to have some of his familial energies diverted to his wife—possibly the second or third one—and her family.

All these characteristics of the future family should reinforce the improved status of women in society in general. Business and government institutions can hardly remain uninfluenced by the spectrum shift from the patriarchal to the matriarchal family. This social trend should produce more women leaders in these and other fields.

Within the baby-boomer generation of family elders, the Early Boomers, born through the mid-1950s, should dominate. Not only will they be older in an era characterized by respect for age, they will also, on the average, be wealthier than their younger brothers and sisters. They are more likely to own a home and to have bought it before the price of houses and mortgage rates got out of hand. They will have a higher net worth than their siblings and might even serve as the family's "banker," lending money to their nieces and nephews as well as their sisters and brothers.

## THE BOOMERS AND THEIR ADULT CHILDREN

Traditionally, Americans have aspired to create a better life for their children. The parents of the baby boomers sacrificed so their children could go to college and have careers that were satisfying and financially rewarding. But the baby boomers' children, maturing in a different, less expansive America, are not likely to pioneer new frontiers of affluence and liberation of the self. We can expect their parents to feel considerable ambivalence about this shrinking of ambitions and expectations.

### Dollars and Cents

In *their* old age New Elder parents have been economically dominant with respect to their children. They have lent money to their Late Boomer children and have taken some of them back into the nest when their young adulthood got a little rough. They have also helped out their Early Boomer children with mortgage down payments. In late middle age many of their boomer children can expect to inherit money from them—notwithstanding New Elder bumper stickers that boast how they're spending their kids' inheritance. But that doesn't necessarily imply emotional closeness. Many New Elders have used their economic independence to declare a kind of emotional independence from their adult children (and their grandchildren).

The boomers and *their* adult children are likely to have a more complicated economic relationship. What it will be like depends partly on how the American economy fares in the next two decades.

If we can negotiate the difficult passage between stepped-up foreign competition and a dangerous trade and budget deficit, all the while maintaining at least moderate economic growth, then we should see the Early Boomers in a relatively dominant position in their families, like that of their New Elder parents now. Under such circumstances, they too will probably give their adult children a helping hand. In fact, the Early Boomers are likely to head their entire extended families, since their younger brothers and sisters might occasionally turn to them for financial help as well.

In the alternate scenario of hard times—a distinct possibility—all generations could find themselves on a more equal footing. A real-estate crash would wipe out the Early Boomer advantage of appreciated housing values. With this outcome, the relationship between elder and adult child would rest even more strongly on the psychological undercurrents built up in the child-rearing years.

## Psychological Undercurrents

Children coming into adulthood in the first few decades of the twenty-first century will have less of a sense of their own importance than their parents did at the same age. These young adults will be fewer in number compared with the extraordinary size of their baby-boomer parents' generation. More important, they will not have enjoyed the kind of parental attention that was showered on the baby boomers, bolstering their sense of themselves. In the early 1980s, the opinion research firm of Yankelovich, Skelly and White asked parents questions related to their willingness to sacrifice for their kids. About two-thirds said they put leading their own lives ahead of spending time with their kids, would not continue in an unhappy marriage for the sake of their children, and thought a good standard of living for themselves now took precedence over leaving money to their offspring in the future.

The contrast between the formative years of the baby boomers and those years for their children will be marked. The number of children living in families split by divorce tripled from the mid-fifties to the mid-seventies, when baby boomers were beginning to raise families. Baby-boom parents may feel guilty about this fracturing of the family. Brandeis University historian Barbara Whitehead, who has interviewed female baby boomers for a book on their generation, has picked up the first notes of this theme. "It's a deeply divided feeling to remember your own childhood with warmth and even longing," she says of what she's heard from them, "and to know that you are creating a very different one for your own children."

This suggests that many older boomers may feel a need to make it up to their adult children by being more emotionally giving with them than perhaps the boomers' parents have been with them. They may be less judgmental about their adult children's domestic struggles, more willing to serve as a stabilizing force for their families. Older boomers may also be able to offer their adult children a vision of optimism and change that the younger generation's more limited historical experience might not readily afford.

About 40 percent of baby boomers' children will spend at least part of their childhood in a single-parent family. Some psychologists believe such children mature more quickly. They often have to take on more responsibilities earlier in their lives, particularly when they are only children, a status likely to be more prevalent than in their parents' generation because of the consistently low fertility rate since the end of the baby boom.

These adult children might have close, almost comradely relationships with their elder boomer parents because they will have been more like their parents' friends and equals during their childhood than kids raised in two-parent families. On the other hand, there is an equal chance that adults could emerge from such a childhood with strained relationships with their single parents, since raising a child under these circumstances can focus family tensions between one parent and a child that might be more diffuse in two-parent families.

Divorced parents now create thirteen hundred new stepfamilies in the United States every day, according to the Census Bureau. There are 4.3 million stepfamilies in the United States, containing 8.7 million children. By the year 2000, contends the Stepfamily Association of America, stepfamilies (including those with adult children) will constitute the majority of all American families. As a result, we will see a rich brew of adult stepparent-stepchild relationships. These are often likely to have the tone of friendships.

Hallmark greeting cards are already foreshadowing this aspect of the family's future. For Father's Day, for example, the store racks carry cards for stepfathers and fatherlike friends, not to mention for single mothers who also serve in a "father" role. In such relationships between adults, the degree of closeness maintained and the nature of the interaction are likely to be more a matter of choice than tradition, although by the year 2020 elder boomers and their families may have spent enough time in the new family to have evolved some customs and rituals for these connections. For example, it may be possible in a brief church or synagogue service to affirm the ties of familial affection that have grown between stepparent and stepchild and between stepsiblings over the years. There might even be a ritual emphasizing ties between the new families of former spouses.

On the other hand, for an important minority of children of well-off professional couples (the fabled yuppie parents), their adult relationships with their parents could be stormy. As young children they have had elaborate toys that played "on the vulnerability of parents who want to be perfect and create a perfect environment for their child," according to noted child psychologist T. Berry Brazelton. Los Angeles psychotherapist Charles Clegg says he's "seeing seven-, eight- and nine-year-olds who are anxious and angry because they're overprogrammed with activities that don't meet their needs." These kids don't want to take risks, says psychologist Bruno Bettelheim. He points out that "the days of most middle-class children are so filled . . . that they have hardly any time to simply be by themselves. They are deprived of those long hours and days of leisure to think their own thoughts, an essential element in the development of creativity."

They could grow up feeling pressured, never able to satisfy some abstract ideal of "goodness." Their parents might feel resentful that their children didn't turn out "better" while simultaneously feeling guilty for having expected too much from their children. That would probably produce a sullen acceptance of elder boomer authority but little true affection or respect.

### Population Growth and the Family

There is one possible wild-card demographic glitch that could have some surprising and unsettling effects on relations between baby-boomer elders and their adult children. According to sociologists Susan Watkins, James Menken, and John Bongaarts, "if current low fertility persists after the baby boom passes out of the reproductive years, the United States will for the first time experience a negative rate of natural increase. Public concern for population extinction may then become as popular as concern about population explosion was in the 1960s."

If we do experience population decline at the turn of the century, we might also see a pronatal policy in the United States. Government subsidies for childbirth could put pressure on the daughters of the baby boomers to have large families, encouraging them to assume the role of the 1950s housewife and mother—the role the baby boomers' mothers played and against which their daughters rebelled. The women of the baby boom have always had some ambivalence about the career/motherhood split. Imagine the complex mix of guilt, ambivalence, and competitiveness that such a turn of events could invoke between *these* mothers as they grow older and their adult daughters.

## BOOMER GRANDPARENTS

Boomer grandparents will feel free to exercise even more choice in their relationships with their children's children. Baby boomers were, after all, a generation that saw having children as an option, not an inevitability. Why would they view grandparenthood any differently?

One phenomenon that will give them that choice—much more than their New Elder parents have now—will be the fact that so many of these grandchildren and their parents will be products of broken marriages. The increasing divorce rate for people over 65—twice now what it was in 1960—will complicate matters further. If boomer grandparents maintain anything resembling their divorce rate as young and middle-aged adults, they will produce family trees that almost defy tracing. And the complex and less tradition-bound character of these families will make relationships between their members more a matter of choice than they are today.

A child of divorced parents whose grandparents have also separated may need a computer program to tell which relatives are where in his or her family. In fact, making family trees may take on a much greater—and more practical—importance for this generation of grandchildren. It would not be surprising to see a standardized form, not to mention computer software, readily available for families that want to teach their children and grandchildren how they are related to everyone else in their family.

We may find that baby boomers will regret that, in pursuit of self-fulfillment and because they concentrated on their careers, they did not spend more time with their own children as they grew up. This could lead them to become doting grandparents, more so than many of their New Elder parents have been.

"Women can expect to spend close to four decades of their lives as grandparents, and men almost as long," Professor Vern Bengston of the Andrus Gerontology Center at the University of Southern California writes of the future. This will be especially true for boomers who did not wait till their late thirties to have children. If they choose to do so, they will be able to forge a grandparent-to-grandchild bond that has more intensity and dimension than the one most boomers experienced with their grandparents. In their later years there will be fewer grandchildren to each grandparent than there have been for many decades, increasing each generation's sense of the special nature of the link between old and young.

What kinds of relationships might this situation lead to? Boomer entrepreneurs slowing down after a long career could take their grandchildren into the business if their children opt for another line of work. In general, we will probably see elder baby boomers serve as guides, mentors, and sources of connections between their grandchildren and the adult world. Grandparents will again become sources of wisdom and practical knowledge about the ways of the world for the young.

Although we now live in a much-vaunted "information age," the most important kinds of information the young have always required have never been available from computers. In the future, as now, the young will need to know how to make ethical choices, set priorities, choose a path in life. In short, they will need wisdom, what was once the traditional province of old age.

The grandparents of twenty to thirty years from now will know vastly more about life than their adult children will. The gap in the experience of these two generations will be wider than usual because of the great social changes witnessed by the baby-boomer generation. As adults in their sixties in the second decade of the twenty-first century they will have known both the years of family stability and the fragmented family. Their lives will also have encompassed a revolution in sexual morality and vast changes in the career and family role options of women. They will have experienced a wider variety of lifestyles than their adult children. As founts of wisdom and experience, these grandparents will be in a unique position to influence the values of their grandchildren—true elders in a society that will place great value on such a role.

Besides serving as mentors for their grandchildren, the new grandparents may also function as their patrons. In a world in which many older people will have wealth, power, and influence—assuming a stable economy—the young will need good connections. Their grandparents are the first generation to experience multiple careers, and they will have a wide network of contacts. We will see grandchildren keeping in touch with their grandparents out of enlightened self-interest.

## GREAT-GRANDPARENTS

As yet relatively unexplored is the present and future role of great-grandparents. According to gerontologist Ethel Shanas, there may be more great-grandparents now (from the Old Guard, the parents of the

New Elders) than there were grandparents in 1900. The present group of great-grandmothers (for they are mostly that) plays a limited role. Just as grandparents usually need their children's cooperation to establish close ties to their grandchildren, great-grandparents must go through their children and their grandchildren to gain access to the fourth generation in the family. Because of this indirect access they are as likely to call these kids "my daughter's grandchildren" or "my granddaughter's children" as they are "my great-grandchildren."

Many of today's young children, born when their parents were in their twenties, can expect to grow up knowing their great-grandparents. But these representatives of very old branches on the family tree are still likely to keep their distance from the greener offshoots. It will be more than the waning energy of old age that will likely hold them back. The generation gap—differences in experiences and values—between these 90-year-olds and their great-grandchildren will be enormous by 2020. In fact, unless we run into a period of extraordinary social stability maintained for decades—giving several consecutive generations similar lifestyles—it's unlikely that great-grandparents will become a significant familial factor in society anytime in the next century.

## THE MANY FACES OF THE FAMILY

The future of the American family will be profoundly influenced by another cluster of unprecedented demographic developments: low birth and mortality rates, high divorce rates, and an increasing number of people who never marry. Taken together, these trends mean that many people will live a substantial portion of their later years without any immediate family because they will have few or no living children or grandchildren. Everyone needs an intimate social support network of one kind or another. Where the family no longer fills this need, other kinds of relationships will have to be invented. Once before, in the 1960s, the baby boomers created their own subculture when the dizzying pace of social change outraced the values they received from their parents. Now they will forge a new adult subculture, replacing the family networks many of them will have outlived.

The culture of black Americans had a major influence on the "counterculture" of white youth in the sixties—on their music, language, and politics, for example—and it may resurface in their lives in old age.

Blacks in this country have had to improvise family when social and economic oppression ravaged their nuclear families. For example, it is common among black Americans for uncles and aunts and even more distant relatives to take in and raise children who have lost or been separated from their parents for whatever reason. As a result, according to University of Michigan sociologist Rose C. Gibson, they tend to arrive at their later years "more fortified, more rehearsed, and better able to adapt to its exigencies."

Women will dominate explorations into the possibilities of new types of kinship. As Alice Rossi, a former president of the American Sociological Association, has written, "In the light of the fact that women are more apt than men to form quasi-kin relationships, it is perhaps fortunate that it is elderly women rather than men who tend to outlive their spouses." Women now married and in their thirties and forties can expect, on the average, to become widows at age 68, with 15 more years of life still ahead of them. If present patterns continue, fewer than 10 percent will remarry. Those who do remarry will tend to link up with men whose ages exceed theirs by even more than did the ages of their previous husbands. The shorter life span of men makes it likely that these women will be widowed again.

In 1984 there were more than eight million people over 65 living alone, according to the United States Bureau of the Census. In twenty to thirty years that number should more than double, and if current projections hold true, about 80 percent of old people living alone will be women. How will they meet their needs for emotional sustenance, security, and companionship? From where will arise the ties that bind, and to whom will these people be bound?

It's important to remember that baby-boom women will have lived considerably different lives from those of their New Elder mothers. Most baby boomers experienced a period of young adulthood in which they lived alone or perhaps shared housing accommodations instead of moving directly from their parents' home into a marriage. Careers have given these women a sense of resourcefulness, and they are used to reaching out to their contemporaries to work in groups to solve difficult life problems. They are likely to see the creation of a supportive family network as a problem they are capable of solving.

The high birth rate that characterized families when the baby boomers were kids will provide many of them with siblings close to their own age as they get older. (And given the population bust that followed, theirs will be the last generation for a while that will have this benefit.) We can expect to see many of these brothers and sisters, widowed or never married, setting up housekeeping together. That's not an unusual practice even today. But the trend toward households based on the relationship between first or second—or possibly even more distant— cousins *will* be novel.

The members of this generation have memories of large family gatherings with their uncles and aunts and their families; it is a part of the boomers' sense of what family means. As they age and experience the death of close relatives and the smaller family networks engendered by the baby bust, they will naturally make the most of the relatives they have. In reaching out horizontally on their family trees to expand kinship ties they will perpetuate the family circles and cousins' clubs so many enjoyed when they were younger. And in doing so they are likely to set important precedents and add to the evolution of the American extended family.

## "JUST LIKE FAMILY"

We are all familiar with people close to us whom we regard as "just like family." These are intimate and long-standing relationships we choose rather than receive through blood ties or marriage. Ella Grant, 74 and a widow, lives next door to one of these "relatives." They have been friends for years. Jackie Morgan checks Ella's living room window every morning to make sure the shades are up, the sign that nothing is amiss. If they were still drawn, Jackie would immediately go next door to investigate. Ella, in turn, has acted toward Jackie's family over the years in a way that we usually associate with aunts and grandmothers. She baby-sat for Jackie's kids, offered advice when the young couple was thinking of buying a summer cottage at the shore, and cooked for Jackie's husband and children when Jackie had to spend two weeks in the hospital.

At some point, neighborly ties can shade into something deeper. When age differences between neighbors mimic the status of parent and child or grandmother and grandchild, there is the possibility of the relationship encompassing the roles of those family members—and the ties of affection and loyalty that go with them. Utah State University professor Gerald R. Adams, an authority on family and human development, has noticed the proliferation of honorary "aunts" and "uncles" as adopted family members. He says, "Their numbers are increasing as our society is increasingly mobile, as the number of extended families diminishes, as fewer people live near their blood relations, as more people remain single or childless and find that they want to re-create a family."

The opportunity to develop such relationships is hardly limited to people who live next door to each other. Total strangers can create close bonds when both parties need them and a framework is provided. The foster-grandparent program in Wayne County, Michigan, is an example of this phenomenon. The relationship begins when older volunteers are paired with teenage parents to listen to them talk about their problems and offer counsel and general support. Many of the young parents do not have extended families of their own and thus find a unique opportunity in the program to learn about life from the perspective of an older generation. The foster grandparents often develop close relationships with these teenagers, forming bonds that are as strong as those between true grandparents and their grandchildren.

The future holds potential for much more of this kind of relationship. People in their sixties and seventies will have fewer grandchildren than they do today, as successive generations produce fewer children. Many elder baby boomers will have the time, energy, and reservoir of affection to develop a supportive network for helping younger people. Youngsters who do not have grandparents will welcome the opportunity to draw on the variety and depth of experience offered by these elders.

Similarly close ties will develop between people brought together even more informally. We already have matchmaking operations for those who seek roommates or potential mates. A New Hampshire program called People Match, for example, introduces individuals who wish to participate in home sharing. Older couples have taken advantage of the service to bring into their homes students who will help them out with household work in exchange for living space and meals. One couple reported that they were beginning to view the student living with them as almost a son.

Matchups by mail have followed a progressive path up the age ladder. They started with pen pals, usually young people of diverse backgrounds and experience, often living far away from each other, who wanted to find new and interesting friends they could not meet in conventional ways. By the 1980s the idea had expanded to personals ads by people seeking romantic partners. The next stage could be ads placed by old and young alike, describing themselves and what they want in a friendship/family relationship.

Picture the possibilities in the newspapers in the year 2020: "69-year-old widow, healthy and active, seeks young couple with at least one child for mutual support, division of domestic labor, intergenerational companionship, and all the emotional goodies that used to come with family life. Willing to consider adopting couple and child as heirs."

That last line carries the matchup progression to the next logical step: It adds the rights of inheritance to the benefits of the "adopted" family. The large number of older people in the coming century who have outlived their family and friends may be in a quandary about what to do with their assets when they die. Adoption is an institution already in place, easily adaptable to "parents" and "children" of various ages.

Andrew Knickerbocker may have had this in mind when he put his ad in the local newspaper. The 88-year-old Texan wants to find a young person—preferably a writer—to move into his house and live with him and his 82-year-old wife, who is in poor health and is sometimes forgetful. Mr. Knickerbocker doesn't need housekeeping help, which he can afford. He wants someone to talk to, "someone to be a member of the family," he says. "We would leave them part of what we have," he adds, "like we would family." If this kind of relationship becomes common, states will have to modify their adoption laws to protect both parties in this delicate exchange of obligations and responsibilities.

## OTHER VARIETIES OF FAMILY EXPERIENCE

The baby boomers have matured at a time of sexual experimentation and increasing acceptance of same-sex romantic relationships. Thus it is no surprise to us to find more openness among the older people for whom a homosexual relationship is their family. In 1985, "Why Is Grandma Different?" appeared in the "Woman Today" section of a prominent women's magazine, demonstrating that lesbian relationships among older adults are becoming more widely accepted. A mother, trying to explain Grandma's behavior to her grandchild, tells the child: "Grandma's not different, darling. You know how Daddy and I love each other? Well, Marina and Grandma love each other the same way." That *Ladies' Home Journal* could look upon this match with such equanimity suggests a growing tolerance for such unconventional relationships.

Groups have been organized to meet the needs of the older homosexual community. Senior Action in a Gay Environment (SAGE), which provides supportive programs and services to older homosexuals, is one of them. Its coordinator of social services says: "The most important thing when one gets older is reminiscing. When straight people are talking [to each other] about their children and grandchildren, who is there for gay people to talk to?" Two gay men in their seventies, whose relationship is now in its fifty-eighth year, said of their experience with the group: "We had a good life but we were reaching that stage when we were losing many of our friends. We were very lonely people. Then we heard about SAGE and found a new family."

And, of course, many family-style relationships will continue to grow from the bonds of old-fashioned friendship. The title of a book by feminist Karen Lindsey that appeared in the early 1980s captured the spirit of this phenomenon: *Friends as Family*. As the baby boomers have developed close friendships, more of them are consciously investing these relationships with a permanence and centrality previously reserved for family. Thus their friendships provide the extended family that the peculiarities of demography may have otherwise denied them.

These *ad hoc* families will open a new branch of family law. Where property and obligations are involved, the law can never be far behind. Before long we should see the development of standardized friendship/family contracts somewhat resembling marriage contracts. What contractual rights are implied when such agreements do not spell them out? Here is much virgin territory for lawyers and judges to clear.

Passing on property within new kinds of families is already creating challenges for people in other fields who must deal with this phenomenon on a professional basis. "The graying of America, the gaying of America, cohabitation, and remarriage now put planners in the difficult position of counseling people whose estate plans are complicated by unusual heirs or beneficiaries," writes sociologist Jeffrey R. Rosenfeld. "It is no wonder that some estate planners are turning to family therapists and social consultants for tips on how better to serve a changing clientele."

An aging population coinciding with an already evolving family will thus continue to reshape the way we live. In the future we can expect this trend to accelerate. If our response to changing family roles and relationships is to satisfy the needs of each generation, we will have to remain flexible enough to accept and take advantage of new ways of looking at hearth and home.

# 3

# Where Will They Live?

"People want to stay where they are."

<small>LEAH DOBKIN, housing expert for the American Association of Retired Persons, describing the direction of the senior-housing industry</small>

In the winter of 1976, 60-year-old Marty Kirsch and his wife Eileen, 54, read an ad in their hometown newspaper for a small retirement community then under construction in Boca Raton, Florida. It was a "Git Acquainted" offer from the builders of Aloha Gardens. For only two dollars plus round-trip airfare, the developers would pick them up at the airport in Florida, chauffeur them to the building site, give them the grand tour, and put them up for a night at a hotel. The Kirsches went, loved the palm trees and swimming pool, and bought a condominium unit. They moved in the next year.

In 1980, the Kirsches left Aloha Gardens. They turned their backs on the shuffleboard courts, community recreation room, and bridge club to move into an ordinary apartment house in a nearby community where the ages were mixed. They did this, they said, "because the ambulance was coming too often."

Marty and Eileen Kirsch's generation had migrated once before to meet their changing needs at a new stage in their lives. But then the trip was shorter. In the 1950s, as they became parents, they asked, "Where is the best place to raise these children?" And they answered in almost one voice: suburbia.

As they came into their retirement years, however, the answers were not so clear. Parenthood—even of the baby-boom generation—was a lot more well defined than this new life stage in which they now found themselves. Their society offered "pitifully few clear guidelines as to how individuals are expected to conduct their lives when they retire," as geographer Stephen M. Polant, of the University of Florida, put it.

With no clear-cut place to fit into society, many older people chose to live apart from younger people, a trend that began in the late 1950s with the rise of the large planned-retirement communities. The president of the homeowners' association in Sun City, Arizona, the country's largest retirement community, was asked why he had chosen age-segregated living. "I'm an outcast because I'm 67 years old," he said bitterly. "I think the whole bunch of us are outcasts who have found a way of living without impinging on anybody, or bothering anybody." "It was an experiment for all of us," one of the first residents now recalls of the first large new town to restrict its population to older adults.

Yet despite the newspaper and TV ads for retirement communities in sunny, often distant climates, and the developers' announcements of new projects for "seniors" in the past three decades, most elders have chosen to age in place, in the house or at least the general area where they raised their children. And that's not likely to change in the future. Kelly Somoza of U.S. Homes, which builds more single-family homes in this country than any other developer, expects that "most people are going to want to stay near their families, not move to Florida."

Every major survey supports this prediction. For example, of fifteen hundred people over 60 who were polled in 1986 by the American Association of Retired Persons, 79 percent had no desire to leave their homes. In 1987, 98 percent of the thirty-five hundred people over the age of 55 questioned by the National Association of Senior Living Industries had the same response.

And even the limited although well-publicized migration that we've seen to Sunbelt retirement communities is likely to taper off as a new generation makes up the ranks of America's elders. Underlying social and economic trends point to a busier future for those in this stage of the life cycle in coming decades. For example, early retirement, which has funneled older people into the Sun Cities and Leisure Worlds, is likely to fade in the twenty-first century, as we shall see in the next chapter.

## THE TIMES THEY ARE A-CHANGIN'

What, then, is the future, if any, of "senior" housing? It's likely that we *will* see specially designed and modified dwellings for older people in the next three decades. Baby boomers figure to play a large part in the growth of this housing in two stages. First, certain kinds of housing arrangements we are about to describe will help boomers assist their aging parents without requiring them to take their mothers and fathers into their own homes. Second, baby boomers will begin to evolve their own elder-housing patterns that reflect the particular values and historical experiences of their generation.

At present, about 90 percent of Americans over the age of 55 live in regular housing, not shelter especially designed or designated for older people. But experts in the mortgage banking industry say this figure will drop to 80 percent in the next ten to twenty years as the top of the population pyramid broadens and greater longevity puts many New Elders in the market for modified accommodations.

The later years, the seventies and eighties, to which so many people are now surviving and which even more will reach in the future, often bring at least minor physical impairments. Totally independent living is not always possible for these older people. Americans now choose a variety of types of housing when this problem arises. Aside from nursing homes, these include congregate and life-care facilities, in which services ranging from prepared communal meals to medical care are included in the price of an apartment; shared homes that bring together unrelated individuals for economy, companionship, and mutual support; and accessory apartments, separate quarters created by renovating part of a single-family house. The reverse mortgage, a variety of home equity loan that enables older people who are cash poor but asset rich to remain in their homes, and Elder Cottage Housing Opportunity (ECHO) housing, in which a small, temporary cottage for elders is placed next to a single-family home, will also play an increasing role in housing older people. None of these has yet become *the* solution, partly because each of these choices meets a different need.

But one thing is clear: Today's elders do not want to move in with their children, nor are elders likely to want to do so in the future. And this is in the American tradition. Contrary to what many people think, the nuclear-family household prevailed even in the nineteenth century. "Families shared their household space with other kin only as a last resort, during periods of housing shortage or severe economic constraint. . . . In most situations, even widows tried to maintain their own household by taking in strangers as tenants rather than live in other people's houses," according to family historian Tamara K. Hareven.

Elders two to three decades from now will bring to their choice of housing different life experiences than do present-day retirees. And since they will be entering their later years in such large numbers, the way they solve their housing problems will go far toward determining what our suburbs and cities will be like at that time.

Elder baby boomers who wish to migrate in their later years will shift the focus of retirement communities from the Sunbelt to college and university towns throughout the country. The congregate-living housing industry, which may be headed for a crash in the next ten years, will be rescued in the third decade of the twenty-first century by aging yuppies. And boomers will impart to elder housing—already taking on more of a communal aspect than most people realize—the singular community-oriented spirit that characterized their generation in their youth.

## Fun in the Sun

The premise behind the Sunbelt retirement communities now occupied by New Elders and the survivors of the Old Guard generation was based on conditions peculiar to the time in which they reached their sixties. "In a society that tends to define an adult male without an occupational role as some sort of deviant, retirement contains an element of degradation, even when tied to an inevitable stage in the life cycle," Carl Gersuny, a sociologist at the University of Rhode Island, wrote in a 1970 study of the rhetoric used to promote the retirement home industry. "There is an inescapable implication of being 'put on the shelf.'" David B. Wolfe, founder of the National Association of Senior Living Industries, put it more bluntly: "In American society, you are what you do. When you retire, in society's view you do nothing—therefore, you are nothing."

Del Webb, one of the leading real-estate developers in the United States in the 1950s, saw this void as an opportunity. If retirees had not yet found their place in society, he would give them one. Webb proceeded to build in Arizona and Florida what are still this country's largest self-contained retirement communities. To promote this new style of living, he redefined old age as something that was decidedly more upbeat, marketing his projects with frequent use of phrases like "active retirement" and "the golden years."

Del Webb's Sun City developments, the destination of many of these migrants, were enormous undertakings. The Arizona unit now numbers about fifty thousand residents living on its 10,500 acres. They have access to eleven golf courses, seventy-two shuffleboard courts, and seven swimming pools, among other amenities. The Sun City in Florida, though smaller, has artificial canals and its own zip code. Each Webb development has its own restaurants, shopping centers, and banks. And they have been models for several other large developments, such as Century Village and Leisure World, as well as many smaller versions. One Leisure World development in California "sprawls across 600 gently rolling acres that are constantly seeded, weeded, and mowed by 170 full-time gardeners," according to an observer.

These palm-treed places in the California, Florida, and Arizona sun—and more than two thousand smaller-scale developments like them—have become almost shorthand for "retirement" in our culture, although they actually house fewer than a million of our elders, not quite 3 percent of all Americans of retirement age.

The developments have also been the subject of a good deal of social criticism. Journalist Frances FitzGerald, for example, visited Sun City. Such places "are without precedent," she marveled; "no society recorded in history has ever had whole villages—whole cities—composed exclusively of elder people." She saw a good deal of emptiness: people who "have no jobs, no families around them, and not very much future." Their surroundings, in FitzGerald's view, were "already so homogeneous as to threaten the boundaries of the self."

*Cocoon,* the only major movie (besides its sequel, *Cocoon 2*) to deal with these communities, concerns the efforts of residents of one of these developments not to sit back and enjoy the good life but to transcend the reason for their community's being: old age. With the shadow of mortality looming larger, they seek the fountain of youth;

they want out. The benign aliens who offer to take them away promise them *more productive* as well as much longer lives.

The specter of eternal rest lurking behind retirement's full-time leisure was a sensitive issue for Del Webb. When the owner of a parcel of land across the road from the eighty-nine hundred acres of farmland that were to become Sun City, Arizona, threatened to open a cemetery, the real-estate magnate knew he was cornered. Gravestones and funeral processions would have threatened the illusion of permanent happiness Webb was trying to sell. So he bought his neighbor out.

But the Kirsches' reaction to retirement-community living—that it was too much of old age—does not speak for everyone who has tried it. Many people thrive in the protected, active life of the self-contained, age-segregated community. They like the insularity. Separated from the rest of society—sometimes by tall, barbed-wire-topped concrete walls and twenty-four-hour manned security gates—they can be with their own.

Retirement is not yet a coherent way of life with distinct and clear roles and values. And these members of the New Elder and Old Guard generations may sense something important in these retirement communities that, under the circumstances, promotes their psychological self-preservation.

The idea that age-segregated living can contribute to the emotional well-being of older people—at least for the present generations of elders—has been supported by research. In 1980 Rebecca G. Adams, a sociologist at the University of North Carolina at Greensboro, conducted a study of friendship among women in both age-segregated and age-integrated housing in a Chicago suburb. She found that "age-segregated housing seemed to enhance the development of emotionally close, local friendships." Since everybody in these communities had moved to get there, well-established cliques were originally absent, and people had to make new friends.

Adams also saw a "leveling effect," caused by relocation. The age-segregated residents "emphasized the similarities of their conditions rather than the differences. Elsewhere in the community, the accumulated differences of a lifetime seemed to have had a larger impact on current lives." For example, in nearby areas where the ages were mixed, widows, divorced people, and those who had never married were not likely to see one another as potential friends. But this was not the case in the age-segregated housing.

Other observers have noted that once retirees in these communities do get to know each other, ties to fellow residents can become so strong that people replace their own children with their new neighbors in their wills.

But as they isolate themselves from other age groups, the residents of Sunbelt retirement communities often limit their access to and sympathy for the wider world. Many of them shut out their families. "Some people here visit their kids out of charity," a Sun Citian remarked. "Do you want to sacrifice five months of good weather for three days—Thanksgiving, Christmas, and Easter?" another replied when questioned about leaving his children who lived up north. "They have a right to their own lives," he added.

Even grandchildren are not above reproach. At Aloha Gardens, young children visiting at Christmastime evoked pointed disapproval when several residents spotted the kids walking on the grass. Another Florida development actually hands out the house rules: "Children require the constant supervision of those responsible for them. They must be kept from interfering in any way with the quiet and comfort of residents."

### Snowbirds

Less massive than the Sun Cities and their spin-offs, the many trailer parks and mobile-home sites dotting the Sunbelt represent a somewhat different approach to retirement living. Their inhabitants, the fabled empty nesters known as "snowbirds," go south and west when winter comes, heading for such favored destinations as the Valley of the Sun near Phoenix, but they leave for home with the first sign of spring.

While they're around, these part-time residents have a major impact on the areas in which they alight. A region's economy may, in fact, depend on them. The two hundred thousand or so who wintered in the Phoenix area in 1986 pumped about $380 million into local coffers. Social Security checks add $11.5 billion a year to the Florida economy. But these seasonal migrants also create traffic jams for part of the year and overwhelm local medical facilities. In some areas year-round residents have to put off elective surgery when snowbirds come to roost and overcrowd the hospitals.

In recent years, the retirement parks at which these transients stay have begun to look more like full-time retirement communities. The management may offer planned recreational activities. Some residents wear name tags stating how long they've been coming down and where they come from. Yet these places maintain an air of impermanence, which is just what their clients want.

### Natural Limits

The nation's popular warm-weather spots have proved to be hospitable environments for the permanent and transient retirement communities that have flourished there in the past thirty years. But the best years in the Sunbelt may already be behind us. Florida has not experienced a devastating hurricane since these retirement developments sprang up, and a big one is overdue, as is a catastrophic earthquake in southern California. Retirees in Arizona may rejoice in their rock gardens, which finally vanquish the implacable crabgrass enemy of their younger years. But they are also discovering that their water supply, which they took for granted where they came from, can be terribly finite.

As development pushes into new areas, we can expect Mother Nature to put up considerable resistance. It's not just alligators foraging in Florida backyards. In New Port Richey, Florida, a retirement community was overrun by black toads. "The whole yard looks like it's moving," one of the community's administrators admitted. "They just completely cover everything. It's unreal."

These areas are experiencing enormous growth—as much because of burgeoning economies as because of the migration of older people. With that growth has come air pollution and bumper-to-bumper traffic. In Arizona, zoning bodies have begun to put strict limits on new trailer parks. Florida may eventually have to take even more drastic measures to halt growth. Should present trends continue, "by 2020 it will take 44 lanes to carry the traffic on I-95 from Miami to Ft. Lauderdale," according to Daniel P. Moynihan, the United States Senate's expert on public works. "Pretty soon there won't be anything left of Florida!"

### Closer to Home

There are already some signs in the housing choices of aging Eisenhower Generation couples and some of the younger New Elders that point toward locations where many retiring baby boomers will migrate, although the boomers are likely to give such moves their own special twist.

As the traditional warm-weather oases slowly become covered with concrete, increasing numbers of affluent older Americans have been willing to pioneer new retirement areas. Seneca, South Carolina, Silver Bay, Minnesota, and Mount Greylock, Massachusetts, are not exactly Palm Beach or Saint Petersburg, but these rural areas are accessible to recreation, and they have not yet been overrun by development. They are also likely to be closer to family and the resident's original home.

Communities such as these couldn't be happier to see an influx of new, older residents. Many have lost old industries, and rural counties can usually anticipate the creation of one service-economy job for every eight new residents they can entice to move in. They go all out to recruit them. Some towns brag about their safe streets, others build roads making natural features such as lakes accessible to retirement housing.

Even closer to home for most Americans are certain rural counties just beyond the suburbs of major metropolitan areas which have become known as "gentrifying counties," partly because of the well-off older people who have moved into them. The Poconos, the mountain country in northeastern Pennsylvania near New York City, is a perfect example. There are five hundred such counties in the United States and, according to Calvin Beale, chief demographer at the United States Department of Agriculture, they may well be the fastest-growing parts of our country in the 1990s.

Many of the high-income people who move here are like Fred Washburn, a 56-year-old television commercial producer, and his wife, Beth, a 52-year-old literary agent, who bought a weekend/summer home in the area and now plan to move in permanently when they retire. They may have been lucky to get in on the ground floor, because the prices of houses in their area are increasing rapidly.

Given their environmental concerns and their experience with gentrification in older urban neighborhoods, the Early Boomers are likely to continue these trends. Closer ties to family, the likelihood that they will continue working at least part-time well into their sixties—the reasons for which we will present in the next chapter—and an orientation toward keeping in touch with "what's happening" in the world beyond retirement ghettos will make the gentrification of rural counties close to cities and of older suburban areas particularly attractive to them.

But we are also likely to see a phenomenon almost completely native to their generation. The destination of many elder boomers who want to retire "to" somewhere is likely to be the outskirts of a college town. This is, after all, the atmosphere in which so many of them matured, unlike their parents' generation. They are much more likely to want to subscribe to folk-music concerts and classic-film series than to engage in community sings, more attracted to prominent visiting lecturers and creative artists and the variety of physical recreation available in a college gym than to arts and crafts and shuffleboard.

Small liberal-arts colleges will probably forge partnerships with real-estate developers to build condominium town houses in outlying areas near their academic communities. With a smaller generation of college students due in coming decades, the schools will need boomer elders and will make class auditing and recreational facility privileges part of the housing packages. These arrangements will encourage developers to endow cultural activities at nearby schools, with the proviso that residents of their projects receive reduced rates on tickets.

We could also see part-time employment for boomer elders tied into housing arrangements. For those whose busy careers caused them to miss time with their own children—or not have children at all—a second chance could loom for them now. Students living off campus might rent rooms in these new developments with elder boomers serving as houseparents or resident counselors.

This kind of housing is, by definition, intergenerational. Rather than shutting themselves off from the young, baby boomers who make such a choice will be able to continue to influence the values and tastes of succeeding generations.

### Living Together

Several years ago, Lina Poleo returned to her seventh-grade classroom in the Cambridge, Massachusetts, elementary school from which she graduated in 1924. At about the same time, another woman her age went back to the factory in Waltham in the Bay State where she had begun working at the age of 14. These women were not just taking a nostalgic trip back to their roots. They have moved in and set up housekeeping.

Across the country, old hotels, hospitals, churches, schools, and factories have been transformed into elder housing through federal grants from the Administration on Aging along with efforts by local government agencies and private nonprofit organizations. Many of these projects provide a community as well as a home. The residents, elders in their seventies and eighties, have access to a variety of services on the premises; in some facilities, they eat one or two meals together daily. The idea is to provide something between totally independent living and a nursing home.

Nonprofit groups have provided for a population of a few thousand at best in various states. Charlotte Muller, a professor of health economics in the Department of Community Medicine of the Mount Sinai School of Medicine in New York City, studied these congregate living facilities, as they are called, in each state in the mid-1980s. She concluded that the influence of this concept on the lives of most older people would be minimal, at least into the mid-1990s, unless the idea attracted considerably more money and attention.

Why not meet this same need among more affluent people through the private sector—but with many more amenities? Both couples and the widowed in this age group who are still living in the family home may feel they don't need a large house anymore. Developers have taken notice. According to real-estate consultant Faye Godwin, "There used to be virtually nothing in the market that appealed to people who were between 75 and 84 years old and were in the middle-to-upper-income levels." But there is now. Some of these hotellike facilities for the well elderly, in which residents live in separate apartments but share one or two meals together, are located in resort areas, but many more aim to draw their population from elders living nearby. The great intangible that comes along with this way of living is the built-in companionship it provides. "Entering an adult congregate living facility is like buying a family," according to demographer Brad Edmondson.

By the mid-1980s, private industry began to put large amounts of money into congregate care. In late 1986, *The Wall Street Journal* noted the trend:

> Retirement housing . . . geared toward affluent "elder seniors" over 75 years old has suddenly become the nation's hottest real-estate market. Dozens of developers as well as major hotel, hospital and nursing-home chains, insurers, banks and even a big cosmetic maker—Avon Products, Inc.—are jumping into a field long dominated by nonprofit groups.

One factor that enticed private capital was that unlike nursing homes, these projects are not regulated by the government. About 70 percent of the congregate-care facilities constructed in 1988 were privately owned.

At Freedom Village, where the average resident is a woman of 78 with net worth approaching $250,000, the director describes the services this way: "We sell love, security, and support, not just housing. This is the final consumer choice. They'll die in our arms." All in all, as one resident remarked, apparently without a trace of irony, "the only place better than this is heaven."

Residents pay for these services in several different ways. Some facilities ask them to put down a large security deposit—perhaps as much as fifteen thousand dollars—and pay a monthly rent, say, sixteen hundred dollars. The basic cost may also include a certain amount of medical care, possibly in a facility on the premises or nearby. Or medical services may be limited to a nurse on the grounds. In some facilities residents have access to full medical services "in-house," and they pay for them as they use them.

In the estimated eight hundred (and growing at the rate of fifty per year) continuing-care retirement communities—a more comprehensive form of congregate living—that now house 250,000 elders, residents pay a lump sum entrance fee and monthly service fees. They can choose from a full continuum of shelter, residential services, and amenities. Long-term health-care services in these communities are available in four different contractual ways.

The first offers long-term nursing care for little or no substantial increase in monthly payments except for normal inflation adjustments.

In the second, only a specified amount of long-term nursing care is included in the monthly payment, with the remainder provided on a fee-for-service basis, sometimes at a discounted rate.

The third offers long-term nursing care only on a fee-for-service basis.

The fourth offers a continuum of housing, residential, and health-care services provided on a fee-for-service basis; no contracts or entrance fees are required.

Will substantial numbers of baby boomers want to live out their lives in this way? One particular group, the yuppies, probably will, but first the industry that created this form of housing will probably pass through a massive shake-up.

Many continuing-care facilities that had committed themselves to supplying residents with lifetime medical services are in trouble, and the worst may be yet to come. "There are a number who have seen the data and figured, 'Oh, they've got to be an easy buck,' " Don Redfoot of the American Association of Retired Persons observed. "Suddenly, 10 years later, you have a population that averages 75, and the tennis courts are empty while the clinics are full." Of 109 continuing-care institutions studied recently by Dr. Hirsch Ruchlin of Cornell University Medical College, nearly 50 percent had either a negative net worth profile or negative net income. Bankruptcies among the more than six hundred facilities of this type could be a snowballing scandal in the 1990s.

Many of the congregate-care living facilities, which probably number about a thousand now (there are no precise figures), have also run into trouble. The problem is that the projects were "overbuilt, overpriced, oversized and undermanaged," according to *Mature Market Report.*

Congregate care is an idea whose time has not quite come—although it will. A close look at the demographics shows why developers jumped the gun. They noticed the coming increase in the number of people over age 75 in the 1990s. But they failed to see that the growth of this segment will temporarily level off beginning ten years from now. The real rise in the post-75 age bracket won't come until the third decade of the twenty-first century, when the baby boomers will be entering their sixties and their surviving parents will be well on in years. Then builders will have a growing primary market, with truly explosive growth just over the horizon.

At that point, elder boomer families in which either the boomers or their parents are fairly well heeled will probably want to take advantage of this kind of housing for New Elders in their eighties to help answer the question, "How can older adults with now-aged parents make sure that their mothers and fathers who can still function have decent housing, adequate services, access to medical facilities if they need it, and companionship—all the while not impinging on the lifestyle of their increasingly elder children?"

By 2020 Early Boomers themselves will be approaching their seventies and some of them are likely to opt for this style of living, particularly in developments built in downtown areas that offer access to shopping and cultural activities. These are the yuppies who may want to continue the lifestyle to which they had become accustomed. They will have passed their working years hiring someone to provide household services, will probably have had little time for cooking, will have depended on restaurants and take-out foods for meals, and may have been so busy with their careers that they relied mostly on their spouses for companionship. The death of a husband or wife could make them prime customers for congregate living.

## Home Equity Loans with a Difference

"Developers hoping to find a lucrative market among the increasing numbers of elderly in the United States are learning that their competition is not with the retirement home, but in the single-family home," reports the United States Senate Special Committee on Aging. Whenever possible, most older Americans want to stay put. As Robert Butler, former head of the National Institute on Aging, put it: "The best place to retire is the neighborhood where you spent your life."

As income decreases past the age of 70 and expenses for services like medical care increase, staying in the family home may become harder to manage financially. But remaining in one's home is so appealing that as New Elders age into their late seventies and eighties, we will see the enactment of many measures to enable them to continue living in their homes whenever possible. Both the private sector and government will respond to this need—and to pressure from their baby-boomer children for whom such proposals will ease the burden of caring for dependents at both ends of the age spectrum.

Although not yet widely known, the reverse mortgage is one example of the imaginative use of financial services to bolster the ability of "asset-rich and income-poor" Americans to stay in their homes as they age. Sometimes called RAMs (reverse annuity mortgages) or IRMAs (individual reverse mortgage accounts), these mortgages are a variation on the home equity loan, aimed at older people who find themselves strapped for funds when their income doesn't keep pace with their expenses. The typical borrower is a widow in her seventies or eighties whose health has declined.

Like other home equity loans, this mortgage converts the value of a house into cash, but in this case the funds are earmarked for a single purpose: paying costs associated with maintaining a single-family house or condominium apartment. The bank pays the borrower a specified monthly amount for expenses such as utilities, repairs, taxes, or the maintenance charge on a co-op or condominium apartment. Repayment is delayed until the owner sells the house or dies.

Many of these reverse-mortgage arrangements are quite open-ended.

The loan can remain in effect as long as the owner lives, with the proviso that the bank gets a share of any increase in equity that a rising real-estate market might bring. For the bank, the payoff comes at the time the house is sold, whether the occasion is the owner's decision to move or his or her death.

In its first three years, this practice has created only about fifteen hundred mortgages because both borrowers and banks have been wary about pioneering such unfamiliar territory. The banks, for example, fear that too many people might outlive their equity in an open-ended agreement and never be able to repay what they owe. But the reverse mortgage's growth potential through the 1990s and into the beginning of the twenty-first century is enormous because federal insurance for these mortgages is in the works—the missing stamp of legitimacy that will put such loans on the map—according to Ken Scholen, executive director of the National Center for Home Equity Conversion.

The reverse-mortgage concept has major implications for increasing the options of both elderly parents and their adult children. For Eisenhower Generation and Early Boomer children it should relieve the fear of having to bail out aging parents if rising expenses related to the maintenance of their house threaten to swamp them and their children. It could provide some insurance against the necessity of having to take the parents in if some combination of setbacks such as medical emergencies or bad investments puts aging parents in a financial hole. But the parents' opting for this financial assistance package will also cut into what the adult children would otherwise expect to inherit. So we can anticipate some very interesting and involved family discussions before older Americans sign on *this* dotted line.

Reverse mortgages, however, are only the wave of the immediate future—the next ten to fifteen years. It's not likely that this way of coping with old-age housing needs will still be of major importance in 2020, when the first of the Early Boomers are in their seventies. Many of the widows who are likely to opt for reverse mortgages today were not eligible for survivors' benefits from their husbands' pensions and so they experienced a decline in their income after their husbands died. But the Employee Retirement Income Security Act of 1974 stipulated that benefits be paid to pensioners' survivors. And the prevalence of boomer women who have worked and qualified for their own pensions also suggests that there will be fewer customers for reverse mortgages in the future.

### "Privacy with Proximity"

What will the bulk of housing built especially for elders look like by 2020? Add up the following: (1) a large stock of oversize housing—too big for most families of the future; (2) many more people age 65 and up than there are now—most of them healthy, although with minor physical impairments, who need a little help with everyday tasks such as shopping; (3) the continuing desire of most elders and their adult children to stay reasonably near each other but not to occupy the same living quarters. This combination of conditions points to one solution: many extended families sharing the same building or grounds but in distinctly separate quarters, each with its own entrance—what the AARP has called "privacy with proximity." The families occupying these houses will include Late Boomers and their aging parents and, eventually, Early Boomers and their adult children.

For some families the answer will be a two-family house in which parents and children each have one of the units. These structures— "mother-and-daughter" houses, as they are sometimes known—already exist in some urban areas and they will be very much in demand. But we probably will not see too much new construction of these models.

Instead, people will be inclined to adapt already existing housing because it will be cheaper. The diminished number of people in their prime house-buying years in the future combined with the trend toward smaller families will put downward pressure on the price of multibedroom houses. Extended families will find it to their benefit, if they don't already own one, to combine their resources to purchase a house and renovate it, creating an accessory apartment within the house. About 40 percent of the single-family houses in America are already zoned for this purpose. Real-estate agents and contractors may work in partnership to create and market these renovations.

Most of the time elder parents will probably occupy the newly created smaller space, but don't bet on it! In many families economic clout and intergenerational relationships (especially if the adult children don't have their own kids) will consign the 30- and 40-year-old children to the apartment.

Adele Smithson's family has already made this move. The 66-year-old Toledo, Ohio, widow was sharing her home with her Late Boomer son and daughter-in-law as they attempted to accumulate a nest egg to set up housekeeping on their own. In Mrs. Smithson's case, rising property taxes and some reverses from investments her late husband had made in the stock market had squeezed her retirement income. With the help of a low-interest loan from a state agency, she was able to have the top floor of her house converted into an apartment with a separate kitchen and bathroom and its own entrance. She chose this space while her son and daughter-in-law took the downstairs. The rent they pay her covers her expenses and then some.

Sharing space in a renovated house is not confined to extended families, even now. People over the age of 50 own more than half the homes in the United States containing five or more rooms. Many of them have already converted part of the home to an accessory apartment so that they can rent it, often to an older person.

Divided housing makes the most efficient use of existing housing stock. This practice is likely to make its mark everywhere, even where zoning ordinances now mandate the single-family house. With the number of older people—especially the very old—certain to increase dramatically, communities that don't ease zoning restrictions will have to come up with housing assistance for the middle class as we move into the twenty-first century. They will find it in their interest to accept this basic shift in our housing patterns that permits family members to help each other and allows nonrelated elders to make practical housing arrangements for themselves.

As renovating housing for elders gains momentum, the building industry will get a boost. Such renovations will sustain demand for doors, wallboard, locks, insulation, and small appliances, even as the sale of some building materials used in new construction, such as shingles and wood beams, diminishes. Look for a burgeoning market for folding-wall dividers that are easy to move and also sufficiently soundproof to create totally separate living areas.

## An ECHO from the Future

An unusually flexible housing option that has been touted for the past decade by the American Association of Retired Persons is something it calls ECHO: Elder Cottage Housing Opportunity. The idea originated with the Australian "granny flat," a small, temporary, prefabricated cottage that goes up at the side or in back of a permanent single-family home. Built on lots of at least six thousand square feet, a 450-square-foot unit of this kind usually houses the parents of the adult children who live in the permanent house.

Such buildings have proved enormously popular in the suburbs of Melbourne in the state of Victoria, where the government superseded local zoning ordinances, paid for the installation and removal of the cottages, and rented the units to their occupants. As the periodical *Aging International* noted:

> It became politically feasible to move forward with the "granny flat" concept in Australia in the early 1970s because of more favorable attitudes towards the aged, the recognition that older people make good neighbors and that families wish to continue to support their older members, and the realization that it was much more cost-effective to keep older people integrated in the community than place them in institutions.

Families split by divorce found them especially useful because the elder parents were around to help with child care while the adult child, usually a daughter, was nearby to offer the parents whatever support they needed. In rural Switzerland, where additions are often grafted onto farmhouses to provide quarters for aging parents, strong intergenerational bonds are also fostered through the custom of having children make frequent overnight visits to Grandma and Grandpa's house.

Companies in California and Pennsylvania manufacture the units, selling them for less than twenty-five thousand dollars, installed. With a little exterior decorating, they can easily be made to resemble the main house. But are suburban Americans ready to permit these additions—about the size of a two-car garage—to their neighbors' lots? Not with any great fervor. They don't exactly conform to the suburban dream of the isolated single-family home on a spacious wooded plot. And of course they often violate local zoning. At the moment, this sector of the housing industry is more a quaint sideshow than a snowballing trend.

ECHO's popularity is by no means assured, but it would be a mistake to assume that such an approach to elder housing will never gain widespread acceptance. When the demand and the need for such departures from the past prove large enough, people are usually willing to let go of all sorts of assumptions. And, in fact, the nuclear family of 2 parents and 2.5 children which is supposed to live in that single-family suburban house is rapidly becoming extinct. So perhaps we will hear a candidate several presidential elections from now appealing for the vote of elders and their adult children with a subsidized ECHO housing program. Besides partial subsidies, the government might offer various kinds of concessions to induce people to opt for this kind of housing for their older members. Under the 1987 additions to the tax code, for example, people who own a second home occupied by relatives from whom they collect no rent can deduct the interest on the mortgage from their taxes. That's just a sample of the kinds of incentives we might see.

Beyond economic incentives, we may see such accommodations become popular if divorce remains as prevalent in the baby boomers' children's generation as it has been in their parents'. For a young or middle-aged divorced mother with children, ECHO housing could be a godsend. Her baby-sitters would not be built-in, but they would be even closer than next door if they occupied a cottage on her lot. And for her elder boomer parents, such an arrangement might be the perfect answer to what to do about remaining close to their grandchildren and providing themselves with housing whose more modest dimensions better fit their needs in their current stage of life.

### Sharing

"I am a recent widow and have a large, older house that I would like to share with another person," a woman wrote to the "What Should I Do?" department of *Modern Maturity*. "I don't know where to start looking for a compatible boarder. Do you have any suggestions?" The magazine referred her to one of the organizations that have sprung up to match people who want to share housing.

Programs to foster shared housing have increased by 800 percent since 1981. Some of the people who wish to share space in their homes are looking for a way to make ends meet, but a substantial number are middle-class. In a 1980 survey, about 30 percent of the clients for shared-housing programs had homes worth more than one hundred thousand dollars.

The most prominent organization fostering this solution to elder housing is the Shared Housing Resource Center in Philadelphia, a service begun by the Gray Panthers. It's a clearinghouse for information about local groups that make housing matches. Many of these housing matchmakers emphasize intergenerational pairing, usually an older homeowner taking in a younger renter or boarder.

It's a growing trend. In the mid-1980s, about 670,000 Americans who were over 65 and not institutionalized were living with people to whom they were not related, a 35 percent increase in this practice in ten years. According to the AARP's Leah Dobkin, the association's poll of its members to determine whether they would consider such a living arrangement produced a "yes" 15 percent of the time. That figure only looks small. "A few years ago," she said, "most older people wouldn't have known what we are talking about."

The growing acceptance of shared housing echoes the past and foreshadows one of the most interesting trends of the future. As late as the 1930s, boardinghouses, which provided both lodging and meals, could still be found in large numbers in American towns and cities. Most New Elders can remember them. They were often run by widows and are still visible in old mystery movies on late-night TV—their variety of residents is the perfect cast for guessing "whodunit." By no means occupied by the rootless or less respectable elements of society, boardinghouses were an acceptable way of filling housing needs, temporary or long-term, for people of all ages and circumstances. An old bachelor, for example, could be in residence, as well as the young working girl who had come to the city from a farm to get her start in the world.

In their heyday, in the mid-nineteenth century, even the well-to-do might live in boardinghouses. "High rents and an inability to find servants at reasonable wages were the reasons usually given for the prevalence of this fashionable makeshift among well-off couples above the Mason-Dixon Line," writes social historian J. C. Furnas. "It might even turn permanent; children were reared in boardinghouses as if in ocean liners never making port."

In every part of the country, strangers often shared housing on a one-to-one basis. Families or individuals who lived in sizable houses and needed a little extra income would think nothing of putting up a "Room for Rent" sign. In Boston one hundred years ago, for instance, people shared quarters with an unrelated individual or family in more than 25 percent of the city's households. At one time or another, especially in the period before marriage, about half the population could expect to live in rented quarters that they shared with strangers.

The building of efficiency apartments and the growth of suburbia undercut these practical ways of coping with the housing needs of single adults. Also, in 1956, single older people finally became eligible for public housing. Today, for the most part, renting rooms to strangers is confined to areas near college campuses. Often these arrangements involve an older person renting to a younger one.

But some elders don't want to share their houses with younger people under any circumstances. The American Association of Retired Persons, in its book *Homesharing and Other Lifestyle Options,* quotes one older woman's reservations: "Young people today only want to have sex, smoke dope, and listen to rock and roll." Anticipating the shared-housing picture twenty or thirty years from now, with the baby boomers beginning to appear on the homeowner's side of the sharing arrangement, one could imagine more of a community of interests—at least on these issues—between elder boomer landlords and their younger tenants.

Looking ahead to the housing expectations of the baby boomers in their elder years, it's both interesting and significant to note that since the 1950s the young have had more experiences with shared housing than any other age group. Baby boomers, who went to summer camp, lived in college dorms, shared apartments in big cities while beginning their careers, moved up to their own condominium apartments and town houses, and then, if they could afford the mortgage, bought a suburban house with built-in neighbors, may take to communal living arrangements with ease. They will feel as if they have come home after a long journey.

## You *Can* Go Home Again

The basic three-bedroom house has been the stock housing-industry product since World War II, but the demand for multibedroom suburban houses can be expected to dry up because the generations that follow the boomers into the prime house-buying years will be smaller. (There may be one last surge in the building of large houses—if the economy holds up—in the early 1990s, as baby boomers reach their forties and early fifties and trade up, sometimes to houses with as many as four bedrooms.) The three-bedroom models were built for the families in which the baby boomers grew up and, interestingly enough, many boomers may end their days in a similar setting—but with a different "family."

Two scenarios are likely: (1) People who have growing children will offer a room and perhaps home cooking to an elder baby boomer who will fill in as a baby-sitter–grandparent. (2) Older boomers living alone will join several of their peers to buy a house to share. (Many multibedroom units will be on the market, sometimes at prices considerably lower than they are now.)

Of the shared housing arrangements we have begun to see, none is more intriguing than these newly created households made up of groups of unrelated people living together. (Older baby boomers might recognize this way of living. In form and in spirit, these groupings resemble the communes of the 1960s—free-form families, islands of experiment in the midst of much more conventional living patterns.) In an early example of this phenomenon, a group of twelve older people sponsored by a religious organization shared a house, each with his or her own room, in the late 1970s. "Sometimes we even fight like a family," said one resident. Another group-house resident, this one in a house financed by a foundation in Westchester County, New York, said almost the same thing about his housemates: "We battle like a family, but we take care of each other, too. It takes a while to rub off the corners, but you get used to each other."

In various government-sponsored independent living centers, where older people live who need some medical or social support but do not require the total care of a nursing home, the residents tend to form affinity groups that resemble the social support networks often found in college dormitories. They look out for one another, set up an informal division of labor to handle chores, and generally come to take an interest in one another's well-being that resembles a familial tie.

By 2020, Early Boomers will all be in their sixties and some will be over 70. Given their experiences with communal living while young, they should have fewer inhibitions about sharing housing than has any previous generation of elders. Many will either live together in arrangements they improvise for themselves or find created by government, or be friendly with people who do and will be considering doing so themselves. Their needs for social support and intimate friendship will engender familylike networks within these communities, even if the stated goal of the undertaking is merely to provide a place for them to live.

### Sharing Becomes Big Business

As sharing becomes an important source of housing for older people, the demand for certain services will rise sharply. Bringing compatible people together in the right surroundings and helping them adjust to their new relationship could require a good deal of support. Matching services may well turn into big businesses, staffed by social workers, counselors, and housing experts.

As the demand grows, entrepreneurs will spot an opportunity. Where government and nonprofit agencies now focus on people with modest incomes, private matchmakers will offer computerized compatibility tests and socials to introduce homeowners and room seekers. Social workers should also find a growth field in serving as part-time consultants to groups of people who buy houses and set up their own communal arrangements but nevertheless need occasional help straightening out interpersonal relationships. This could engender a new category of social service professional: the adjustment counselor. Elders may also found successful businesses based on the creation and management of private group residences.

Certain durable goods will be required by this new lifestyle, as well. We should see a demand for modified home appliances, such as large refrigerators with dividers so that each resident can have a section exclusively for his or her food. Shared homes will need similarly compartmentalized medicine chests. And these elders are likely to be in the market for small sets of personalized flatware and place settings and the like to avoid the air of institutionalized togetherness.

The lawyers will be busy. New insurance policies will have to be written. New law may be needed to cover the intricacies of these novel personal and property relationships, and many will wish to describe their intentions in contracts of various kinds.

As shared accommodations become a much more significant part of our total housing, the transition will require changes in present housing and zoning laws. Until the idea of shared and group housing gains respectability, opposition from neighbors and from local government will probably continue. The 1986 experience of a nonprofit suburban group that bought a large old summer house with several guest cottages with the intention of renovating the property for use by elders in a joint living arrangement is typical. "Not here you don't," responded the local zoning board. The head of the sponsoring organization was frustrated: "We've got a big, vacant property, and we've got lots of solid, responsible elderly people who need homes. Sadly, some of the neighbors seem to think we are talking about bag ladies."

Another battlefield in the same war is the question of allowing suburban houses to be subdivided. Government policy involving services for lower-income people has begun to break the ice here. Since 1983 the Department of Housing and Urban Development has accepted for rent subsidies units in which nonrelatives share a bathroom or kitchen. But many communities still forbid accessory apartments in their single-family homes.

The prospect of changing zoning regulations to create suburbs and cities much different from the ones we know now may seem farfetched. But consider this: "Single family zoning is virtually unique to this century and this nation," as gerontologists Carol A. Schreter and Lloyd A. Turner have pointed out. Such zoning was not handed down from the mountain engraved in stone, and the particular social and economic circumstances that gave rise to it in this country are passing. As the population ages, changing the rules will become a matter of self-interest. Enough people either will be old enough to sympathize with the practice of sharing or will have old parents who need to share, and resistance will diminish.

Already the climate is changing in areas such as the suburbs of New York City. Localities are just starting to approve middle-income housing projects in their midst, something they never would have done in past years. "Basically, it is because we are talking about the children and parents of the middle class," says a sponsor of one of the developments about this change of heart. "It's not just low-income people any more." The Supreme Court gave this trend a further boost with a 1988 decision striking down a Huntington, Long Island, zoning law that excluded lower-cost housing.

### A Return to Community?

Much of the housing occupied today by elders—the well-off and the middle class as well as the poor—involves fairly high-density, cooperative living. The rest of us are just beginning to notice this phenomenon as the number of elders increases. The Sunbelt retirement communities, trailer parks and mobile-home developments, congregate facilities, accessory apartment renovations, and house sharing are all different from the separate, single-family houses we're used to. Getting old, often of necessity, has come to mean drawing closer to other people, often strangers. And older Americans are gradually coming to accept this new lifestyle as natural, providing role models for younger generations when they age.

It is, however, a real change. Living together with your age mates in housing you rent or own collectively just goes against the grain of that part of the American spirit embodied in the ownership and sole occupancy of a single-family house on its own plot of land. "The single-family tract house—post World War II style—whatever its aesthetic failings, offered growing families a private haven in a heartless world," according to urban historian Kenneth T. Jackson, our foremost authority on the development of suburbia. ("Haven in a heartless world" is a phrase Jackson borrowed from fellow historian and social critic Christopher Lasch, who sees the nuclear family as a refuge from what many perceive as the breakdown of community in America.) The image provides some continuity between the immediate past and the immediate future, between the ways we are living now and what will be ahead for us when the baby boomers age.

To go back a generation: For the parents of the baby boomers, suburbia was an escape from the city and its rough edges, an attempt to find a gentle and nurturing geographical counterpart to the spirit of child rearing represented by Dr. Spock. Their houses epitomized the protectiveness in which they tried to envelop their children. Within this fortress of love they felt comfortable in exercising the famed "permissiveness" that everyone now remembers.

But the "haven" didn't last any longer than did the primacy of the nuclear family. Today suburbs are no longer so protected. In the new suburbs, the "heartless world" has somehow managed to get within the gates. Gwinnett County, Georgia, the fastest-growing county of more than one hundred thousand population in the United States, is a case in point. It is typical of the newer, larger, more self-contained suburbs that are growing all over the country. In the midst of their office parks and subdivisions, people "drive alone to work and then drive home and turn on their VCRs," notes sociologist Mark Baldassare. He sees this life as "much less centered on community, and more on work, entrepreneurship, the private life." Parents worry less about equipping the Little League team and more about their elementary-school kids who might be experimenting with drugs.

Social critics who saw alienation in the suburbs of the 1950s and 1960s have been almost at a loss for words to describe the desolate aspects of this lifestyle. The inhabitants probably have a better handle on it. "It's getting to the point around here where you're going to have to hire somebody to cry at your funeral," lamented one longtime Gwinnett County resident.

But in the older suburbs, there is an undercurrent of change that eventually might provide a countertrend. Housing patterns are evolving that feature a greater mix of types of shelter. There are more apartments for singles and young couples who can no longer make the payments on a single-family house. Town-house condominiums are springing up all over, some of them designed for a particular market niche, such as Eisenhower Generation empty nesters or tennis and golf players.

Since 1980, a majority of Americans over 65 have lived in the suburbs—particularly the older areas. It is not unreasonable to suggest that a different generation of elders with life experiences and values unlike those of the present occupants of this age bracket will encourage more communal housing and help to create a new, more community-oriented society.

It won't happen overnight. For many people the acceptance of communal housing requires a basic shift in values. When the Minnesota Board on Aging sought to promote congregate-care development outside the state's biggest cities, its deputy secretary acknowledged it was an uphill battle because "it's not even fully accepted by the elderly that apartment living is a good thing." But on the whole, the trend is toward more shared living.

"Living communally is an adventure at our age," remarked Joan Erikson about the arrangement in which she and her psychologist husband, Erik, share their large house with a student and two other scholars. It is perhaps fitting and a sign of things to come that the person who did most to develop the idea of the stages of life should be one of the pioneers of the stage that is still evolving—the time in one's later years when it becomes necessary to build bridges to others.

As we move into the twenty-first century, aging baby boomers may help restore a sense of community to our society by choosing to live differently. In their youth in the 1960s, they reminded us of how far from that ideal we were straying. As much older grown-ups, living in communal settings in such numbers as to serve as an example to the rest of society, they could finally help to humanize that "heartless world."

The generational experience and psychology of the Early Boomers in particular has prepared them for such a task more than any of us probably realize. They were raised mostly in what were then new suburbs in the 1950s and 1960s. In 1956 sociologist Ernest R. Mowrer noted that "homogeneity and social integration seem to be characteristic of the initial stages of suburban life succeeded later by diversity and anonymity. . . ." Early Boomers were grouped together right through adolescence in scouting, team sports, and the community life that is a natural part of college. And a small but influential minority of them lived in communes even after college and into their twenties, trying to create by intention a utopian world based on communal living.

But what has attracted less attention is the extent to which even as adults a large number have continued to live a form of communal life. It was only in 1961 that the government first supplied an FHA mortgage for a condominium, and not until 1979 that the building of condominium units outpaced the construction of rental apartments. Today, condominium residents number more than forty million. They govern themselves through 125,000 owners' associations.

For many, particularly those who have not had children, this has become a way of life, not just a way station on the road to the purchase of a single-family home. Rising real-estate values and high interest rates have seen to that. Thus, millions of Americans of the baby-boom generation will reach old age having lived virtually their entire lives in one kind of communal setting or another, the only twentieth-century generation to have done so.

The communal aspect of condominium living is likely to take on greater importance as the baby boomers reach their later years. In middle age, condominium residents are not likely to act in concert on much of anything beyond housing and grounds upkeep. But as elders, with more leisure and fewer career pressures, the cooperative spirit could come to the fore. Accustomed to acting together on housing particulars, they may find themselves reaching out to one another in a spirit of mutual aid as increasing age creates the need for such relationships.

Brandeis University sociologist Shulamit Reinharz, reflecting on planning for housing older people, has remarked that so far, on the whole, even communal arrangements such as shared housing "are experienced as communities of convenience, not commitment." There is no guarantee that elder baby boomers will bring the communal spirit as well as its form to their living arrangements. But their past suggests the possibility that the return to community could be the story of their future.

# 4

# An Early End to Early Retirement

"Sixty-five is a Mickey Mouse number. Somebody made it up years ago when they invented Social Security, and now we have it etched on the brain."

DIANNE McKAIG, lawyer

In 1950, about half of all men in the United States 65 and older were working. By the mid-1980s, only about 15 percent of men in this age group still worked. American men now retire at a median age of 62, compared with 65 as late as 1970.

For the Old Guard and New Elder generations, retirement from work is an institution that has involved mostly men. The federal government defines retirement as "the act of leaving paid employment. The retiree, upon reaching a predetermined age, is usually provided some regular payment such as a pension and/or a Social Security payment." Old Guard and New Elder women were in and out of the work force if they worked at all, and generally did not have the kinds of work histories that entitled them to pensions or Social Security other than as the wives of retirees. As a result, their statistics are not useful for comparison.

The later working years of the baby boomers will differ substantially from those of their New Elder parents. Contrary to what most people assume, the boomers are not likely to experience early retirement. Women of the baby boom have had careers as a matter of course, and they will not be relegated to a footnote in retirement statistics. They will collect pensions and Social Security benefits on their own.

Elder boomer workers will also change work patterns by:

- turning old age into a period of independent entrepreneurship;
- spending much of their later work life working part-time or on project work as part of phased-in retirement;
- altering the work-life cycle to the point where the word *career* takes on new meaning;
- transforming work benefits through an intergenerational coalition with younger women workers to respond better to the needs of female employees.

## EARLY RETIREMENT: "A UNIQUE EVENT"

Some have called it "the golden handshake." Corporations entice their workers to leave their jobs at increasingly younger ages. Fred Weldon, an engineer at one of the *Fortune* 500 companies, calls it a good deal. When his company decided to "downsize," cutting its staff to enhance efficiency, Fred was able to get out at the ripe age of 56. His company's offer was a percentage of his sixty-thousand-dollar salary just high enough to make him think that he could make a go of the part-time consulting he had always wanted to do.

Consistently in the 1980s, major corporations have underestimated how popular early retirement would be. When Du Pont made its early retirement offer to employees in 1985, for example, the planners figured that a maximum of 6,500 employees would take the company up on it. But instead, 11,500 of its workers called it quits. One study of retiring employees in big companies found a steady increase of those leaving before age 65: 62 percent in 1978, 70 percent in 1979, 80 percent in 1983, and 84 percent in 1986. "It's socially acceptable to retire," observed Du Pont's senior vice-president for employee relations, in what was clearly an understatement.

The trend toward early retirement has seemed relentless. However, it's a much more unstable phenomenon than it appears to be. By the first decade of the twenty-first century, "people will be retiring later than they are now," says James W. Walker, vice-president of the management consulting firm of Cresap, McCormick & Paget. Other experts agree. They see a reversal of the recent early-retirement trend over the next twenty to thirty years, with new patterns emerging: workers staying at their jobs after 65, staying with their old companies but in new positions commensurate with the skills and talents that develop with age, leaving long-term positions to work at part-time jobs, or working on job-sharing teams.

Early retirement "may eventually emerge as a unique event in our economic history," says Jon Moen, an economist for the Federal Reserve Bank of Atlanta. Particular demographic and economic circumstances brought it into being, not the inevitable march of progress toward a better life. The conditions that created it are already starting to change, and the institution of retirement is likely to change with them.

## THE ROAD TO THE "GOLDEN YEARS"

"Retirement is no longer a luxury, it is now an institution," reports the United States Senate Special Committee on Aging. A look at the way that retirement as we know it has developed shows just how much this institution has changed in response to the changing needs of the economy. Very little of this history has been motivated by a wish to provide a better life for older workers. People have been able to stop working and collect pensions because it has suited the interests of both management and labor.

Industry began providing pensions at the end of the nineteenth century because companies needed to stabilize their work forces. As one manager put it at the time, "The pension operates as an incentive to hold men between the ages of forty and fifty when they have acquired the experience and skill which makes them especially valuable and prevents their being tempted away by slightly increased wages." If a worker quit, he lost the pension credits he had built up.

Mandatory retirement at 65, which appeared about the same time as pensions, was originally management's response to union demands to base layoffs on seniority. With a mandatory retirement age, employers could ensure that seniority did not go on forever for their older workers, who tended to make higher wages. Mandatory retirement also dealt with management's fears that older workers, protected by seniority, would continue working even when they could no longer handle the ten- to twelve-hour days of heavy labor.

Until the turn of the century, these problems were somewhat theoretical on both sides, since many workers did not live to age 65. The average life expectancy at birth in 1900 was 46.3 years, and industrial accidents took the lives of many who did not succumb to disease. But from 1900 to 1930, people started to live longer, and that created problems. With a large pool of cheap labor available from immigration and young men moving to the cities from the farm, older workers were less in demand. When the production line speeded up work, management claimed that older workers couldn't keep up. Theories were developed to explain how older workers simply "wore out" and couldn't handle the new, quicker pace. Want ads put it bluntly: Anyone over 40 need not apply.

Most workers did not receive pensions; those who did got stipends small by today's standards. And, of course, there was no Social Security. Retirement thus became associated with poverty. About 23 percent of older people needed welfare (private charity and state programs) in 1910, 33 percent in 1922, and 40 percent in 1929. The Great Depression began for older people well before it hit the rest of the country.

In the 1930s, Social Security began to provide for the growing number of impoverished elders, although the program was aimed at keeping older workers out of offices and factories so as not to aggravate unemployment as much as it was at easing old people's poverty. Thus Social Security penalized retirees by lowering their benefits if they earned more than a minimal amount.

World War II brought about drastic changes in both production needs and the labor pool. With many younger men in the armed forces, other workers were desperately needed on the production lines. Government and industry discovered that older people do not necessarily wear out after all. Suddenly needed, they could still do good work. (With industry operating under the gun, employers were even willing to admit that women could be good workers in fields that had not been deemed suitable before—witness "Rosie the Riveter," the symbol of the productive woman worker.)

The end of the war brought the boys home—and, of course, they wanted their old jobs back. Both women and older workers were forced out. A recent report from the Task Force on Employment and Aging, sponsored by the Brookdale Foundation and the Community Council of Greater New York, describes the immediate postwar climate:

> There was a general belief that there were not enough jobs to go around. Various policies were established to ease the older worker out of the labor market. Early retirement, expansion of pension systems in private industry, the expansion of Social Security all came into being. Training, promotion and hiring opportunities for older workers closed down. Negative stereotypes about older people began to appear in the media, in literature and in the work place. Older workers were pictured as slow learners, difficult to get along with, poor performers and generally infirm. . . .

After World War II, retirement became separated from concerns about poverty, and began to resemble the institution we know today. Both management and labor came to view pensions as deferred wages, a natural part of collective bargaining. Between 1945 and 1955, the number of workers covered by pension plans more than tripled. By the mid-1980s, private pension plans covered more than half the work force.

Through the 1950s and 1960s, annual increases in productivity provided enough money to pension off workers. The baby boomers descended on the workplace as an army of job seekers starting in the late 1960s, and retirement was promoted as a legitimate stage of life and a good bargain for everyone. It made room in the work force for the new baby-boom employees and afforded older people a life of leisure. The anticipated reward of healthy years free of work, beginning for many in their fifties, also served as a powerful incentive to keep people at jobs they didn't like. "People had learned to want retirement, and to be willing to bear economic sacrifices in order to have it," as gerontologist Robert C. Atchley put it.

Today mandatory retirement no longer exists in most lines of work. Congress legislated it out of existence in a series of measures enacted from 1967 through 1986. Retirement had become so popular that it no longer needed a mandate. New Elders have come to expect that they will stop working, their positions thus becoming available to the younger workers who want them. "Our experience is that very few workers stay past age 65 anyway," a lawyer for AT&T remarked when the law repealing mandatory retirement took full effect. In fact, the current mean age of retirement for blue-collar workers is 55.

## CHANGING COURSE

Widespread early retirement is unlikely to last, however. By 2005, when Early Boomers begin to reach the ages at which New Elders have been retiring, changing economic facts will create incentives for many boomers to continue to work. For example, according to the schedule of Social Security retirement benefits now in effect, workers born in 1960 or after will not be able to collect the full amount until age 67. And the decreasing ratio of workers to retirees at that point will cause a shortfall in tax revenues that will require raising the qualifying age even more, as we will explain in the next chapter.

Pensions for workers retiring in the future will almost certainly be less generous than the ones current retirees collect. Over the past decade the emphasis has been away from paying specific amounts according to salary and years of service and toward worker contributions matched by employers, as in the widespread 401(k) programs. These matching plans guarantee nothing and are vulnerable to sharp decreases in the assets in which they are invested. Workers who can't afford to contribute to them end up with no pension at all.

Small companies, which are generating the most new jobs in the economy, are less likely to offer pension plans than are larger firms. Pensions cover only 43 percent of full-time employees in smaller businesses, compared with 90 percent in plans in larger organizations. (Eighty percent of all employment is in firms of fewer than 100 people.)

Early retirement has created the potential for enormous pension liabilities in corporations in which many workers take advantage of this benefit. Professor James H. Schulz of Brandeis University, author of *The Economics of Aging,* estimates that a pension for a worker who retires at 60 can end up costing a company *twice* as much as one for an employee who leaves at 65. Should the economy suffer a serious recession in the next few years, underfunded pensions could become the scandal/tragedy of the 1990s. During October 1987, when the stock market crashed, $210 billion worth of pension-fund assets—almost 10 percent of their portfolios—vanished. Despite federal guarantees of pensions under the Employee Retirement Income Security

Act of 1974 (ERISA), widespread bankruptcies combined with bank failures might make it difficult for the government to reimburse everybody completely.

Many employees count on company health insurance benefits to cover medical expenses for their early retirement until they become eligible for Medicare. American companies now have more than $100 billion worth of potential health insurance claims by their retirees that are neither guaranteed by the government nor backed up by funds set aside in reserve by the companies (unlike money put aside to fund pensions, medical insurance reserve funds are not tax-deductible). If his or her former employer runs into financial difficulties, a retiree can lose these benefits.

Some early retirees are already starting to feel the pinch. Matt Willis retired from a Pittsburgh machine company a few years ago when he was in his late fifties. His pension provided him and his wife with a decent income; when combined with Social Security, it also gave them good medical insurance. But then his former company went under. Although the government guaranteed his pension, it did not assume his insurance coverage. Unfortunately, his family was hit by a medical disaster. His wife developed emphysema, entailing a twenty-thousand-dollar hospital bill. Matt was forced to return to work until he and his wife could qualify for Medicare.

Workers can lose their medical insurance without their firms going bankrupt. Some companies have been unilaterally cutting back on health insurance because it has cost them so much. Experts in the field predict that many companies that can still afford to pay for these benefits will have to reduce them in the future. As a result, in the next decade we will be seeing a parade of lawsuits filed by retirees against their former companies.

## ELDER WORKERS BACK IN DEMAND

In 1987, three million people over 65 were employed in the United States, only about 16 percent of the population between ages 65 and 75. Roughly half of them work full-time, the other half part-time. About one-third of our older people are employed at some time after they begin to receive Social Security benefits.

Baby boomers are likely to experience an employment rate in excess of 50 percent when they reach this age bracket, and they will work in jobs with more power and responsibility than do New Elders. Besides personal economic need, other factors will encourage elder boomers to remain employed. More elders will stay in the work force because demand for their services will grow. In recent years, small start-up companies of fewer than one hundred employees have supplied two of every three new jobs in this country, and this trend should continue. Full- and part-time jobs have been opening up for older people in these firms because the firms need experienced, knowledgeable workers to get them through the first few years that capsize many new businesses. This trend should continue well into the future.

The service sector, the fastest-growing part of our economy, can be expected to continue its leadership role in job creation into the 1990s and probably beyond. This bodes well for elders who are especially well suited to fill these jobs. Services such as banking, counseling, retail trade, and health-care administration involve face-to-face contact, in which people are most comfortable dealing with someone like themselves. Since there will be increasing numbers of older people in America, more and more customers will be in their fifties or older, and these people will prefer to be assisted by their peers.

Clothing-store and drugstore owners who have hired older workers have already discovered the importance of this age matching, as have a growing number of financial-service companies. Tommy Lasseigne, manager of two Baton Rouge, Louisiana, hardware stores, has learned it from experience. "A middle-aged man [customer] isn't going to ask a teenager [clerk] how to do a home repair job, and he won't listen if the kid gives him advice," he says. "But if the clerk is a 60-year-old who's done the job a dozen times, he'll listen."

New demographic factors will also shape retirement. The Reagan Generation baby bust has already produced fewer younger workers and an increased demand for older employees to fill in the gap. The trend toward smaller families and couples with no children will continue to diminish the number of young workers starting careers in the future. According to the Bureau of Labor Statistics, the annual growth rate of the labor force is only about half what it was in the 1970s, and that shrinkage should continue. By the year 2000, we will have a million fewer workers aged 16 to 24 than we do now. As this smaller cohort moves through its working years, a shortage of qualified workers at every skill and experience level will persist well into the twenty-first century, creating a demand for older workers to stay on the job.

One dramatically visible consequence of the decline in new workers now is the older person serving up hamburgers at McDonald's. Fast-food restaurants and similar businesses have found themselves competing for a smaller pool of teenage workers, and they have reached out to the other end of the age spectrum for help. McDonald's has instituted its "McMasters" job-training program especially for New Elder workers. This company has found that the food is just as fast when it's cooked and served by older people as when teenagers dish it out.

But this doesn't mean that elder baby boomers will be working under the McDonald's golden arches in 2020. Hiring elders is a stopgap measure for fast-food businesses. "The fast food industry has no alternative; it will have to robotize," according to John Durocher, a food industry expert at the University of New Hampshire School of Business. In fact, McDonald's and Arby's are already installing automated systems that will eventually eliminate many employee positions.

The demand for older workers has also increased because they have the basic skills, such as reading, writing, and arithmetic, that many Reagan Generation workers, for whatever reason, have not fully developed. About a third of all large United States corporations have to train their employees in the most fundamental reading and math skills. And even simple tasks are becoming more complex, thanks to technology. A cashier's job, for example, once required only honesty and a little counting ability. But cash registers aren't what they used to be. Some machines handle credit-card purchases and update inventory, and require the skills of a computer operator to run them. In 1975, United States jobs required a median 12.5 years of schooling. Now it's up to 12.8 and by the year 2000 it should hit 13.5, according to the American Society for Training and Development. The skills of the well-educated baby boomers should thus remain marketable in the workplace as long as they are capable of working.

## SOME DON'T QUIT

Some New Elders are fortunate enough to enjoy engrossing, creative, even exciting work, and early retirement has no appeal. Many lawyers, editors, artists, chief executive officers, musicians, and physicians work well past the age when others would have retired. Or they may take advantage of the savvy they've built up over a career and apply it to a new field or a business. Other retirees leave their jobs only to join the millions of volunteer workers who have changed the traditional composition of the unpaid work force.

Still others start their own businesses after retirement—perhaps the ones they fantasized about while sitting behind corporate desks. Most people who go into business for themselves do so in their late twenties or early thirties. But "there definitely is a trend toward older entrepreneurs," says Jeffrey A. Timmons, a professor of entrepreneurial studies at Babson College. "I think we're going to see it continue."

A banker who had dreamed of trading one kind of liquidity for another opened a marine-book store. His shop was part of a franchise operation, a type of business that has attracted many retirees. Franchisees do not have to spend years building up experience and contacts in a particular field. They pay a company that has already done so for the use of its name, its supply system, and continual advice about how to run their enterprise. In return, they pay the company a percentage of their profits. The opportunity to buy a business as a package, and the low failure rate that characterizes franchise operations, makes them just right for many of today's older people.

We can expect this trend toward second careers in one's own business to achieve widespread popularity by 2010. It was, after all, baby boomers who made a success of magazines like *Inc.* and *Venture.* As their generation ages, many of its members who did not give in to the entrepreneurial urge in their early adulthood will get a second chance to see if they can make it on their own.

While the franchise system will probably still be around, boomers are likely to want more independence in their businesses. *Creativity* has been a byword of their generation—"doing your own thing" implies individuality in addition to freedom—and franchising limits entrepreneurial self-expression. Their generation has worked for organizations more than has any other birth cohort—even boomer professionals like lawyers and doctors have made their careers in groups—and when many of them finally get the opportunity to strike out on their own, it's likely to be *on their own.* Old suburban downtown areas may be renewed by the return of the corner store. Semiretired boomer lawyers might return to the storefront individual practice. The desire of their age mates for more personal service than large organizations can offer will bolster this trend.

One largely baby-boomer-created trend that we should see burgeon with the aging of the boomer generation is the home-based small business that depends on a personal computer for its functioning. One can see this phenomenon already developing in the changing name of one magazine: *Family Computing* (1983) to *Family and Home Office Computing* (1987) to *Home Office Computing* (1988). Baby boomers have taken to personal-computer technology quickly—they were, after all, the first generation to mature with consumer electronics. Many of them will leave the corporation and work from home part-time as consultants by the time they reach their mid-fifties, commuting electronically over fiber-optic telecommunications lines.

## VOLUNTEERS

Of all the ways that the present generation of retired older Americans keeps busy, none compares with the activity that is as American as the cherry pie served at a church supper: volunteer work. A Gallup poll showed that between 1977 and 1986, the number of Americans who did volunteer work increased from 27 percent to 36 percent. College graduates over 50 did more of this unpaid labor than anyone else. Another survey reported that almost 44 percent of those between ages 50 and 74 do volunteer work.

A retired doctor in Saint Petersburg gives five hours of his time every week in a clinic. A Toledo widow works at a community center as a counselor for the recently widowed, thus relieving her own loneliness as well as helping others. Their stories are repeated daily all over America, and in them a new social trend has taken shape. "Today the face of volunteerism is changing," an article in *Modern Maturity*, the magazine of the American Association of Retired Persons, declares with evident pride. "Where once its ranks were almost exclusively filled by young or middle-aged socialites or homemakers, today's volunteer is often the retired or semiretired woman or man."

Volunteerism is often seen as a kind of charity, good deeds performed by people who have time on their hands; nice enough, but less than serious work. Consider, however, the views of Peter Drucker, probably our most respected analyst of business management and Clarke Professor of Social Sciences at the Claremont Graduate School. He says volunteerism more and more is coming to resemble big business.

The American Heart Association has 2.5 million volunteers; the Red

Cross, 1.5 million. Altogether, nonprofit organizations in the United States use the services of 30 million or more unpaid workers, many of them New Elders. These organizations have huge budgets, and they are starting to treat their volunteers like employees. "They are increasingly being managed as unpaid staff," Drucker notes of the volunteers, "rather than as well-meaning amateurs." When they don't perform up to par, they may find themselves with more leisure than they had anticipated.

This is not likely to be the picture of elder boomer volunteerism. One can't imagine them willing foot soldiers, regimented yet again by large organizations such as the ones that have constrained their freedom since the schools and colleges of their youth—not when increasing age finally offers them some options. Instead, we can expect them to demand a voice in how their services are used, opting wherever possible for working alone or in small groups on projects that provide them with tangible results of their efforts. We should not be surprised, for example, to find them engaged in activities such as tree planting, or other environmental actions over which they can maintain personal control. The environment is far more likely to be the area in which they will work because it is a central concern of their generation and many of the diseases that prompt current volunteer work will be cured by the second decade of the twenty-first century. (Elder boomers will, however, be extensively involved in volunteer home care of the chronically ill, as we will discuss later in this book.)

One kind of volunteer activity that we see only a little of now will play a much larger role in elder boomer volunteerism, and women are likely to be in the forefront. As the first generation of women to pursue careers in corporations, they have coped with old-boy networks by forging their own intergenerational ties. Typically, a young aspiring manager will seek out an older woman further along in her career, making the more experienced worker her mentor. In the midst of their harried work years, some of these women are developing similar relationships in volunteer work. For example, in the five hundred Big Sisters programs nationwide, women, average age 30, serve as mentors to girls, many of whom come from female-headed single-parent families. With approaching old age and more leisure, the familiar pattern of mentoring is likely to be the model of the intergenerational volunteer work in which many baby-boomer women will engage. One manifestation of this trend will probably be mentoring relationships between elder boomer women and young single mothers.

## LESS THAN NINE-TO-FIVE, MORE THAN ZERO

In the future, one of the most significant changes in work in the later years will be not *what* elders do but *when* they do it. The biggest area of growth will be in the number of part-time and project workers at all levels of the work force, from clerks to managers.

More than ten years ago, government analysts in the United States Departments of Commerce and Health, Education, and Welfare foresaw that "the ability to continue working in old age will bring pressure for gradual, not earlier retirement." Despite the popularity of part-time work among older workers, the number of firms that now allow retirees to reduce their schedule step by step to part-time status is virtually nil. Workers who are nearing the time when they will want to leave their jobs entirely will come to prefer a phased-in approach rather than abrupt retirement. This preference will encourage the already growing phenomenon of part-time employment.

Part-timers already make up 25 percent of all employees, according to Conference Board economist Audrey Freedman. Their numbers have increased at a rate of about 25 percent per year since the 1982 recession. Of those over 65 who are now employed, 47 percent of the men and 62 percent of the women are part-timers.

Corporations continue to create part-time jobs for the most basic of reasons. Two part-time workers cost less than one full-timer does. Additionally, companies that resist this trend risk being undercut by foreign competitors that embrace it and thus lower their labor costs. For example, part-time employees make up 17 percent of the United States work force, while 21 percent of British workers do not work a full shift. And part-time work is growing faster in Japan than in the United States.

Part-time and temporary jobs, which many older people should find attractive, are also opening in large numbers because of changes in the typical career path. Employee commitment to one company throughout a career continues to lessen. This creates gaps in staffing that provide more openings for part-timers and for workers hired for a single project. Here's one tip-off that this trend is expected to grow: The Bureau of Labor Statistics predicts that one of the ten fastest-growing jobs in the next decade will be that of *employment interviewer*.

Structural changes in the American economy—particularly downsizing to "lean and mean" along with corporate takeovers and the inevitable bumps in the business cycle—all point to fewer full-time career jobs with great futures. "We don't want people to come to us as a marriage," says one bank human-resources manager. "We want them to think of it more as dating." He is blunt with prospective employees: "Don't come here for security, come here for excitement."

New Elders have had numerous chances to fill slots as temporary office workers, but they have been slow to take advantage of the opportunity. Two of the nation's largest "temp" firms, Kelly Services and Manpower, Inc., have more positions than they can fill. They've been specifically targeting their appeal for workers to older people, trying to convince them to reenter the labor force. Kelly calls its program "Encore." Its ad in a recent issue of *Modern Maturity* proclaims: "Want To Work Again? Kelly Lets You Say When. . . . And don't worry if you're a bit rusty. You can use our equipment to brush up."

By 2010, many of these temp firms will focus on older workers, and they will have no trouble recruiting baby boomers to their ranks. The agencies will create insurance packages to cover their older workers and they will lease elder boomer workers to corporations whose insurance rates will not be affected by their temporary employees.

How will this change to a large and permanent part-time work force affect productivity and quality? Management's experience with part-time employees over the past decade or so has provided some very positive answers and bodes well for the employment outlook of elder boomers. Lois F. Copperman and Frederick D. Keast of the Institute on Aging at Portland State University in Oregon, citing a study by the Conference Board on this subject, say:

> Almost half the organizations that utilize permanent part-time employment report that the job performance of their part-time workers is better than their full-time counterparts. Productivity is often improved due to less fatigue and the ability of a worker to keep up a faster pace for a shorter time—especially in repetitive jobs or those which are emotionally or intellectually taxing. Productivity may also rise because the part-time workers themselves are better than the full-time workers. In one-third to one-half of the cases studied absenteeism, tardiness, and turn-over records of part-time workers were actually better than those of full-time employees.

In Lexington, Kentucky, the Lexington Central Bank & Trust Company began bringing in older people part-time to process monthly statements. Michael Otter, the bank's operations officer, was delighted with the arrangement. "They walked in, took their coats off and—

boom!—went right to work," he said. "It's been like that every time." The bank has saved money and the work has been done with fewer mistakes than before. "They have too much life experience to be ignored," Otter has concluded of older people like these former teachers, clerks, and insurance company workers.

Some companies have already realized that their own retirees form an excellent pool of temporary and part-time workers. The Equitable Life Assurance Society, one of our country's largest life insurance companies, decided to tap its own retirees for temporary help after totaling up the cost of securing such assistance from outside sources in the 1980 fiscal year and discovered that it added up to $3 million! By using its former employees, Equitable could avoid agency fees and the cost of training a new group of workers. Its program to bring back its own retirees began then. The Travelers Companies, an insurance group, are also leaders in this trend, as are the Grumman Aerospace Corporation and IBM.

Changes in the organization of work—already under way—will also create the need for many more part-time managers, whose leadership will provide the only efficient way to oversee certain kinds of work. Markets are becoming more and more segmented and, wherever possible, companies must move quickly to exploit every niche they can to stay ahead of the competition. In manufacturing, for example, the use of computer-aided design and computer-aided manufacturing (CAD/CAM) is enabling firms to profit from short production runs of specialized products.

This new technology requires many small production teams and creates minibailiwicks with decentralization or even fragmentation of authority. These operations will require managers with specialized knowledge and experience—too much for one person or even a few people to handle efficiently. It's a perfect situation for many semiretired, part-time managers.

## BETTER WITH AGE?

Would an older work force be up to the challenge of restoring America's competitive edge in the world economy? Is it unrealistic to expect workers now entering middle age to buttress American productivity when they are in their sixties and early seventies?

One of the most astute political observers in America described the place of older workers in the economy of the 1970s this way:

> Old people get older and usually less productive, and they ought to retire so that business can be better managed and more economically served. We should treat the elderly with respect, which does not require treating them as if they were not old. If politicians start inventing "rights" that cut down productivity, they infringe on a consumer's right to a product at the lowest cost. . . .

Many people would still agree with this assessment by William Safire. Yet virtually every study done in the past two decades shows that most older workers not only maintain their productivity but even, in some ways, improve with age. These studies have appeared in periodicals as diverse as *The Harvard Business Review, The New York Times, The American Journal of Sociology, Psychology Today,* and *The Wall Street Journal,* as well as in local newspapers and on television. But still we cling to our stereotypes—and we will probably continue to do so until the need for older workers reaches a critical mass and necessity makes us reexamine our views. That should occur by the year 2005.

To find out whether our stereotypical view of the older worker is valid, the Bureau of Business Management of the University of Illinois went right to the people who know best about productivity. They asked more than three thousand supervisors in more than eighty organizations in all fields of work to rate the performance of their employees who were over 60. These supervisors reported that most of their older workers were as good as or better than their younger colleagues.

Many of those who suggest that age diminishes work skills point to what they say are declines in problem-solving ability and frequent memory lapses by those in their sixties and seventies. Is there anything to this?

People in their fifties, sixties, and seventies do score lower than younger people. It has been shown, however, that these differences have more to do with test-taking experience than with declining intelligence. The younger cohorts had more formal schooling and thus more exposure to the format of the tests. In other words, the differences had to do with the varied generational experiences of each age group.

Beginning about the year 2005, the media will begin to report healthy increases in the scores elders are making on these exams. These high scores will not represent an evolution in the intelligence of older people; instead they will mean that the baby boomers, test takers *par excellence,* have begun to sit for the tests.

Many of the qualities we associate with aging can be seen as having positive value in the workplace. Older people may take longer to make a decision on the job, for example, because they are more likely to weigh the risks of a negative result. But that can be a positive trait when mistakes resulting from hasty judgment cost money.

Memory loss is another liability often held against older workers. There is *something* to this. Older people may develop short-term memory lapses. For example, they might forget a co-worker's name momentarily or not remember where they put something. But they are better than the young in recalling facts and concepts they've known for a while. Also, when older people remember something they are more likely than the young to interpret it, give it significance, and put it in a context—a valuable trait in many lines of work.

What of the future then? In a recent editorial, *Science,* the journal of the American Association for the Advancement of Science, tried to put the problem of age-related work limitations in perspective.

Age by itself does not bring wisdom, nor does youth automatically bring a fresh viewpoint: some individuals are born doctrinaire, and others embrace new ideas until the day they die. Each profession will have to think of the criteria that justify continued employment. Early retirement for some and late retirement for others may well average out to a more productive society.

If anything, baby boomer workers are even more likely than New Elders to preserve the height of their powers as they age. More than any other generation, the boomers have been obsessed with maintaining good health. They also have had access to better nutritional information on subjects such as cholesterol, caffeine, and alcohol than was available to today's elders when they were younger.

Their generation was less likely to work at manual labor than was their parents', so the waning of strength that comes with age will be less of a factor in their ability to work (although it's worth noting that the safety records of older employees are no worse than their middle-aged co-workers'). Also, their familiarity with computers throughout most of their work careers will make it easier for them to adapt to electronic commuting should they experience minor disabilities in their later years.

If these elder baby-boomer workers end up boosting American productivity with their wisdom and job experience it will certainly be ironic, since some analysts attributed the drop in our productivity in the 1970s to the baby boom's entry into the labor force! The sudden flood of inexperienced people into offices and factories at that time may have dragged down output, but boomers will have a chance to help the economy to accelerate later in their lives.

## YET ANOTHER TEST

Since age brings impairment to some people, the greater number of workers remaining employed in their later years as we enter the twenty-first century will require employers to devise objective criteria to make good hiring decisions and appropriate job assignments. The baby boomers, probably the most tested generation in history, will face yet another exam when they reach their sixties. Those who need or want to work can expect to undergo periodic mental, psychological, and physical checkups to see if they can still do the job. The manipulation of blocks and other procedures requiring physical and mental agility will become as common as the office baseball pool.

Preemployment screening has already established a precedent for this kind of qualifying test. About 50 percent of all companies now give physicals to prospective employees, and 25 percent test for drugs. Cincinnati Bell, Inc., even administers a memory test to applicants for jobs involving interaction with customers. By the beginning of the twenty-first century, job applicants past the age of 55 will probably have to take additional tests to establish their "functional" age, a more important measure of ability than their chronological age. These tests may also be used to "force" retirement.

## BACK TO THE CLASSROOM

"We're living longer and longer today," says Robert O. Snelling, Sr., chief executive officer of the Snelling & Snelling employment agency. "What's wrong with having a couple of careers?" Richard Nelson

Bolles, author of the best-selling *What Color Is Your Parachute?*, the guide to changing jobs used by tens of thousands of baby boomers, thinks that three or more careers will be the norm for those just now starting out in the working world.

Bolles could be erring on the conservative side. Ten different jobs in a person's working life is now the average, and it's typical to have gone through four of them by one's mid-twenties, according to economist Robert E. Hall. But the generation of 1946–1964 may revise this pattern. The rate of change in the workplace is accelerating, making employment increasingly less stable. Baby boomers could hold a substantial percentage of their total positions after the age of 45. And the nature of those jobs could change so rapidly that the very word *career* may lose much of its meaning.

In future decades, workers will come to their later years expecting change in their employment experience. They will shift lines of work and make continual readjustments to the rapid pace of technological change—particularly the computerization of many office tasks. According to a Yankelovich, Skelly and White survey, management sometimes complains that older employees today have difficulty adapting to new technology. But the advent of more user-friendly machines such as inexpensive computers that respond to anyone's voice commands should help to reduce these difficulties.

During the New Elders' work life, there was only one basic change in the technology of the office: the advent of the copier—and its widespread use came late in their careers. Every other technological change, such as the electric typewriter, was merely an improvement on already existing machines.

The baby boomers, on the other hand, have experienced constant technological change in the workplace. They are the tech-literate generation of workers. Not only are they comfortable with machines such as computers that their parents still approach warily, they are also at ease with innovation itself: They expect it. In less than a decade, for example, they have seen the original IBM PC become virtually an antique. They have accepted *fax* as a verb as easily as they've gotten used to the idea that overnight delivery of documents, itself only a few years old, is okay as long as you're not in a hurry.

Companies will become more active in assisting their employees through these transitions. Control Data's "preventive maintenance" approach for mid-career course correction is typical of the program of the future. Through retraining this corporation helps its employees to adapt to the use of new technology and other changes in the nature of their jobs.

An increasing number of older workers amidst a constantly changing workplace and work force suggests explosive future growth for retraining programs and the number of workers employed to administer them. By 2010, retraining should be one of our most important service industries. Boomer elders themselves may see an entrepreneurial opportunity here, particularly in the retraining of members of their own cohort who are more likely to feel comfortable being instructed by someone their own age. In an effort to stay lean and competitive, companies may farm out such work to small, flexible consulting firms that will have specialists under contract in a number of fields.

The retraining companies will work closely with a corporation to get a picture of its employment needs, and then develop courses and materials that will turn out employees with new skills and knowledge. A visitor peeking into one of their classrooms will see a worker seated at a terminal, responding interactively to a program of instruction contained on a laser-read disk. The scene or problem depicted on the terminal screen will change according to how the employee responds to questions, creating an almost real-life scenario in which the retrainee will be "walked" through the problems he or she will face in a typical workday on the new job.

By 2010, the prominent role that elder boomers will play in society compared with the lesser influence exercised by their New Elder parents should make wisdom the valued attribute of elders it was in previous centuries. The wisdom amassed by elder boomers may prove useful to them when they apply their experience in a different area from the one where they were first employed.

We are only now starting to see the first glimmer of these opportunities. In certain fields, especially education, those empowered to hire are beginning to look beyond rigid job requirements. Already facing shortages of people who can do the job, they are coming to think that perhaps talent, broad experience, and proven ability ought to overshadow the criteria in job descriptions. In New Jersey, for example, the State Board of Education is reaching beyond the pool of teachers from which it has traditionally picked school principals. It's opened the competition to those with graduate degrees in a management field, proven competence, the ability to pass a written test, and the willingness to teach for up to two years in order to qualify for the job. The Carnegie Foundation sponsored a study to see if retired scientists and engineers could be the answer to the serious shortage of science and math teachers. Why not accept their professional experience and accomplishments in lieu of the many education course credits they would normally need to qualify to teach? The report, *Education's Greatest Untapped Resource: Second Career Scientists and Engineers*, found that the scientists and engineers looked favorably on the prospects of teaching if the authorities involved would relax the usual requirements for the job. Both a school chancellor and the head of a teachers' union approved the report's conclusions.

## RETOOLING THE WORK-LIFE CYCLE

Multiple careers and employee retraining throughout the work life will be just two aspects of the gradual relaxation of our work-life cycle expectations. Traditionally we have seen the life stages as progressing in lockstep fashion from school to work to retirement. As the population in general ages and more older workers remain in the work force, this rigid concept of the employment cycle will become obsolete. The newer, more varied use of time in one's later years should serve as a model for more flexibility in other stages of the life cycle.

As we move farther from the notion that work should automatically end by the time a person reaches his or her sixty-second birthday, we will see changes on every rung of the career ladder. With less leisure at the end of life than they have now, for example, people may be more inclined to demand increased free time earlier.

In the next twenty years, employees are likely to get more control over the path their work lives will take, according to a recent survey of corporate managers and others specializing in benefits. Karen Geiger, the career development director of NCNB Corporation, a North Carolina bank holding company, thinks employees will have the option to "move up, down, or even out (temporarily) and still be part of a corporation." Unpaid leave will become available for a variety of reasons, including child care and care for an older, dependent relative.

Corporations will be more liberal in offering such benefits because the "birth dearth" in the Reagan Generation will leave them with a much smaller pool of potential managers than they have now. This will put all experienced personnel, including older boomers, in a position to insist on such benefits.

When Sue Roland, age 39, turned down a promotion her supervisor knew she had hoped for, began making mistakes she had never made before, and started coming in uncharacteristically late, he knew something was wrong. Finally she came to him in despair. Her 82-year-old father had recently been disabled by a stroke, and Sue was having a hard time keeping up with her job while simultaneously supervising his care.

About 25 percent of all employees have some responsibility for the care of aging parents. A few major corporations, including Colgate-Palmolive, Aetna Life, and Kodak are already granting unpaid family leaves lasting several weeks for what has come to be known as "elder care." They're also bringing in consultants such as the Senior Partners group in Massachusetts and the Institute for Human Resources in Washington, D.C., to advise their workers about how to tap all possible resources for help with this family responsibility. Funds to help with elder care are becoming available as part of worker benefits at some firms.

Sue Roland's company had just installed such a program. It set up a hot line that Sue and others like her in the firm could call at any time to get expert advice on available elder-care resources such as home health aides and respite care. Sue's company also began offering employees lunchtime seminars on issues related to caring for aged relatives, giving her a chance to pick up information that helped her to feel more in control of her situation. When her father recovered sufficiently from his stroke, Sue was able to drop him off at the company-sponsored adult day-care center, an experimental program the corporation ran in a suite of rooms next to its day-care center for its employees' young children.

At present, Sue's story is the exception. Few companies have anywhere near the programs and facilities for elder care that hers provides. But her experience does foreshadow the future benefits that both middle-aged and, increasingly, older employees can expect to have available when they must cope with very old parents in failing health. By 2015, all union contracts will provide for them and managers will expect to be offered them at least as an option.

By then we will see much more of the cafeteria approach to benefits, already instituted by some corporations. Under such plans workers are allocated a certain amount of money that they can "spend" on benefits ranging from adult day care to extra-long vacations. The key element here is options—each worker chooses which benefits he or she wants most. For example, a woman in a two-income family covered by her husband's medical insurance might forego that benefit at her company to opt for adult day care for her aging mother.

Baby boomers were raised in a suburban culture that put a premium on leisure. The youth culture of the sixties reinforced this value. But as adults, boomers have been squeezed in a vise of time constraints. They are the generation that has learned to "work hard and play hard." By the time they reach their late fifties, they are likely to want to slow down the pace.

Influenced by older workers who will place their work in the larger context of what they want from life, workers of all ages may elect to take leaves of absence at regular intervals just for reeducation, soul-searching, and contemplation. The work sabbatical could become an institutionalized part of the employment cycle.

Almost twenty years ago, Xerox took the first small steps toward creating this new feature of work life. It chose about twenty people from its payroll of thirty-eight thousand to receive a paid yearlong "social service leave" for nonprofit work of the employee's choice. It did not set a precedent or change the lives of New Elders, but we can anticipate much larger programs of this type in the new workplace, with much of the time off unpaid.

The redefinition of careers and the increased role of the corporation in providing services such as day care and elder care could eventually produce a typical workday we hardly recognize. Jolie Solomon, a reporter for *The Wall Street Journal*, envisions this scenario:

It's Wednesday, Sept. 4, 2008, and another day at the office. You drop off your daughter, 12 years old, and your father-in-law, 80, at the first-floor Family Care Center. In your office, you look over yesterday's mail (you aren't working Tuesdays this summer), and you find a message from the company's school services: They've received the tuition bill from your son's freshman year in college and have paid it. You write a memo to your boss, outlining your plan for a three-month unpaid sabbatical to work with homeless children.

## READJUSTING SOCIAL SECURITY

As demand for older workers increases, and more elders find it desirable or necessary to stay employed, the laws affecting retirement will change. To make working into the later years a practical proposition, we will have to lessen the penalties in lost Social Security benefits for those who work after the retirement age. Workers 62 to 64 years old now lose $1 for every $2 they earn over $6,480 in one year. Maximum benefits will have to be adjusted to a higher percentage than is now the practice for each year people work full-time after 65. At present, they receive a 3 percent increase for each year worked between 65 and 70, with a scheduled increase to 8 percent by the year 2008. Private pension plans will also need adjustment so that nobody loses money because he or she rejoins the work force.

## LABOR-MANAGEMENT CONFLICT

These changes in the workplace will bring new strains to the labor-management relationship. A work force made up of many older employees working part-time schedules will look like a nightmare to labor unions. Such workers are notoriously difficult to organize.

We can anticipate a period of tension between labor and management as both sides maneuver to regain their balance with a changing work force. The equilibrium that will eventually result is likely to involve altered union strategies. Older employees will want more non-monetary benefits, so their unions will probably stress sabbaticals, tuition subsidies, access to the full range of jobs in the company, and the like. It's conceivable that older part-timers may form their own unions, thus presenting organized labor with a split comparable to that in the 1930s between craft unions that were represented by the American Federation of Labor (AFL) and industrial workers who were members of the Congress of Industrial Organizations (CIO).

On the other hand, unions may also be able to organize a class of workers now off limits to them. Some companies avoid a commitment to big salary and benefits packages by renting managers when needed, usually for periods ranging from three to nine months. New temp firms springing up to service these needs, including Management Assistance Group, Corporate Staff, and Interim Management Company, send retired managers out on assignment. Are these managers really part of *management?* If the rent-a-manager trend, now a minor part of the employment picture, should grow with the aging of the baby boom, the legal definition of who can be organized—which now excludes managers—may have to be changed.

Also looming on the horizon are possible management strategies to loosen the tight labor market of the future. Three significant ones include the use of telecommunications to give service industries instant access to cheaper foreign labor, the fostering of immigration to enlarge the work force, and the introduction of advanced computer software that would emulate the experience of elder workers.

Future demand for elder workers in this country may be influenced by improvements in computers and telecommunications that now make it possible for businesses to tap the foreign labor pool. Some service industries, for example, handle much of their office work abroad, where labor is cheaper. If this trend continues, at the end of the typical workday at an American financial securities firm, the last person out of the office will press a button that will automatically send all of the data involving the day's transactions to back offices in countries where skilled labor is cheaper than here. There workers will credit and debit customer accounts, and have the data ready for instant transmission back to the home office at the beginning of the next business day in the United States.

"This is a phenomenon that has just begun," says D. Quinn Mills of the Harvard Business School. "You'll see a lot more of it. And there are very few real limits to how far it can go." The limit, as in the export of factory jobs, will be how much of this practice labor will tolerate without demanding some type of protectionist law. It's a significant trend that bears watching.

Businesses could also fill some of their need for more skilled workers by getting the government to alter the criteria we use for admitting immigrants to the United States. Now preference goes to people who already have relatives living here, but in the future we may see legislation creating more slots for people who have skills that are in demand or high levels of education. The need for a larger base of taxpaying workers to support Social Security for retired baby boomers could attract widespread support for such measures.

Some firms have already tried to replace experienced workers who retire with computer software, creating a technology that mimics the wisdom and "smarts" these seasoned employees built up in years on the job. This phenomenon is part of the research and development of what is called "artificial intelligence." The Gartner Group, which follows such trends, reports that in 1987, businesses were developing twenty-seven hundred software systems designed to imitate human behavior on the job. In 1988, the figure leaped to eighty-five thousand.

Southern California Edison, for instance, has been trying to put engineer Thomas Kelly's talents into its computer. The 55-year-old

Kelly's specialty is dealing with the idiosyncrasies of the huge Vermilion dam in the Sierra Nevada Mountains. Much of his work overseeing the condition of the dam is seat-of-the-pants analysis. (He only gave up his slide rule for a calculator in 1987.) The company has spent three hundred thousand dollars on two experts in artificial intelligence who have tried to capture the essence of Kelly's thought process. But as one of the experts acknowledged, "Tom is very intuitive, and that is the toughest problem to deal with."

Such software has not yet proved to be the wisdom machine that futurists are predicting. It has had only limited success as a substitute for experienced workers and, if anything, this technology has brought home to many businesses the advantage of keeping their older employees. But given continued improvements in computer speed and memory, the next two to three decades could bring some amazing advances in this field.

## A MATRIARCHAL ALLIANCE

One of the most notable characteristics of the elder boomer work force figures to be the role that women will play in it—there is nothing similar among New Elders. Boomer women will have their own agenda. It will include pensions for themselves comparable to those their male counterparts receive and benefits including maternity leave and child care for younger women workers, who are likely to be their confederates in an alliance cutting across age and class lines.

There are no current estimates that would have baby-boomer women reaching retirement age at salaries equal to those of men in their cohort. This raises a sticky question: Will these older women also draw proportionately smaller pensions from their jobs? The shape of things to come may be seen in the current move to secure equal pay for equal work. This involves the idea that salaries for women's jobs have been kept artificially low, even when the jobs were as difficult or required the same skills as higher-paying "man's work." It's likely that court cases and political pressure will bring the equal-pension issue to the fore, probably between 2005 and 2010, when enough boomer women are facing the prospect of unequal retirement payments.

This issue will probably create as many problems for labor as for management. What position can unions take if comparable pensions mean reducing the stipends that men can anticipate? If the issue of

securing equal access to union jobs for blacks in our time is any indica-
tion of what we can expect, there could be a period of turmoil in the
union movement.

One factor causing lower pensions for many women may be their
need in the course of their work-life cycle to take maternity, child-care,
and elder-care leaves. This experience will make them especially sensitive to similar demands on younger women workers and will probably
generate ties among female elder boomers, middle-aged women workers of the Reagan Generation, and women employees of the boomers'
children's generation. The position of older women in their families,
discussed in chapter 2, will also create the grounds for this alliance.
These women will agitate for equal treatment in their unions, with
their employers, and in the realm of politics. Their fight could be a
landmark in the social and political history of the early twenty-first
century.

## ALIENATION IN THE TWENTY-FIRST-CENTURY WORKPLACE

As we come to the twenty-first century, more people in all fields will
be working part-time with progressively fewer hours and longer vacations. Add to this phenomenon the increase in flextime and job sharing
in many companies—where two part-time people who add up to one
full-time employee may never see each other—and you get offices
where people are working on increasingly divergent schedules.

What happens to the office social life? Relationships forged on the
job play an important part in many of our lives, and they will certainly
be changed when there's less nine-to-five. Aside from hurting office
morale, all this coming and going could result in the further atomiza-
tion of our society—more loneliness and increased indifference toward
others.

On the other hand, and on a more positive note, the addition of large
numbers of part-time elder employees to the work force could promote
more intergenerational friendships than exist now. Friendships are
usually confined to members of an age cohort who are in a similar stage
in the life cycle and work at the same level, live in the same place, have
children of about the same age, and so on. But elders working part-time
off the career ladder will interact with younger workers as equals,

providing the opportunity for friendship and socializing outside of work.

Paradoxically, the computerized office of the future could reawaken community consciousness in the generation of 1946–1964. Just as the cold megauniversities of the 1960s provided the basis for their own reform by bringing disaffected youngsters together in such large numbers, the computerized office may plant the seed of greater egalitarianism at work by changing work relationships. Professor Sara Kiesler of Carnegie-Mellon University sees these machines as undercutting the very distance they seem to create. She's spotted something inherently democratic about them: They "make people less aware of the status of others—so they can cross organizational lines." This will be especially true in the future as electronic mail becomes the main channel of intracompany communication. Elder baby-boomer employees, most of their working lives behind them, should be in sufficiently secure positions to pay less attention to protocol and more to getting the job done.

Older workers could also be a force for other changes in the office atmosphere and ambience. They are likely to be less driven and more relaxed because their schedules will allow more time to think, to pursue interests outside of work, even to fantasize. With their increased interest in health as they age, they are less likely to exhibit Type A behavior. In the interests of productivity as well as psychological health and fitness, they may encourage regular meditation breaks.

The elders' influence could show up in something as specific and basic as how people dress for business. They will be leading a more informal life that could set the tone for the office of the future. For example, there's nothing sacred about business suits. They first came into use in the eighteenth century, when gentlemen in England wore jackets resembling today's suit jackets in order not to be mistaken for common people. (The slits at the rears of their jackets permitted the garments to go over their saddles—a vestigial feature of today's suit jacket.) As an office uniform, the suit gained popularity in the nineteenth century because it separated the managers from the laborers. But today so many people wear them as to render that function almost extinct.

Nathan Edelson, director of the Center for Office Health and Productivity Enhancement in Silver Spring, Maryland, writing in *The Wall Street Journal*, suggests:

Let the standard of today's business dress be that of contemporary sportswear. Stylish, well-coordinated and not necessarily inexpensive sportswear outfits far better "suit" the conditions of the modern office than a uniform designed hundreds of years ago for the vagaries of the English moors. Such outfits would also encourage the healthful movements of limbs and very likely inspire the more lucid expression of thoughts.

If this seems too radical a departure from common practice to be believable, recall the adoption of "stylishly" long hair—and sometimes even Nehru jackets—in the offices of the late 1960s and early 1970s in response to the energy and power of the youth culture of the time. In the twenty-first century the same people who inspired that trend will be spending as much time wearing loose-fitting, comfortable clothing as they will business dress. There will be a lot of them, and they could become the tastemakers in office corridors and boardrooms.

Thus baby boomers could return to a familiar role. Pressured as youngsters to score high on college entrance exams, then thrown into competition with their huge age cohort in vast, impersonal universities, they finally forced these institutions to show a more humane face. They also created the youth culture as a response to the alienation they found in the rest of society. But then, out in the "adult" world, competition, pressure, and the demands of making a living in the 1970s and 1980s narrowed their vista again. Might they as older workers repeat their college experience of the 1960s and early 1970s? It's not out of the question.

# 5

# Social Security and Medicare: Defusing the Time Bomb

"[It is] the most complex program that God and the Congress ever made."

Social Security Commissioner Dorcas Hardy, on the system over which she presided.

In the summer of 1988, the Social Security Administration offered all workers a personalized analysis of the estimated retirement benefits they could expect to receive. Overnight its phones were "ringing off the hook," according to the agency's commissioner. To cope with the response, she ordered the installation of one hundred new lines. Within three weeks, the agency logged more than 1.5 million calls, half the total of such requests received for all of 1987.

According to a 1985 Yankelovich, Skelly and White poll, 66 percent of nonretired adults believe they will never receive Social Security retirement checks. Americans are understandably jumpy about what they can expect from Social Security when it's *their* turn to collect; after all, they've been hearing mostly bad news about their prospects for several years. "It is not yet possible to determine who will be the last recipient of Social Security benefits," claims Peter Young of the Adam Smith Institute, "but it is fairly safe to say that he or she is alive today."

Nothing is as sobering as the statistics that point to a possible future disaster. When the Social Security system was set up in 1935, there were forty workers to pay taxes to support benefits for each retiree. That ratio has steadily diminished to the present three workers for each current beneficiary, and taxes have risen to meet the costs. By 2020, should the Early Boomers be collecting under the presently constituted benefit structure, the ratio will be approaching only two workers for each retiree. At that time programs for older people will consume more than 65 percent of the federal budget—assuming no changes in entitlement programs—about double what they do today. And, it would seem, staggering payroll taxes will all but consume the workers who will have to pay them.

But baby boomers need not write off their Social Security retirement benefits. We *will* see a resolution to the impending Social Security crisis. And as has been the case all along with Social Security, the government will not make the necessary adjustments to carry the program well into the twenty-first century until an impending crisis makes it possible to extract at least some concessions from everyone affected.

## SOCIAL SECURITY

### Where It All Began

The Social Security system came into being slightly more than fifty years ago. The people who set up this system would be surprised to hear the hostility expressed toward today's retirees. Current critics say Social Security is not fair because elders get too-generous cost-of-living increases in their retirement benefits and enough services from all entitlement programs to be able to live better than many younger Americans. The original framers had something else in mind.

Born of the Great Depression, the 1935 Social Security Act had as its first goal not to make a better life for older people but rather to get them out of the labor force to open more jobs for the young, according to historian William Graebner. The enticement was a modest pension for those who worked in private industry. The money to pay these pensions was to come from a tax collected from both worker and employer. The legislation's supporters also hoped that the economy would get a boost by making consumers of older people who were not spending enough money.

As they wrote and debated about the new law, its advocates laid the groundwork for future misunderstandings about how Social Security works as well as what it was really intended to do. Those who created the system referred to it as "insurance"; they called the tax workers paid "contributions"; and they designated money used to pay retirement benefits the "trust fund." A. Haeworth Robertson, the Social Security Administration's former chief actuary, says that "they gave people a false impression that money was being put aside for them in their own retirement accounts."

Wilbur Cohen, one of the act's creators, says this linguistic smoke screen was thrown up deliberately so that people would not view the program as welfare. Older people thus became *the only group* "exempted from the Calvinist screenings which are applied to other Americans in order to determine whether they are worthy of public assistance," says gerontologist Robert H. Binstock. But in the long run, this strategy backfired. As beneficiaries of the one big program pegged to age rather than need, the retirees could later be singled out as the culprits when government benefit obligations began to outrun revenues substantially.

Congress began to expand Social Security almost as soon as the ink had dried on the original legislation. The government extended coverage to children and spouses—in effect, wives—early on. It added disability benefits in 1956, then increased them and included provisions to bolster the income of the poor, with the Supplemental Security Income (SSI) program of 1972, which was financed through general revenues. In 1956 and 1961, Congress lowered from 65 to 62 the age at which women and men, respectively, could begin to collect retirement benefits.

All along the number of categories of workers who were eligible for Social Security steadily increased. At the outbreak of World War II, the system covered about 60 percent of the work force, compared with about 95 percent today. In a major expansion of the scope of the program and the benefits that it would pay out, the Great Society gave us Medicare in 1965.

Also, from time to time, Congress raised benefits to allow retirees to keep up with inflation. In the 1950s, the nation's big corporations, such as Ford Motor, were strong supporters of these increases. Pensions were becoming part of their collective bargaining agreements with labor. The amount the company had to pay was often the difference between an agreed-upon amount and what the worker collected from Social Security.

In 1972, the Nixon administration introduced the idea of tying benefit increases (cost-of-living allowances, or COLAs) to changes in the consumer price index—a practice that has never been implemented for other kinds of government supports, such as Aid to Families with Dependent Children. Making Social Security increases automatic—"indexing" them—seemed a good idea because it placed the process above politics. But it also came close to putting the cost of Social Security beyond control. This problem became especially clear in the late 1970s and early 1980s, when inflation kept boosting benefit levels at a rate that was higher than the wage and salary increases of the average worker. In fact, the political appeal of pleasing elderly constituents has been strong enough that several times in the 1980s, when inflation did not reach high enough levels to trigger automatic increases in retirement benefits, Congress voted them anyway.

None of this was free. In 1972, the Social Security payroll tax rate was only 5.2 percent and wages over nine thousand dollars were exempt; now employees pay 7.65 percent on wages up to fifty thousand dollars.

The positive role Social Security has played in our society is clear. Robert Ball, who headed the agency from 1962 to 1973, points out that "the old poorhouse, with all its horrors, was very real. Old people, disabled people, widows, motherless and fatherless children frequently lived in desperate poverty. Social Security changed all that." And Robert N. Butler, chairperson of the Department of Geriatrics and Adult Development at Mount Sinai Medical Center in New York, and winner of the Pulitzer Prize for his *Why Survive? Being Old in America*, celebrates Social Security for its positive transformation of the American family. He says it has allowed children and parents to act toward each other "out of affection, not financial obligation."

The United States Senate Special Committee on Aging put the enormous contributions of the program in perspective when it reported:

The 1985 poverty rate of seven percent for families headed by older persons would have risen to 39 percent if Social Security and other transfer payments were not available. Likewise the poverty rate for older unrelated [single] individuals would have increased from 26 to 67 percent. Seven of every ten older families who would have had incomes below the poverty level without such benefits in 1985 were raised above the poverty line by transfer payments.

## Promises to Keep

Social Security today is a program with some enormous promises to keep. Most Americans have come to believe that they are entitled to certain benefits at predetermined points in their lives. We feel we have something coming to us. And we expect the program to be fair and equitable—everyone should be treated reasonably and the same as everyone else.

That's why Jack Doran, age 72, is angry. Jack's older brother collects a larger pension from Social Security than Jack does—for no good reason. Jack is a "notch baby," one of a group of retirees whose birth years condemn them—they feel—to perpetually unequal treatment. The "notch" refers to the dip in benefits paid out to people who were born between 1917 and 1921.

Who carved this notch? Why were Jack Doran and his cohort singled out? Congress was the culprit. The deed was done in 1978 when the legislators fine-tuned Social Security benefits. The hyperinflation of the 1970s was producing annual cost-of-living adjustments way beyond anything envisioned in 1972. To keep the program from going bankrupt, Congress phased in, over several years, new, lower increases. This change did not affect retirees already collecting benefits. But those people who entered the program during the transition to the new rate schedule—Jack Doran among them—received less per month in cost-of-living increases than those born just before them. To this day, Mr. Doran complains bitterly because his brother, a year older, receives $150 more per month than Jack gets.

This episode in the reshaping of retirement benefits suggests something important about the outlook for Social Security in its date with destiny as the retirement time of the huge cohort of baby boomers approaches. When runaway cost-of-living adjustments threatened the financial health of the program, Congress did the unpopular thing and took back some of the promises it had made. Taking advantage of public awareness of the shortfall in revenue, the legislators bit the bullet and modified the "entitlement."

But the plight of Jack Doran is bound to be repeated in the corrections the system will need in the future to keep it afloat. It's virtually impossible to tinker with such a system without hurting somebody.

In 1983, the government took still bolder action when, again, benefits were threatening to outrun resources. This time, Congress looked further into the future, and, eyeing the huge bill for retirement benefits that would begin to come due in 2010, fundamentally altered Social Security.

It took a crisis to make basic change acceptable. When it got to the point that the Social Security Administration had to raid its Medicare funds so as not to bounce retirement checks, Congress acted. Out went pay-as-you-go, the system that had current workers paying taxes to provide just slightly more money than the government needed to write checks for today's retirees. The legislators replaced the small cushion built into Social Security revenues to keep the benefits flowing during brief downturns in the economy with a major surplus financed by higher payroll taxes. Invested in treasury bills and government bonds, this surplus would protect the system against that rainy day forecast for the second decade of the twenty-first century, in effect making Social Security a kind of funded pension plan.

Perhaps ultimately more significant, Congress also made benefits received by wealthier retirees taxable, opening the way to a system that will ultimately be based on a means test. A person with an income of at least twenty-five thousand dollars (thirty-two thousand dollars for couples) would now pay income tax on half of what he or she received from Social Security. The age at which retirees could begin to collect full benefits was raised very gradually from 65, and will reach 67 in the year 2027. Congress also increased the tax rates and the cap on income subject to the payroll tax.

## Social Security and the Economy

Will the surplus created by the 1983 legislation save the system as it was designed to do?

An exuberant Senator Daniel Patrick Moynihan, who served on the National Commission on Social Security Reform that authored the revisions, recently wrote: "If we don't blow it, [the surplus] will put the Federal budget back in the black, pay off the privately held Government debt, jump start the savings rate and guarantee the Social Security Trust Funds for a half century and more." In 1988 the surplus amounted to more than $100 billion. If the economy holds out, Social Security taxes will add $80 billion a year by 1993, about double what Congress estimated in 1983. So why is everybody so worried about Social Security? By the time the baby boomers come to collect their retirement benefits, the surplus will enable the system's computers to write checks to cover its obligations without bouncing a single one.

If only it were a sure thing. Unfortunately, the amount of the surplus several decades from now is unpredictable. Under the best scenario put forward by the trustees, the surplus set aside for the Old Age, Survivors, and Disability part of the Social Security fund will climb to $12 trillion by the year 2025. But that's assuming the economy will experience *no* recessions, an audaciously rosy view of the future.

The odds are better that the surplus will take a beating in the short run. With budgetary and trade deficits acting as drags on the economy, unemployment will probably increase from the low level it reached at the end of the eighties, and a recession—possibly a serious one—is widely predicted for the early nineties. So sitting back and waiting for a rising tide of cash to carry us over the mountain of obligations ahead would be foolish and irresponsible. If the surplus is ravaged and the baby boomers feel cheated at retirement time, we could be looking at intergenerational warfare between elder boomers and the Reagan Generation, who will be forced to support the older generation through payroll taxes increased yet further.

## In Search of Solutions

The United States is not the only country in the world facing a future of more retirees and fewer workers, increased demands for Social Security benefits and diminished tax revenues to support them. Western Europe and Japan also have aging populations. They, too, face declining ratios of workers to retirees. Perhaps we can learn from their experiences and adapt some of their strategies to our situation.

Unfortunately, other industrialized democracies are not doing even as well as we are. West Germany, for example, has one of the oldest populations in the world. More than 15 percent of all West Germans are over the age of 65, and about 17 percent of the population should be in that age group in the next decade. By 2030, West Germany will have one pensioner for each worker. At current benefit rates, to support those retirees, that country's equivalent of the Social Security payroll tax would have to rise to about 33 percent. What's more, government retirement benefits make up about 90 percent of a typical German retiree's income, as opposed to 50 percent for the average retired American's. You would think that the first industrialized country to introduce government-sponsored pensions would be working day and night to find a way to meet its future obligations. But about the only thing the West German government has done to avert a future catastrophe is to cut back on a widow's right to collect a full double pension, hers and her husband's.

"No European nation has grasped the nettle," says Edwin Bell of the Organization for Economic Cooperation and Development. "They're all postponing their decision about what to do about it." In Italy, pension reform proved so unpopular a few years ago that the government had to abandon its efforts to put the system on a sounder footing. Great Britain has taken some small steps. In line with Margaret Thatcher's conservative policies, the government has lowered retirement benefits and offered tax incentives to get people to invest in private pensions.

The aged in Japan now make up about 11 percent of the population, and should comprise 20 percent of the total by the year 2020. One is not likely to hear the Japanese speaking of their elders as members of an affluent leisure class, since many of their old face hard times. Our image of the Japanese family as a tight-knit institution in which adult children lovingly care for their aged parents is moving farther from reality every year. While 80 percent of those over 65 lived with their children in 1960, the figure has since declined to 65 percent. Japanese law still compels blood relatives to support one another, and anyone supporting someone over the age of 70 receives a tax break. But in practice, many elderly Japanese have had to leave their property to the offspring willing to care for them, in effect buying peace of mind from their children in their old age.

In response to a squeeze on pension funds brought about by increased numbers of older people, the Japanese government cut back benefit increases and raised from 60 to 65 the age when retirees can collect full government pensions. Since the mandatory retirement age for full-time career positions at Japanese companies is typically 60, many retirees face several years during which they have to find low-paying, menial jobs (although the Japanese often prefer to work past the usual retirement age even when it's not a necessity, a 1981 survey showed). According to demographer Linda G. Martin of the University of Hawaii, the Japanese government encourages the hiring of older workers for these jobs through wage subsidies. The lack of retirement benefits comparable to ours, and not an exceedingly frugal nature, is the explanation for the extraordinarily high Japanese savings rate, reports *The New York Times*.

## Saving Social Security

How *can* we assure the best resolution of the potential Social Security crisis? What combination of policies is likely to be most acceptable to young and old?

Lowering the benefit level is not practical because the amount that most people get is already minimal—a supplement to whatever other sources of retirement income they have. Nor is privatizing the system—dismantling Social Security—an option. It's probably not politically feasible. Americans are not likely to tolerate a return to a system in which everyone is solely responsible for saving for his or her own retirement. Individual retirement accounts and Keogh plans notwithstanding, such a scheme would falter on its inability to guarantee the middle class a financially stable old age. The last time we had such a system, the Great Depression wiped out what people had put away for their retirement. "You really can't save enough now to cover old age," Martha Holstein of the American Society on Aging points out. "Almost everyone will need some public support."

We have only to look at the erratic performance and management of private pension plans to see the danger of putting too much faith in the solidity of this income source for future retirees. "Pension funds are piling through the door to invest in real estate—at a time when real estate investment fundamentals have rarely been worse," read the lead sentence in a recent article in *The Wall Street Journal*. Pension-fund managers were desperately looking for a shelter for these vast sums in their trusts because the safe haven they previously favored, the stock market's blue-chip stocks, had been swept by a typhoon in the crash of '87.

Saving Social Security will require a two-pronged attack. It will involve pumping up the national economy so we can pare down the national debt, reduce the trade deficit, *and* fund the baby boomers' retirement benefits. Steady economic growth will provide the tax revenues to fund Social Security. But there will also have to be changes in the Social Security system itself.

Fostering economic growth could be as simple as altering tax policies to encourage business to concentrate on long-term productivity gains rather than on short-term profits; such a strategy aims to heighten America's competitive position with respect to Japan and a united Europe. But that's only effective given the scenario of continued prosperity. It's likely that we will have a more difficult time, and that at least parts of the following scenario will come to pass:

Sometime within the next ten years, the next serious recession will reduce tax collections and conjure up images of the well running dry. At that time, no matter which party controls the White House and Congress, it will become clear that our economic engine will have to be fine-tuned, if not completely overhauled, so that it delivers the power to get us where we need to go.

We will have to invest the Social Security Trust Fund surplus, putting it to work to raise our economic capacity. If we experience sharp and prolonged economic decline, the scope of this enterprise could resemble the New Deal of the 1930s, a period of government activism also preceded by a conservative, laissez-faire era. Congress will authorize the creation of an agency to coordinate government investment in new and old industries, as well as in our infrastructure of bridges, roads, and communications systems. The government will encourage the formation of entirely new high-tech enterprises, retrain the labor force to shift workers from backwater industries to businesses on the cutting edge of progress, and, in general, step in, acting directly or indirectly, to make American business more efficient and competitive.

In this more controlled economy, the government will use powerful economic incentives to steer workers toward the jobs that will most benefit the economy. The watchword will be *productivity*, with educational benefits available at reduced tuition or free when such training will increase a worker's output. Vast sums of money will also go toward improving the education and vocational skills of black and Hispanic youth, who will form a proportionately larger part of the work force than they do now.

A more flexible immigration pattern will emerge, with the government opening and closing the doors to suit the changing labor needs of favored industries. These foreign workers, predominantly from the Third World, will pay Social Security taxes without being permitted to establish permanent residence or eligibility for retirement benefits. This new immigration policy will bear some resemblance to the European "guest worker" programs of the 1980s. Accompanying it, unfortunately, may be a similar rise in racial tensions and a further stratification of our society into rich and poor. Older workers may have mixed feelings about such a policy, since on the one hand it may crowd them out of some jobs while, on the other, buttressing the system that will eventually pay their retirement benefits.

And Social Security itself? The cap on earnings subject to the Social Security tax will be gradually lifted until there is no cap at all (but the tax rate will level off). In effect, Social Security will be based on the general income tax. Retirement benefits will be taxed even more than they are now. Also look for a decrease in the schedule of benefit reductions for those who continue to work after the retirement age, diminishing the penalty for continuing to work. This will do several things, all helpful. It will reduce the underground economy—many older people work off the books—thus recovering income-tax revenues now lost completely. It will also increase the tax base from which Social Security funds come, and it will encourage older people to work later into life, helping to compensate for the growing shortage of younger workers.

Finally, a healthier, longer old age and a shortage of younger workers will make possible—in fact, inevitable—an increase in the minimum age at which workers can begin to collect full retirement benefits. The 1983 legislation that scheduled an increase from 65 to 67 in very small increments has set a precedent for a still further postponement of that important milestone in the life cycle. The only thing preventing this postponement is the fact that we have not determined how to do it fairly. For people to accept this boost as legitimate, the government will have to convince them that it is not only necessary but just.

In a little-noticed recent article in an academic journal, Yung-Ping Chen, professor of economics and holder of the Frank M. Engle Distinguished Chair in Economic Security Research at the American College in Bryn Mawr, Pennsylvania, discusses the framework within which the new retirement formula is likely to be worked out. The government paid the first retirement benefits in 1940, when 65 was set as the age of retirement, Professor Chen points out. Since that time improved life expectancy has increased the number of retirement years and medical advances have made those years healthier. On the average, people spent about 7 percent of their lives in retirement then, compared with 23 percent now. Longer retirements have meant that the government pays more in benefits than the original act intended it to. That law's creators assumed that people would work from roughly 20 to 65 and then collect benefits for fewer years than they do now.

The arrangement for an equitable rise in the retirement age will go something like this: There should not be a monetary reward simply for living longer. A longer and healthier life is itself the prize. So we can preserve the spirit of the Social Security Act by keeping the ratio of years worked to expected years in retirement much what it was in 1940. By Professor Chen's calculations, that makes 70 the approximate present equivalent of the 1940 retirement age of 65. Assuming still further improvement in mortality rates as we move into the twenty-first century, the retirement age under this schedule could reach 73 by mid-century.

By increasing the funds available to pay retirement benefits, decreasing the amount well-off elders collect, and raising the eligibility age for full benefits, Social Security will muddle through. There are bound to be many echoes of the notch-baby phenomenon since transitions in the workings of the system will single out and squeeze some groups and individuals. But a basic tone of fairness will prevail. And through these changes, Social Security will continue to ensure at least a minimally decent standard of living for all Americans in their later years.

## MEDICARE

### Bigger Trouble

The problem of providing retirement income under Social Security will be overshadowed at the turn of the century by concern about another system: Medicare. When it comes to paying for medical care, the stakes are even higher. Cutbacks in the Social Security pension system might impose some hardships. Reductions in Medicare coverage or eligibility could be deadly. Intergenerational warfare over Medicare spending could produce real casualties.

As we look at the options available to those who will be restructuring the Medicare system in the twenty-first century, we can anticipate that we will keep the basic system now in place with some form of rationing and a modification of the way the health-care system delivers certain services.

### The Price Keeps Rising

Contrary to what many people believe, the cost of medical care in the United States did not start its ascent with the passage of Medicare legislation in 1965. The rise began around 1950 when medical insurance such as Blue Cross and Blue Shield became widely available to the middle class. With more people able to spend more money on their health, the price of health care began to go up.

But the coming of Medicare did boost medical costs considerably. At the behest of the American Medical Association, which spent $115,000 a day on lobbyists to influence Congress while it debated Medicare, the final legislation did not impose effective controls on hospital costs or doctors' fees. In hindsight, the consequences were predictable. With still more people suddenly able to afford even more medical services, the costs of those services took off. Over the next decade hospital charges increased at an annual rate of 14 percent, double what they had been until 1964, and physicians' fees rose 7 percent a year.

The frequency of visits to doctors and the length of hospital stays for everyone covered increased. Those eligible for Medicare now paid a smaller percentage of their bills than they would have before, while the government took care of the rest. But because the price of medical care went up so much, patients ended up with greater out-of-pocket expenses than they would have had before Medicare, even taking inflation into account. The upshot, concludes historian Allen J. Matusow, was that the program "primarily transferred income from middle-class taxpayers to middle-class health-care professionals."

As we enter the 1990s, Medicare has been partially reined in by the establishment of cost controls absent from the original legislation, but it still threatens to surge out of control. The medical miracles we've witnessed in recent years—ever more daring cardiac surgery, joint replacements, CAT scans—represent advances in cost as well as increased capacity to heal, cure, and improve the quality of our lives. According to Dr. William B. Schwartz, who teaches at the Tufts University School of Medicine:

> The artificial heart, new drugs for heart attack victims, genetic engineering and a host of other advances promise to accelerate the rate of technological change while raising health-care costs.
>
> Moreover, because most of our new diagnostic services are non-invasive, and thus painless and risk-free, virtually all barriers to their use have been removed. Even technologies that are cheaper per unit of service than the old technologies add greatly to costs because they are used more widely.

Also threatening the system is the sheer increase in the number of older people, since they have greater medical needs than the rest of the population. Particularly troublesome is the prospect of providing care to those over 80, the fastest-growing segment of the older population, and the group whose needs are greatest of all.

In recent years the Hospital Insurance Fund and the Medical Insurance Trust Fund, the two Social Security reservoirs of money dedicated to paying Medicare's bills, have occasionally had to borrow from the other Social Security fund—Old Age, Survivors, and Disability—to meet hospital and doctors' bills. In 1988, the Medicare funds' trustees reported: "Growth rates have been so rapid that outlays of the program have doubled in the last five years. For the same time period, the program grew 40% faster than the economy as a whole. The growth rate shows no signs of abating despite recent efforts to control the growth of the program."

Medicare no longer hands over a blank check for treatment. Since the mid-1980s it has specified how many days of hospital care it will pay for specific illnesses and what fees it will pay surgeons for operations. For the moment, these measures have slowed the rate of increase of the system's hospital costs. Nevertheless, by the year 2000 the budget for Medicare may exceed that of the Defense Department. Surpluses built up in the program could run dry a few years later.

There is disagreement over whether there is room left for cost cutting in hospital charges. But doctors' fees may be another story. The AMA is still a potent force in Washington, but popular sentiment that doctors charge too much increases as we move toward the millennium. (The average doctor earned $116,440 in 1987.) William Roper, who heads the administrative body that manages Medicare, says that

"Medicare physician spending has been and will continue to be out of control." From 1983 to 1988, the amount Medicare paid out for doctors' fees, outpatient procedures, and diagnostic tests went up about 15 percent a year. "Over the next 10 years," Roper adds, "even without any program expansions, we project that Medicare spending for physicians' services will triple." But there's a good chance that Congress will slam the lid down before that.

The price of medication could also be the focus of cost-trimming efforts. The drug industry is an inviting and obvious target for restrictions. Prescription prices have soared to the point that patients can measure the cost of their drugs in dollars per pill—three dollars a swallow for one new form of penicillin—so the drug companies have good reason to worry about price controls in their industry. We may see such controls well before the end of the 1990s if Congress can arrive at a formula that will allow for research and development costs.

Some people have suggested that the solution to the threat of a bankrupt Medicare is to shift more of the burden of retiree medical insurance to employers, which for many years have added this fringe benefit to their pension plans to the point that such plans cover about one-fourth of all retirees and one-sixth of those over 65. These plans have insured employees who retired early, before they became eligible for Medicare, and have provided supplementary coverage for those services not paid for by the government after the age of 65.

But now the trend is going the other way, as we pointed out in a previous chapter. In an effort to cut costs, corporations are *reducing* their liabilities in this area. Often this involves less coverage for people who have been with a firm for fewer than a specified number of years. With multiple careers and job mobility becoming the norm, fewer people will qualify for full benefits. TRW, for example, recently began such measures, diminishing coverage for fifty thousand employees. Pillsbury's economizing will mean greater out-of-pocket expenses for twelve thousand workers. An additional problem presented by this cost containment is that companies will no longer have the incentive to pressure doctors and hospitals to hold down their fees.

How about offering companies more tax incentives—like the ones they already get for building pension funds—to encourage the continuation of insurance plans for retirees at present levels? Don't expect it. That course would cut tax revenues, aggravating the federal deficit.

Medical IRAs in which people put away money for potential doctors' and hospital fees incurred after they reach 65, as they do now in special accounts for general retirement expenses, are a possibility. But that again runs into the problem of privatizing insurance in such a way that a large percentage of the population who can't afford to buy policies will end up insufficiently covered.

## The Health-Care Rationing in Your Future

Great Britain, which has socialized medicine, spends a bit more than 4.5 percent of its gross national product on health care—not unusually low for an industrialized nation. We now spend at the rate of about 11 percent of GNP, and in ten years the rate is expected to reach about 15 percent. Why does our medical care cost so much? According to Robert H. Blank, associate director of the program for biomedical research at Northern Illinois University, it is because we have chosen to spend our money on heroic and costly measures to deal with illness rather than promoting good health early on in life. He puts the choice facing us in the future this way: "Do we invest in preventative and primary care or do we continue to spend it on curative medicine? Do we emphasize care for the young or the old?" Blank calls for a national commission to be appointed now to deal with this question. "The commission must set priorities and it must also set limits and reduce expectations."

Several years ago Colorado governor Richard Lamm framed the problem much more dramatically when he said that those who were very old and sick had "a duty to die and get out of the way." Few social philosophers would put their views that starkly, although it is the gist of what they write. Dr. Mark Siegler, director of the University of Chicago's Center for Clinical Medical Ethics, says we will have to decide which patients can benefit most from expensive care. For example, he would have society pay for the treatment of painful and chronic arthritis of people who were alert, creative, or contributing in some way to their families and their community—in other words, still leading worthwhile lives. But he questions the value of heroic measures to save an 85-year-old woman barely hanging on after a massive heart attack. Where to draw the line? "I don't know," he writes. "You don't know. Nobody knows."

Daniel Callahan is one of the most prominent spokesmen for setting limits on how much we should spend to keep sick old people alive.

Author of *Setting Limits: Medical Care in an Aging Society* and director of the Hastings Center, a think tank that investigates ethical problems, he writes that the escalating cost of medical care strikes at the belief "that old age and good health are biologically compatible and financially affordable. It [the increasing cost of medical care] may turn out to be no less unsettling morally, forcing choices that could well corrode values and principles that are centrally important and deeply cherished."

According to Callahan: "Other countries have been far more successful in controlling health costs because they are willing to accept stronger government involvement, like Canada. And other countries are less enamored of endless medical progress. They're more prepared to accept illness and death."

Callahan applies utilitarian standards when it comes to drawing the line. The young offer the prospects of future productivity, the old don't, he reminds us. It's the quality of life that's important, not its length. He suggests that people reach the end of a natural life span at around the age of 80. Beyond that we owe it to the patient to relieve suffering, but nothing more.

Sociologist Amitai Etzioni, a visiting professor at the Harvard Business School, points out the danger inherent in rationing medical care by age. What if our economy hit the skids in the 1990s? Would that reduce "the 'maximum' age to 72, 65—or lower? And should the care for other so-called unproductive groups be cut off, even if they are even younger?" Etzioni asks. "Should countries that are economically worse off than the United States set their limit, say, at 55?"

Those who would be most immediately affected by age rationing have some strong opinions on the subject. "The people that are saying that medical care should be reduced at a certain age don't realize that they're going to get to the point where *they* will need such help," says Estelle Brown, a 71-year-old Florida resident. She is alive today because of open-heart surgery to replace a valve damaged by rheumatic fever when she was young. Such talk enrages her and members of her cohort.

We already have a hint of what a policy like age-based health-care rationing might produce. About forty million workers in the United States have no medical insurance. When one of them or one of their dependents needs dramatic, life-saving surgery, such as an organ transplant, the only hope is Medicaid, the joint federal-state program to pay the medical expenses of the poor that came into effect with Medicare.

This is a welfare program in which the federal government and each state pay part of hospital and doctors' fees.

The states decide for themselves how much money they will spend and on what procedures they will spend it. In 1988 Oregon shifted the money it had been spending on organ transplants to prenatal care. As a result, Oregonians witnessed a stream of TV commercials, news features, and wall posters featuring children in need of donations for transplant surgery. The lawyer for one of the children, a 7-year-old who died when his family's pleas for money for a liver transplant did not bring in enough, was bitter. He said: "It's degrading, really horrible. He was forced to spend the last days of his life acting cute; he had to become an actor to save his life. What about those people who don't look so cute . . . ?" What about people who are gray and wrinkled?

Rationing health care by age would be problematic for many reasons. In the worst-case scenario, anyone beyond the age limit would buy care as long as he or she had the cash, if not here then abroad. Rationing would also encourage the rise of a black market in medical care in this country—just as abortion was available for those who could afford it before it was legalized. Only the poor would no longer be considered candidates for cardiac surgery at age 76.

With the ranks of the 50-, 60-, and 70-year-olds expanding, and the advance guard of the baby boom poised to join them, the Callahan approach to apportioning our limited funds by age appears doomed. It threatens the interests of too big a part of the electorate. Unlike the system that ensures old people's retirement benefits, this entitlement program has little room for compromise—their lives depend too much on access to such medical care.

What then? The worst case would be an age war in which electoral might made right. That would mean either younger people depriving their elders of high-tech medicine or older people maintaining a tight grip on a large share of the resources our society could devote to medical care. The alternative is to find a way to spread any sacrifice equitably across the life cycle.

While there is little doubt that in the future we will devote more of our resources to preventive medicine, there is still the problem of the generations already too old to benefit fully from it. And under the best of circumstances, even with an excellent preventive medicine program in place, the deterioration often experienced in the last few weeks of life in old age will still be susceptible to heroic and extravagantly expensive measures to hold off death.

We do not yet have an appealing and widely acceptable solution to the problem of stratospheric increases in the cost of medical care. But the dilemma won't go away; as the population ages, the need to find a solution will become more pressing.

According to Larry R. Churchill, who teaches in the Department of Social Medicine and Religious Studies at the University of North Carolina, "No society has been able to avoid rationing its health care services. The only question is how to do it justly." As with the modification of retirement benefits, the key to the resolution of the problem will be to find a way that most people accept as just, legitimate, and fair. Churchill's own answer, rationing care by limiting the use of extreme measures throughout the life span, at least has the advantage of not saving money by withholding medical resources from one group.

The outlook is that as the year 2000 and the Medicare crunch approach, we will eventually adopt measures such as these to rein in medical expenses:

1. A campaign to encourage acceptance of the idea and use of living wills to place self-limitations on medical care in terminal illnesses. Older people often seem to favor the rejection of heroic measures to keep them barely alive for a few more days, but when the time comes they are often incapable of communicating their wishes. In the vacuum, their families usually ask doctors to do all they can to "save" their dying relatives. A shift to living wills will require legislative action in states that do not permit such documents.

2. A much tighter rein on government grants for research on the development of technology and techniques involving the practice of medicine at the "extreme"—life-threatening situations involving aggressive measures to stave off death. The young automobile-accident victim might potentially lose out as much as the 83-year-old cancer patient, but at least it will be easier to accept these funding cuts since they will deprive us only of medical miracles we have yet to experience.

3. A more critical look at the success rate of certain expensive medical procedures, such as coronary bypasses, whose efficacy has been questioned. For example, a recent study conducted by the Rand Corpo-

ration contended that 44 percent of heart bypass surgery was unnecessary. We can expect the government to set up panels of doctors to develop objective criteria against which we can measure the results of different approaches to dealing with specific conditions.

4. Tax incentives and changes in Social Security to encourage people to work longer, producing a net gain in payroll taxes collected by the government.

### In the Long Run . . .

David Samson, 73, had worked hard all his life. At age 63, with the nest egg he had built up and Social Security to supplement it, he and his wife, Eileen, then 59, retired to Arizona. For a few years they lived the life of leisure they had pictured when they made their retirement plans. But then David, who had begun to develop a shuffle when he walked, was diagnosed as having Parkinson's disease, a degenerative neurological condition. Eileen's chronic arthritis meanwhile worsened and the diabetes that ran in her family surfaced in her. Complications from diabetes eventually reduced her eyesight. Over the years David's condition worsened. With increasingly impaired mobility brought on by his disease, David became harder to care for. Eventually, Eileen had to put him in a nursing home.

Their three children did what they could. The youngest, Linda, the Samsons' 40-year-old daughter, who was the assistant director of public relations for a medium-sized company in Duluth, Minnesota, took on most of the burden. She flew to Tucson several times a year, sent her parents whatever money she could afford, and offered moral support to her mother on the phone. But she had a husband and 9-year-old daughter of her own. There were limits to what she could do.

Within two years of David's becoming institutionalized the $2,400-a-month nursing-home bill had wiped out the Samsons' nest egg. Medicaid stepped in, although Eileen Samson still had to turn over her husband's $459-a-month Social Security check to the nursing home, leaving her with an income not much above the poverty line.

This sad story will become more familiar as time goes by. Traditionally, the family took on the job of caring for their older members when they became dependent. Most of the time that is still the case. But with geographical dispersion of families, and with women, the traditional caretakers, now working, such a solution often imposes immense hardships.

While there are measures we can take to reduce exorbitantly expensive medical procedures to prolong life at the end, there's little we can do, short of decreeing a Nazi-like age limit to life, to avoid the cost of caring for the chronically ill and the debilitated old. One way or another we will have to deal with it. The question is how. The experience of baby boomers like Linda Samson who will increasingly have to care for, or supervise the care of, an elderly parent or other relative guarantees that enough pressure will be put on government to bring about some answers by the beginning of the next century.

## The Rising Issue of Long-Term Care

In 1988, Congress considered two proposals to change Medicare. One, a bill to finance care for "catastrophic" illnesses not then sufficiently covered under the program, became law. It covered expenses that more affluent elders were protecting themselves against by buying private, supplementary insurance, popularly called "medigap" policies. Congress designed this addition to Medicare to be self-financing, with those older people who could most afford it paying a supplement to their bills based on their income-tax liability. Coverage for prescription drugs and some nursing home and hospice care was also included in the legislation, which the AARP played a major role in getting passed.

At the same time, Congress turned down a bill that will define the battleground over the extension and cost of Medicare in the 1990s and beyond. Its provisions will weigh heavily on the mind of every American in the coming years, but it will most dramatically affect the baby boomers and their parents. The proposed law would have provided payments for long-term home health care and thus answered the challenge of the coming nursing-home crisis.

At any one time 5 percent of old people are in nursing homes—22 percent of those over 85. The head nurse at one nursing home said that her nursing students "are always astounded that the proportion is that low." (The rate was 2.5 percent before the coming of Medicaid.) Everyone who passes the age of 65 has about a 40 to 50 percent chance of being in a nursing home at least temporarily. In 1985 there were 1.3 million nursing home residents. But in ten years, the United States

Administration on Aging projects, that figure will reach 2 million. It will rise to 2.4 million in 2010 and almost 2.8 million in 2020.

Nationally, nursing-home costs average $2,200 a month. (After the advent of Medicaid, the costs increased at a rate of 15 percent a year from 1966 to 1982.) Within three months 70 percent of all new nursing-home residents who are single exhaust their savings; 50 percent of couples in which one member enters a home run out of money in six months.

Even if we had enough nursing-home beds to accommodate the number of people who will need them in the future, paying for the intensive care characteristic of such institutions will be a daunting task. Medicare pays only a tiny percentage of the cost, primarily limited to posthospital care and rehabilitation. Private insurance also covers a very small part of the tab—about 1 percent. Americans now spend about $42 billion a year for nursing-home care, with the government paying $20 billion of it, mostly through Medicaid—but only after the recipients of aid first spend down their assets. According to Dr. Joshua M. Weiner, who headed a recent Brookings Institution study of the problem, by the year 2020, assuming the continuation of present policies, the government's share of that bill will be $65 billion.

"Private insurance can play a much larger role," says Dr. Weiner, "but will never be a panacea because only 30 percent to 40 percent of the elderly can afford it." *Consumer Reports,* which surveyed the kinds of insurance policies available (including that offered by AARP), found them inadequate in their coverage and inefficient in their use of financial resources. According to Gail Shearer, manager of policy analysis for Consumers Union, which publishes *Consumer Reports,* "The private sector will divert about half of the premiums collected to pay for marketing, administrative costs and profits. In contrast, the Medicare program returns 97% of revenues to benefits for enrollees."

For many families, possibly the majority who finally must place a loved one in a nursing home, affordable home care would enable them to keep an elderly mother or father at home. Similar help for people who live alone would permit them to retain their independence. A policy that would finance the services of nurses and nursing assistants, home health aides, physical therapists, homemakers, and companion-workers to stay with chronically ill patients, offering frequent respite to their family caregivers, would also be a less expensive way of meeting the challenge of caring for the growing number of people over 85.

As it becomes clear that we cannot continue to increase the number

of nursing-home beds to keep pace with the growth of the aged population, our approach to dealing with chronic illness and debility will
change. In the next decade the increase in the number of nursing
homes will slow considerably. Their function will become more specialized. Within a decade or two we will regard nursing homes only as the
last resort when a person's condition makes it absolutely impossible to
care for him or her in any other way.

The state of Oregon offers an early picture of how necessity will force
Americans to change the way we care for the dependent and semide-
pendent elderly. The same state administration that redirected its
resources from transplant operations to prenatal care has also looked
into the future of nursing homes and found it limited. Dick Ladd, head
of Oregon Senior Services, says, "All these nursing homes sprang up
to chase all that Medicaid money." Too many people were ending up
in them who could get along outside if they could just get sufficient care
and medical attention—and if their families who were caring for them
at home could get enough help and frequent respite from their responsibilities. There had to be a cheaper and more efficient way of solving
this problem.

The task was to get the Medicaid bureaucracy to rethink the way it
allocated its funds. Oregon asked for a waiver on the expenditure of this
money, receiving permission to try a program in which revenue went
instead for home care. The result? Over the past decade the number
of nursing-home residents has remained the same, while the number
of those receiving home care has doubled. In 1987, the state spent an
average of $230 per month per person on home care, while its share
of the cost of nursing-home care was $962. Just as interesting, people
who have too much money to get Medicaid assistance but not enough
to afford private insurance or the bill for a nursing home or home care
can get help based on their ability to pay, on a sliding scale.

The nursing homes don't like it, but it's impressed other states.
Already most of them want the same type of waiver, and Mr. Ladd has
become very popular as a consultant on this subject.

New York is another state that sees home care as the wave of the
future. The Empire State spends 70 percent of the money Medicaid
sets aside for this purpose. In 1984 in New York, almost twice as many
chronically ill and debilitated patients were cared for at home as in
nursing homes at one-third the cost.

What does that mean in human terms? Anne, 67 herself, was at wit's
end. Her 91-year-old mother-in-law, who lived with her and her hus-

band, was still spunky and very much a member of the family. But an accumulation of infirmities made caring for her ever more complicated and burdensome, and it looked as if she would end her days in a nursing home. But thanks to regular visits from a nurse, daily help from a home health aide, and fifteen hours a week of someone who just comes in to watch over the patient, letting Anne and her family "get away" for a while, this extended family will stay together and the older woman can live out her life at home.

The home health care industry, which now grosses $7 billion a year, should more than double in size by the early 1990s, bringing in $18 billion annually. It will provide health care to the chronically ill and elderly in the future on an even larger scale. H&R Block's purchase of Medical Personnel Pool, the largest network of proprietary home health agencies in the country, highlights the potential for growth in this field. A more comprehensive Medicare program will absorb the cost of chronic care for the aged, taking over that function from the states and the Medicaid system. And Congress will authorize a means test for such care.

Workers who provide this care will push for higher wages and salaries. Older people have been a low-status group, and those who take care of such people are not traditionally well paid. As elders take a more central place in the scheme of things, those who care for them for a living may want to have their own status and pay reevaluated.

Government will have to regulate these health services more closely. By definition they are delivered in a decentralized manner, away from the watchful eyes of anyone responsible for seeing that the workers properly accomplish their tasks. While families will, of course, recognize mistreatment of their relatives, they might not be able to judge worker competence. A carefully worked-out licensing and inspection system will have to be created.

Despite the increased bureaucracy and greater federal and state intervention in the details of the delivery of health services it will involve, home care (hopefully bolstered by the enactment of a national, comprehensive insurance coverage program) is the only way we can afford to care for the chronically ill without being swamped by the multitudes that will otherwise be knocking on nursing-home doors as we turn the corner of a new century.

Paradoxically, increased government involvement will strengthen the role of the family in caring for its older members. The program will make some adult children more responsible for the care of their elderly parents than they might be now. A nursing home will no longer be a ready option, except in extreme cases. With funds for such expensive care less available and the beds in these institutions filled to near-capacity, a person who wishes to place a parent in a home may have to fulfill the government's stringent criteria before having the mother or father admitted.

While this may seem like a prediction of future heavy burdens, that is not necessarily the case. With much of the hard work of caring for the aged patient taken over by home health aides and other outsiders, family members will get a chance to interact without feeling the resentment and guilt that such care often entails. Boomers getting on in years themselves will thus have more of a chance to deepen their relationship with their aged parents, as we have already suggested. And at least part of the Medicare crisis may thus turn out to be a blessing in disguise.

# ⓑ

# Age Wars?

"... future forms of age-ism toward both young and old and the relations between age groups may well be one of the 'sleeper' problems of our times, perhaps in the way that race relations was a sleeper problem no more than twenty years ago. . . ."

Gerontologist BERNICE NEUGARTEN (writing in 1970)

"Why should I care about posterity? What has posterity ever done for me?"

GROUCHO MARX

The gray-haired urban guerrillas steal out of their retirement ghetto late at night and cross the forbidden zone into an area of streets containing schools, day-care centers, and playgrounds. Walking briskly and keeping to the shadows to avoid the Generational Police, they near their target, the National Institute of Youth. A 71-year-old woman, her arthritic hip forcing her into a somewhat measured pace, steps forward, pulls an old Geritol bottle full of gasoline from a shopping bag, lights the wick, and heaves the vessel against the side of the building. "Off your asses!" they yell, echoing the war cry of the venerable Maggie Kuhn, founder of the Gray Panthers. Several weathered fists punch the air in triumph as the bottle explodes against the wall, bursting into flames.

Silly? Sure. This scenario is as unlikely in the coming decades as the imprisonment of everyone over 30 was in the 1960s. Yet today's magazine and newspaper headlines, TV news reports, and documentaries speak of the War between the Generations.

Is this much ado about nothing? Hardly. Social Security and Medicare *are* in trouble. We will have to struggle to make the necessary adjustments to keep the money flowing in from today's workers and the benefits paying out to the future old, as we showed in the previous chapter. And there *is* reason to worry about whether everyone will be treated fairly in the process.

But the way the media have framed the issue, as young battling old, is a distortion of reality. Future relations between young and old present some complicated problems that need solving, and it isn't particularly helpful to polarize. Stories of young good guys who must vanquish greedy old bad guys to protect the children of today and the widows of tomorrow make great reading, but it isn't that simple. Humphrey Taylor, president of Louis Harris and Associates, testifying to the House Select Committee on Aging in 1986 about polls taken by his organization, said: "I must report conclusively that this hypothesis of intergenerational conflict is absolutely invalid." Polls conducted by the *Los Angeles Times,* the Gallup organization, Cambridge Reports, *The New York Times,* and NBC News point to similar conclusions.

Today's youth, as middle-aged adults in the early twenty-first century, *will* have to grapple with intergenerational matters the likes of which none of us has ever confronted. The presence of a much larger proportion of older people in their time will force them to ask and answer questions about what old and young owe to one another—and to examine ideas and values we have never really needed to consider seriously. But the political alignments of the future may also offer some surprises, with the formation of intergenerational connections now barely visible.

## "GUNS VS. CANES"

The idea of an Age War has not suddenly materialized out of thin air. A comparison of population projections for the next thirty years and

Social Security and Medicare benefits now mandated by law can be pretty sobering, as we have noted. Rising doubts about the future of Social Security and Medicare have opened a Pandora's box, and the accumulated fears and anxieties are flying out, helter-skelter. Hostility toward the New Elders and their "selfishness" at monopolizing so much of government expenditures has burgeoned. The controversy has been expressed in caricature: Greedy geezers grab for all they can get through a host of "entitlement" programs with no regard for what they leave the future old. This view has old people sponging off a gullible society that had better put an end to their nonsense before they empty the public treasury.

One writer, Henry Fairlie, suggested derisively in *The New Republic* that older people waste much of the medical expenditures devoted to them on "psychiatrists, therapists, and cosmeticians. . . . If one needs a psychiatrist by the time one is 65, one should take the quick way out: jump off a bridge." He confided to his readers in an aside: "When I was in the hospital not long ago, the nurses told me that the medical care for many elderly patients was really cosmetic, to disguise the natural process of aging."

A decade ago no national magazine would have published such a piece. Could older people have changed *that* much in ten years? What has made such a high level of contempt suddenly acceptable?

Strong, objective differences do exist regarding how best to allocate limited resources among social programs that often benefit only one group. But misunderstandings, mythology, and deliberate misrepresentations about the place of older people in our society—some of them spread by those who are advocates for older citizens—play a significant role.

Advocates for the rights and needs of older people have found success in the evocation of a negative image: the poor, frail, isolated, friendless, politically impotent, mentally slow, and forgetful older person who is deserving of society's assistance because she or he is helpless. In examining the passage of the Older Americans Act, the 1965 law that encouraged states and localities to plan comprehensive services for the elderly, for example, one scholar concluded that using "demeaning images of the aged" was the best way to get funds appropriated for their benefit. At its extreme, this technique made use of horror stories: desperate old people eating dog and cat food because they couldn't afford anything else. The stories may have been true, but they were made to sound as if they described the conditions under which a large percentage of old people lived.

Presenting the older members of society as "the deserving poor," as Robert H. Binstock, director of the Policy Center on Aging at Brandeis University, put it, helped get around the strain of puritanism in American culture. If the old could not help themselves, they were not responsible for their plight and deserved the help of society. "There is no reason why a wealthy American society should not do more for them," Binstock pointed out.

Social scientists describe this strategy as indulging in "compassionate stereotypes." In one Congressional debate over Social Security benefits in 1981, it ran rampant. According to a study made of that debate by political scientist Slava Lubomudrov, only about one-third of the arguments offered on the floor of the House were free of these stereotypes; almost one-half consisted exclusively of them. "Political support for the aging appears to be greatest among legislators who express misperceptions about the aging," Lubomudrov concluded of this early 1980s legislative fight.

Some older people do (and did) fit these stereotypes. They are needy. So what's wrong with exaggerating a little to pass some good legislation? Plenty. Romanticizing or otherwise misrepresenting any group can cause a backlash if the group is later perceived to be more powerful than previously thought and thus "undeserving" of social support. The road from "the needy" to the scapegoat can be perilously short.

A sudden shift in public perception of the old began in the late 1970s. By the early 1980s, unrealistically rosy assumptions about old people were in place. Magazines and television touted "the new ageism." Within a few years, the public image of the aged had all but turned on a dime. No longer eating pet food, old people were instead depicted as riding high in the saddle—too high for many people's tastes.

According to Professor Binstock, this was the new picture presented by the media:

(1) The aged are relatively well off—not poor but in great shape.
(2) The aged are a potent political force because there are so many of them and they all vote in their self-interest; this "senior power" explains why more than one-quarter of the annual federal budget is expended on benefits for the aged.

(3) Because of demographic changes, the aged are becoming more numerous and politically powerful and will be entitled to even more benefits and substantially larger portions of the federal budget. They are already costing too much and in the future will pose an unsustainable burden on the American economy.

That's a remarkable turnaround in the conventional wisdom—pathetic victims to powerful parasites—in just a few years. The shift was rooted in the growing awareness that our economy was no longer a treasure chest. People began to see our resources as limited, particularly in light of the Social Security crisis of the early 1980s. Giving to one group might mean deprivation for another. Anybody who has ever taken Introductory Economics has heard this described as the choice between "guns and butter": If government spends more on one, it can afford less of the other. We can't have it all, even when times are good. A sign of the times appeared in 1982, when an analyst for the Congressional Office of Management and Budget posed the trade-off as "guns vs. canes."

Since then, TV documentaries, local newspapers, and *Time, Newsweek,* and *U.S. News & World Report* have treated us to a steady stream of stories suggesting that the future will bring a polarization of American society along generational lines. It's all going to come to a head when the first baby boomer blows out the candles on his or her sixty-fifth birthday cake, according to these sources. *Is* that where we're headed? Are we in for an intergenerational Armageddon or is the Age War only a ploy? Let's get beyond the manipulation of politicians, the exploitation of a dramatic image by various interest groups (old and young), and the media's melodrama.

## The Drama and the Players

In 1984, in the wake of a scare over what some perceived to be the imminent collapse of the Social Security system, Samuel H. Preston, director of the University of Pennsylvania's Populations Study Center, gave an address that was later published as an article in *Scientific American.* Titled "Children and the Elderly in the U.S.," it was widely discussed and is still often cited.

"The conjugal family is the chief source of support for children," Preston said. "In recent years it has begun to divest itself of its responsibility for the young, just as earlier it abandoned much of its responsibility for the elderly." But the government, through retirement insurance and Medicare, was now shouldering much of the burden of caring for older people. On the other hand, especially after the Reagan administration's cutbacks in social welfare programs in the early 1980s, government was doing less to make up for the lack of support and nurturing experienced by many children. Their plight resulted from living in families that the father had deserted, or from the lower standard of living that often accompanies divorce and maternal custody.

Preston made the connection between the unequal status of these two age groups at either end of the life cycle, suggesting that one was benefiting at the expense of the other. He claimed that people have a natural tendency to favor older Americans in this competition for government spending. For one thing, "the elderly, unlike some other special interests, make up a group we all expect, or at least hope, to join eventually." With declining mortality rates, more middle-aged people have parents still living and taking advantage of Social Security. Another significant factor is that the disadvantaged children in question "are increasingly from minority groups with whom the majority have trouble identifying."

He concluded by casting the problem in terms that would come up again and again: "Whereas expenditures on the elderly can be thought of mainly as consumption, expenditure on the young is a combination of consumption and investment." In other words, older people no longer work; they are not productive, and money spent on their needs will never be seen again. But the young, who will become workers, will pay future dividends on any funds diverted to them when they ultimately add to the national wealth. The obvious conclusion is that we should spend less on older people and more on children.

The battle was joined by forces that aligned along conservative versus liberal lines. On one side stood Americans for Generational Equity (AGE), an organization among whose sponsors are major corporations that hope to reduce their participation in the Social Security tax. AGE's goal is a smaller Social Security system, with Americans supplementing diminished government retirement benefits with private pensions, IRAs, and the like. Across the battle lines Preston helped to draw, AGE faced the American Association of Retired Persons (AARP), which is the largest old-people's advocacy group in the country and has its own business interests.

## AGE versus AARP

AGE was formed in 1985 to publicize the view that people in their twenties, thirties, and forties were in danger of being ripped off by social programs that benefited older people at the cost of depleting resources that should be held in reserve for the future old. One of its first major activities was to sponsor a national conference on the theme "Tomorrow's Elderly: Planning for the Baby Boom Generation's Retirement."

AGE's mandate is to "promote greater public understanding of problems arising from the aging of the U.S. population and to foster increased public support for policies that will serve the economic interests of next century's elderly." Its view is that the "excessive" benefits the current elderly receive from the government have played a big role in the ballooning of the federal deficit. According to AGE, not reducing the benefits will create "the potential for real generational warfare in the next century."

Republican senator David Durenberger (Minnesota) and Democratic congressman James R. Jones (Oklahoma), chairman of the House Ways and Means Subcommittee on Social Security, headed the group at its founding. Its membership includes corporations such as Equitable Life Assurance, Metropolitan Life, the U.S. League of Savings Institutions, General Dynamics, ITT, B. F. Goodrich, Ford Motor, USX, (formerly U.S. Steel), Chrysler, and Exxon, and health-care companies such as the Hospital Corporation of America and Beverly Enterprises, whose chain of nursing homes is the nation's largest. Representatives of conservative think tanks such as the Heritage Foundation and the American Enterprise Institute serve on its board of directors. Sources of funding include the Cato Institute, one of whose main activities is to work for the privatization of Social Security.

Opposition to AGE's point of view comes largely from advocacy groups concerned with issues of aging and from old-age membership groups, the largest of which, by far, is the AARP. Twice as large as the AFL-CIO, with twenty-eight million members, the AARP has signed up almost 25 percent of all registered voters in the United States— most of them white and middle-class. Only about 3 percent of its membership comes from minority groups. It has a $235 million annual budget, an eight-story headquarters building in Washington, D.C., and its own zip code, and it sent out about 1.5 percent of all nonprofit third-class mail in the country in 1987. The association represents close to 40 percent of all Americans over the age of 50, the minimum age for membership, lowered from 55 in 1983. In 1996, the first baby boomers will be eligible to join. AARP communicates with its members through its magazine, *Modern Maturity*, which has the largest circulation of any magazine in the United States.

Where did this giant come from? Founded in 1958, it came into being to fulfill a specific need. The National Retired Teachers' Association, started by Los Angeles high school principal Ethel Percy Andrus in the late 1940s, had begun marketing reduced-rate life insurance policies to its members in 1955. Insurance companies had been rejecting them as poor risks because of their age. Other retirees wanted to take advantage of this service, and the AARP was formed to allow their participation.

The annual five-dollar membership fee covers only one-third of the association's expenses. Group purchasing power—and the service fees retained by the organization—form the underpinnings of the association's activities. Its mail-order pharmacy service is the world's largest run on a private, nonprofit basis. Its catalog features a large variety of goods aimed at older consumers. In dealing with the companies whose products it sells, AARP is very hard-nosed in securing good deals for its members. To companies that would offer products in its catalog, the association has stipulated: "Your product will be featured at a reduced price or not at all. . . . We are not easy to do business with . . . but no one else can offer you the target market of 50+ as well as we can."

AARP also continues to sell a variety of insurance. Health insurance, from Prudential, represents the largest segment. The association, which serves as the collecting agent, holds the premiums long enough to keep an interest float of $15 million per year and also collects a 4 percent service fee. It offers home and auto insurance through the Hartford Insurance Group. Members may also take advantage of a special investment fund (and they do—the fund totals more than $3.5 billion) and a wide variety of travel services at substantial discounts. In 1988, in an effort to become a major provider of general financial services to its members, AARP started its own credit union.

AARP staffs its projects with 250,000 volunteers. There is usually a waiting list of several thousand to join this army of unpaid workers. Its services include income-tax counseling for older people (in cooperation with the IRS) and grief counseling for widows and widowers through a one-to-one support network.

"What they do affects the whole country," says Paul S. Hewitt,

AGE's executive director. With a Washington-based legislative staff of 125 and 20 registered lobbyists, AARP is "the most powerful lobby on Capitol Hill," not to mention a formidable force at any of the nations' fifty statehouses when the need arises. It is a major power in the struggle over what to do about providing for older people in the future.

On one side of the battlefield, then, we have AGE, which claims to represent the interests of today's young (and tomorrow's old); on the other are the forces of the AARP, which represents the interests of those 50 and older.

### Youth versus Age: A Red Herring?

Not all analysts agree that this is where the battle lines will be drawn, however. Some say that pitting the old against the young is just a red herring. William R. Hutton, executive director of the National Council of Senior Citizens, for example, says that while AGE "claims to be working for increased fairness and cooperation between the generations . . . [it] promotes divisiveness, not equity. The organization's solution to poverty among the young is to attack programs that help the old. This strategy poses a danger to needy citizens of all ages."

In answer to AGE's claim that it speaks for the interests of the young—the retirees-to-be—Hutton points out that without generous Social Security benefits for their parents, "the burden of support would fall largely among younger family members. At precisely the time that adults are struggling to rear and support their children, the responsibility for dependent parents would create enormous family stress, not to mention substantial costs." Thus, transferring the burden of support back to the family would impoverish more children because their parents would have to spend large sums to support *their* parents, money they would ordinarily devote to their children's needs.

Ronald Pollack, executive director of the Villers Foundation and a former dean of Antioch University Law School, agrees: "It is the growing disparity between rich and poor, not between old and young, that tears at the fabric of America." Pollack emphasizes that many older people have incomes that are only slightly above the poverty line (which, because of entitlement programs, is set at about one thousand dollars below the poverty-level income for other people). About 42 percent of America's elders have an income less than twice the poverty level. He decries the stereotype of "the tanned senior citizen lounging in a Ralph Lauren polo shirt at a sumptuous Florida 'gold coast' condominium with nothing to worry about other than his latest golf score."

Picturing money spent on elders as funds taken away from children shows the problem in a crooked frame. Meeting one group's needs does not necessarily exclude the other. One way to do justice to both would be to spend less on the military, for example. Why is the ratio of taxpaying workers to retirees so often brought up, while we never ask how many workers it takes to support the building of an aircraft carrier?

The idea of a coming age war depends upon the assumption that old people will stick together, acting in concert to force their will on the rest of society. The specter of a monsterlike AARP, lying in wait to crush any proposals that would limit benefits to older people and always ready to propose new entitlement programs, makes an especially powerful image. The Age War idea also assumes that younger Americans will see their elders as the enemy and act together themselves to thwart the efforts of older people to monopolize the national wealth for their own needs. In other words, it assumes that *the* old and *the* young are largely monolithic groups that know just what they want and will single-mindedly pursue it. Is that the way it's going to be? Let's look at the potential for turning the two generations into effective voting blocs.

## The Politics of Age

"Politics," social scientist John R. Weeks has written, "is one of the few social institutions in modern society in which age is often equated with wisdom, sound judgment, and power." In Congress, the forces who speak for the interests of older Americans were (until his recent death) led by Representative Claude Pepper. This former New Deal senator rose phoenixlike from an earlier political defeat to become the favorite villain of everyone who thinks that old people are getting more than their share. He had a second career, and then some. In the 1982 Congressional election campaign, when a looming crisis in the Social Security system threatened to cut into retirement benefits, he campaigned in twenty-five states, helping seventy candidates. He made sure that an increase in the Social Security payroll tax would be an important part of the solution.

When 72-year-old Irene Herbert visits the Pennsylvania state capital, she's not there to sightsee. To get there, she rises at 5:00 A.M. to catch the bus chartered by her senior citizens' advocacy group; her sister, with whom she lives, knows not to expect her back until nine that night. Ms. Herbert spends the day buttonholing state legislators, making sure they know how her group stands on issues such as the expansion of Medicaid and the regulation of nursing homes. She takes breaks only to have lunch—a half hour—and to down a nitroglycerin pill when dizziness from her heart condition threatens to temper her zeal.

Although the number of politically active people her age is increasing, Ms. Herbert is still something of a dramatic exception. Older people of her generation tend to be less active than people of other age groups in trying to influence how their representatives vote. They also participate at a lower rate in election campaigning.

However, they *are* more likely to vote than members of any other age group. The most powerful voting bloc, as every politician knows, is the 55- to 74-year-olds. More than half the older people in this country live in eight states that are crucial in presidential elections: California, New York, Florida, Pennsylvania, Texas, Illinois, Ohio, and Michigan. So anyone who wants to occupy the Oval Office had better pay some attention to what these people want. They will make up an even bigger share of the electorate in those states in the future, and their influence can only grow.

It would be a mistake, however, to draw conclusions too quickly about how older Americans will exercise that influence. There is very little precedent for their age group exercising collective power. It was not some irresistible gray voting bloc that secured the entitlement programs we have today. As political scientists John B. Williamson, Linda Evans, and Lawrence A. Powell have pointed out, "Such legislation as the Social Security Act, Medicare, and the Older Americans Act, which are often interpreted as major victories for the aged, are largely the product of efforts of others on behalf of the aged, rather than being due to the political influence of the elderly themselves."

Older people have begun to take their fate into their own hands in the last ten to fifteen years, however, particularly through the activities of the AARP. Of all the groups and individuals speaking up for the retired and their interests, none is accorded more political respect—though some would call it fear. The AARP Voter Education Fund, begun in 1986 and now active in eighteen states, promotes voter registration among its members and lets them know how candidates stand on issues related to aging. Financing comes from voluntary member contributions, not the membership fee; the association keeps the donations in an account separate from that paying for other AARP activities. The fund also has a nonprofit tax status. John Rother, the association's director of legislation, has declared himself well satisfied with its initial efforts. For its first year of operation, he claims, 5 percent of the people it reached changed their vote.

Yet even the AARP's political power is less than monolithic. The organization's membership includes 20 percent who consider themselves political independents and the rest are evenly split between Democrats and Republicans, so no single party can claim their loyalty. People in their early fifties do not necessarily have a lot in common with those in their nineties. A glance at the letters to the editor in *Modern Maturity* reveals that even on issues such as Social Security and Medicare, for which self-interest would seem to dictate a united front, there are differences of opinion about obligations to the young, further government intervention in people's lives, and the responsibility of AARP to act with the interests of society as a whole in mind and not just those of its members.

"For all its supposed clout," writes Landon Y. Jones, managing editor of *Money*, "AARP is unwilling and probably unable to mobilize its members behind its policy positions."

### Elder Boomer Politics

But will American politics change as the baby boomers age and older people become a proportionately larger part of the population? "The big challenge for A.A.R.P. is to provide leadership to meet the needs of 77 million baby boomers coming on line," said Cy Brickfield when he recently retired as AARP executive director. In which direction might the organization lead, and would the boomers follow? Is there a political persuasion "natural" for older people, which would enable us to predict how the huge cohort of baby boomers will act politically decades from now?

According to political scientists John C. Campbell of the University of Michigan and John Strate of Brandeis University, the results of their study of the attitudes expressed by voters in national elections from 1952 to 1980 showed that, compared with the young, older people "are more likely to cling to traditional social values, are less in favor of racial equality, take an isolationist position on foreign affairs, are concerned about law and order, and tend to oppose most governmental services that do not benefit themselves directly."

But a close look at these results show how tricky it can be to try to predict people's politics by their age. What the study demonstrated was that the historical experience of a generation, not its age, determines its politics. These parents and grandparents of the baby boomers were raised with values that are significantly different from those learned by today's generation of young and middle-aged adults. The baby boomers will reach their later years assuming that divorce is an acceptable solution to a marriage that has soured, for example. Their parents have much more ambivalent feelings about divorce, and their grandparents find it even harder to swallow. Racial attitudes, too, are a product of generational experience. Most of the older whites in the Campbell-Strate study were taught—either overtly or by observation of their parents' words and actions—that blacks are socially inferior. White baby boomers have been raised at least to pay lip service to notions of equality, and they have matured in a more racially integrated society. Attitudes toward foreign policy have much to do with how the world was when a person matured. And law and order is a matter of self-interest to those whose physical ability to avoid assault is beginning to diminish.

So, for the most part, there is no inherent political stance that comes with the territory in this part of a person's life span. Campbell and Strate concluded: "The political orientations of older people are not peculiar. Knowing that someone is old will not help very much in predicting how conservative he or she is, in most important respects. The elderly are very much in the mainstream of American political opinions."

Nor do the more conservative leanings of the baby boomers since the 1960s necessarily predict their politics as 60- and 70-year-olds. Their move to the right was a response to the times and a sign that they were passing through a point in their lives when building careers and families clouded out everything else. Had they reached the edge of middle age in the 1930s, their political outlook might have been a different story. Their future politics will very much depend on what sort of society they confront in their later years and the total life experience they bring to it.

But there is still the matter of self-interest and the implicit threat of an age war that lies behind it. Will the huge cohort of baby boomers as elders, in an effort to get age-related benefits from the government, come on like a political juggernaut in the twenty-first century, ramming their pet programs through state legislatures and Congress? Robert B. Hudson, professor of social welfare policy at the Boston University School of Social Work, says it could go either way:

> Should able elders emerge with a common consciousness built around age, ability, or other life circumstances, their being a group with vast personal, economic, and social resources would make them, in the parlance of a younger generation, awesome. At the other extreme however, is the possibility that the future able elderly will have so little in common, will be so numerous, and will have so many identifications with people not so labelled that their differential political impact could be virtually nil.

Certainly the elderly baby boomers will present a potentially more formidable group of voters than the present old do. They will be better educated, and those with more education have a higher voting rate. In 1980, at the last census, 44 percent of those aged 65 to 74 were high-school graduates and 10 percent had completed college. But by 2020, we can expect about 86 percent of this age group to have high-school diplomas and 24 percent to be college graduates. Baby-boomer women will bring with them into old age less passivity and a much more extensive work history than did their mothers and grandmothers. Issues such as the ERA, abortion, and child care have made them a politically aware and mobilized generation.

The prominence of women among baby-boomer elders and the developing matriarchal tone of the family suggests the future importance of gender-based coalitions. Elder boomer women will share with their daughters and granddaughters a common consciousness on issues like child care and abortion. Therefore the decade 2010 to 2020 is likely to see a woman's right to choose whether to bring a baby to term written into the Constitution. Day care will also be guaranteed by law, with sufficient funds provided through a combination of government appropriations and the requirement that businesses supply such care for the families of their employees.

Improvements in communications technology will allow baby boomers to remain politically active well into their old age. Two of the reasons that older people now tend to take a smaller part in political activism are the minor infirmities and diminished energy that accompany aging, especially from the mid-seventies on. But by the time the baby boomers are the nation's elders, new communications technology will provide all age groups with an equal opportunity for increased political participation. Interactive television will make it possible to respond instantly to polls taken by representatives simply by pushing a button on the set, for example. This development is already upon us. Cable TV now makes it possible for a voter sitting in his or her living room to respond to a question on the screen by pressing a "yes" or "no" button on a device connected to the cable. By the time most of today's 30- and 40-year-olds reach their later years, political uses for interactive communications will be commonplace.

### Intergenerational Politics:
### The Wave of the Future

It's November 2020, and the people have spoken. The Dan Rathers, Peter Jenningses, and Tom Brokaws of their day are wrapping up their presidential election coverage. Will their analysis include what the elder bloc of voters did at the polls? Or will the diversity of the baby boomers defy easy generalization?

The anchormen and -women will look at which candidates promised most in the way of legislation benefiting older citizens. But they will also examine the role of the aging baby boomers in coalition politics.

Demographic developments within our country present the possibility of a complicated series of intergenerational relations in the twenty-first century, something much more complex than just young versus old. For the first time, racial minorities will be represented in substantial numbers among our country's aging population, for example. About 90 percent of those now over 65 are white, but by 2020 nonwhites will constitute about 21 percent of older Americans, making their interests a much more significant factor in considering the needs and desires of the aged (in 1985 the AARP finally got the message and established its Minority Affairs Initiative).

Older Americans from ethnic minorities will see a disparity between their Social Security retirement benefits and those of the white majority. Since the amounts on their benefits checks will depend on lifetime earnings, minority retirees will receive consistently less than their white counterparts. At the same time, more minority workers will be employed in the labor force and the taxes they pay will go to support retirement benefits. The Hispanic segment of the United States population is growing five times as fast as the rest of America and will supply a much greater proportion of workers in the next century. Ethnic origin, race, and class may be just as important as age when commentators discuss Social Security issues in the year 2020.

Even now the spread between rich and poor is greater among older people than in any other age group. For the most part this is related to age and gender: Lower income is more likely to be the case if a person is older and female. The widening gap between income groups in the rest of the population will probably carry over into succeeding age groups as the population ages. There is thus a greater chance of class warfare than there is of open and unremitting struggle between well-defined age groups.

Intergenerational coalitions will be as much a part of the political scene as will concerted efforts by older people to protect the interests peculiar to their age group. One cross-generational issue that the TV commentators will note in the wake of the voting is the environment. By the second decade of the twenty-first century environmental concerns will have resurfaced from their premature retreat in the early 1980s. Productivity and economic competition notwithstanding, enough people may have choked to death in killer smogs and succumbed to bacterial infections and tumors brought on by polluted drinking water to raise ecology out of the domain of reformism and into the realm of bread-and-butter politics. In this movement, the anchormen and -women will observe, the generation of 1946–64 has always been active.

While Vietnam and civil rights were as much the leading themes of their older brothers and sisters of the Eisenhower Generation in the 1960s as they were baby-boomer causes, environmentalism was the quintessential boomer issue. On Earth Day, April 22, 1970, ten thousand elementary and high schools and two thousand colleges dispensed with regular classes to focus on ecological issues. Ecology is a motif in their consciousness that has never faded. When former senator Gary Hart was a front-runner for the presidency and widely considered the candidate with high appeal to their generation, it was his stand on environmentalism that most endeared him to voters in their thirties and forties.

Why should this subject take on such vital importance in the baby boomers' later years? "Old people are, by nature, conservationists," say psychologists Erik and Joan Erikson and Helen Kivnick. "Long memories and wider perspectives lend urgency to the maintenance of our natural world."

It is, of course, in every age group's self-interest to preserve the environment. Indiscriminate dumping of wastes may imperil children's play areas. Pregnant women could miscarry because of substances that should not be in the drinking water. But elder baby boomers are likely to have an even more *immediate* reason to lead the fight to preserve the environment. Just as the threat of the draft made many young men particularly zealous antiwar activists in the 1960s, so will environmental dangers that create immediate life-threatening conditions mobilize elder boomers. They will, for example, be at an age when access to prescription drugs becomes a more important part of life—people over 65 now fill three times as many prescriptions per year as do younger patients. And because of environmental degradation, that access will be in deadly peril.

According to British botanist Hugh Synge, an organizer of a recent conference sponsored by the World Health Organization, the World Wildlife Fund, and the International Union for Conservation of Nature, the destruction of rain forests and vegetation all over the world threatens extinction for "one in every four of the world's medicinal plants." In this country, 25 percent of all prescription drugs are derived from plants. For anticancer agents, that figure approaches 40 percent. Varieties of foxglove, used to produce heart medicines like digitalis, are among the plants threatened. With increased medical interest in the healing power of plants, extinction could also snuff out potential cures not yet discovered. For the future old, environmentalism will be a matter of life and death.

Similarly, the levels of air pollution produced by atmospheric inversions threaten older people with more than just raspy throats: they kill. It happened in Donora, Pennsylvania, in 1948, taking the lives of twenty residents, most of them elderly, and forcing the evacuation of cardiac patients and those with respiratory conditions. A killer fog in London wreaked similar havoc, but there four thousand died. Imagine how baby-boomer elders will react to the first deadly Los Angeles smog.

Is there a scenario that could produce intergenerational conflict here? Environmental activists in the future could face an opposition that, while encompassing some elders, is likely to be predominantly younger, most likely based in Reagan Generation adults who will then be approaching or entering middle age. The crux of contention would be ecology versus jobs. Foreign competition, if anything, could make it even more painful in the future to choose between cleaner air and water and the maintenance of industrial production. There will be enormous pressure on the American economy to turn out goods as cheaply as possible, even it means environmental degradation.

## An Intergenerational Coalition Based on Disabilities

An even more important coalition will emerge sometime after the year 2000 involving the great number of Americans who are disabled. This intergenerational alliance could encompass more people than AARP and substantially change the appearance of our cities and towns as well as alter our political landscape.

Estimates of the number of people in this country who have a disability vary, depending on how the term is defined. The United States Census Bureau says there are thirty-seven million Americans with impairments, the majority of which are physical. People over 65, who may typically experience severe arthritis, other mobility impairments, or hearing problems, make up a significant segment of this population. We don't know exactly how many, but a 1984 survey of those needing long-term care conservatively put the figure at close to seven million.

The development of antibiotics and other improvements in medical technology that coincided with the beginning of the baby boom have increased the number of disabled people. Many who would not have survived illnesses at birth and during childhood were saved and have gone on to live a normal life span.

Many people with disabilities have important problems in common: difficulties with access to buildings and other facilities, the experience of prejudice, and varying degrees of social isolation. They have begun to articulate their special needs in a movement of protest, demanding social change. It was only about ten years ago that a cross-disability coalition of people with different impairments first came into being to stand up for the rights of all disabled persons. Disability consciousness, an awareness of the rights of people with disabilities to be respected and treated equally, has risen steadily among the young for the past decade or so—witness the successful 1988 protests at Gallaudet College for the Deaf in Washington, D.C., which forced the trustees to appoint a deaf president for the institution.

But disabled people have not yet made common cause across generational lines. New Elders and the Old Guard are more likely to deny their increasing disabilities. They have not been open to seeing themselves as members of a minority group who have been denied their full rights in society. Confronting their impairments, they tend instead to focus on their feelings of incompetence, shame, and dependence. For example, an older man who loses his right to drive because he can't pass the vision test is more likely to see the restriction as a personal trauma than as an incentive to demand better public transportation.

But the current generations of younger disabled people will change this sense of shame, simply through the process of their aging. They see themselves as a minority group with special needs that give them a common identity and a reason to be politically active. The National Council on the Handicapped sponsored a 1986 Harris poll of one thousand noninstitutionalized disabled Americans age 16 and up, the results of which articulate the emerging identity of an intergenerational disability rights movement:

> This survey included two attitudinal questions not asked before of a national sample of disabled people:
> - the extent to which they feel a sense of common identity with other disabled Americans, and
> - whether they feel that disabled people are a minority in the same sense as blacks and Hispanics
>
> The results show clear signs of an emerging group consciousness, particularly among younger disabled Americans.
> - An overwhelming majority (74%) say they feel at least some sense of common identity with other disabled people
> - A 45% plurality expressed the view that disabled Americans are a minority group in the same sense as blacks or Hispanics
> - Fifty-six percent of the younger disabled people and those disabled from birth (largely the same group) see the emerging group consciousness increasing among the younger disabled generation

Even among the young this kind of identification would have been considerably weaker a decade ago, when the disability-rights movement was still in its fledgling stage. No wonder the present generation of older people lacks it almost entirely. A marked increase in such sentiments and accompanying political activity by older disabled people seems inevitable in the near future. A first hint of the agenda of such an intergenerational coalition came in the unsuccessful 1988 Congressional fight to pass Claude Pepper's long-term home health care bill.

That legislation, besides benefiting older people, would have extended Medicare home health care benefits to disabled children under the age of 19, thus linking the needs of disabled people of all ages.

Among the planks of the platforms of both parties in the presidential election of 2020 will be promises to accommodate the needs of people with physical impairments. We will see wheelchair ramps everywhere (and not hidden away on the sides of buildings), curb cuts for wheelchairs in sidewalks at every crossing, widespread accessible public transportation, stiff fines for employment discrimination, braille counterparts of signs wherever feasible—like the braille floor numbers that now appear on the control panels of many office-building elevators—teletypewriters (TTYs) installed next to pay phones for people who are hard of hearing or deaf, sign-language interpreters at most public meetings, and wheelchair-accessible bathrooms. And all of it will be mandated by strictly enforced building codes. The presence of both young and old people with disabilities as models in TV commercials and print advertising will be commonplace.

### Lobbyists in the Twenty-first Century

Will the AARP be the most powerful lobbyist in twenty-first century Washington? Maybe, and maybe not. Any big group is in danger of splintering simply because it includes people with so many divergent interests. Its politics may also end up tripping over its business activities. How effective could the AARP be, for example, in a fight over regulating the insurance industry when it is one of the country's largest insurance agents?

Activist elders twenty to thirty years from now may think of AARP as "Uncle Methuselah": stodgy, top-heavy, one-dimensional, and substantially out of touch with the times. To find a model for their intergenerational activism, they might look instead to another group: the Gray Panthers.

The United Presbyterian Church created the Gray Panthers. It didn't intend to, but when it forced Maggie Kuhn to retire as the editor of its magazine because of her age, it angered the wrong person. A social worker/activist who once said that she wanted her tombstone to read, "Here Lies Maggie under the Only Stone She Ever Left Unturned," Ms. Kuhn founded the group that is today's model of intergenerational politics.

About one-third of the Gray Panthers' seventy thousand members are under the age of 35. College students helped launch the organization in Philadelphia in the early 1970s. (It was first called the Coalition of Older and Younger Adults.) Among the Gray Panthers' aims is to promote job sharing, learning sabbaticals, better child care for workers, and zoning laws that promote intergenerational housing. They have also fought for better regulation of the hearing-aid industry, nursing-home reform, banking regulations that favor the small depositor, and an end to mandatory retirement. Naomi Howard, an 81-year-old Gray Panther and former vice-chair of its steering committee, played a major role in the recall campaign against Governor Evan Mecham in Arizona in 1988.

Maggie Kuhn has often criticized AARP for not looking out enough for the welfare of all age groups. "A healthy society," she says, "is one in which the elderly protect, care for, love and assist the younger ones to provide continuity and hope." Her emphasis on intergenerational cooperation seems a world away from the Age War predictions with which we began this chapter. And she may be on to something important. There are, in fact, as many signs of increased intergenerational cooperation and mutual aid between young and old as there are of conflict:

• In 1978 the University of Pittsburgh Center for Social and Urban Research established Generations Together, a popular program in which people 22 and under are paired with older people in all kinds of institutions, from schools to senior-citizens' centers.

• In Illinois, the state's Department of Aging has begun the Gate-keeper program, in which utility company employees, who often have occasion to come in contact with older people, including the very old who live alone, keep a watchful eye out for their well-being. Similar programs exist in about twenty-five other states.

• In Brooklyn, black and Hispanic retirees have volunteered to work with ghetto children in a program called They're All My Kids. Dr. Harry R. Moody, deputy director of the Brookdale Center on Aging of Hunter College in New York, says the program is "the first we know of that specifically attempts to transmit values from old to young in the minority community."

A 1986 Yankelovich poll of two thousand randomly selected Americans reported that more than 90 percent wanted Medicare to continue, and 75 percent wanted it extended to cover long-term care. More young adults in the survey supported increasing government help for elders than did older respondents. Almost 90 percent of the young said children should be there to support their elder parents if it became necessary. Most people gave high priority to lowering the poverty rate of children and extending Medicare to cover catastrophic and long-term illnesses.

The older people surveyed did express a lower rate of support for education than did the general population, a reminder that self-interest-inspired tunnel vision *does* exist among elders, as it does in every age group. But all in all, Madelyn Hochstein, executive vice-president of the Yankelovich Group, concluded of the survey, "The young worry about the old and the old worry about the young."

### Flash Points

While the potential for pitched political and economic battles between the generations in the twenty-first century is nowhere near as likely as some would have it, that's not to say that generational conflict is out of the question. There are some issues and a few possible scenarios that could cause trouble.

On one issue adult baby boomers have shown themselves to be clearly on the conservative side: crime. In fact, they are almost as likely to support capital punishment as are the current old. Those who commit the most violent crimes tend to be under the age of 35. As elders, baby boomers are likely to feel even more vulnerable to physical assault than they do now in their urban and suburban neighborhoods, perhaps moving even further to the right on this issue. We can expect them to be prime consumers of security devices of all kinds, in some cases turning their homes into miniature forts.

If nothing is done between now and 2020 to remedy the education and income gap between minority youth and the rest of the population, we could see boomer elders focusing their anger and fear on minority youth, who in turn could scapegoat elders, blaming them for their living conditions rather than injustice on the part of society as a whole.

In the Yankelovich poll, some sentiment against older people was expressed, mostly by those who were poor and poorly educated—a possible danger sign if demagogic politicians in the future seek to create and exploit intergenerational tensions at a time of economic distress. Should the difficulties most economists anticipate over the next ten years or so get out of hand and contribute to a full-fledged depression, one could imagine a dismal scenario for America by the year 2015. People in their twenties, despairing of ever getting a leg up on anything resembling a career ladder, with little money and no hope, cut loose from whatever ties they may possess to their elders, may give in to the enticements of neofascist demagogues. What starts out as the American Association of Young People (AAYP), an organization to secure discounts for unemployed youth and to lobby in Washington for their interests, begins to take on the air of a group of skinhead elder-bashers. Exploiting their resentment, young opportunistic politicians of the generation that was in elementary school in 1990 could slash entitlement programs "for the greater good of all." They might also appeal to young people's sense of nationalism, claiming that the Social Security Trust Fund really ought to be applied to restoring America's defense establishment so that the United States might once again achieve the world prominence from which it has fallen. In the face of impending persecution, more affluent elders emigrate.

While this scenario is not likely, it is not nearly as farfetched as the one that opened this chapter. On a small scale we have already seen this kind of thing happen in some working-class areas in England, an aging industrial country fallen from the pinnacle of international power, where disaffected youth have clashed with immigrant minorities. And there have been hints of a similar phenomenon in some blue-collar neighborhoods in this country. One could easily imagine older people, especially elders who seem to be doing better than the young, providing convenient targets by the second decade of the twenty-first century.

## A Question of Values

We needn't wait for 2015 and a possibly dramatic generational crisis to see some potential fissures growing between young and old. They are all around us and could cause trouble if we ignore them.

A man in his early sixties was about to cross a busy intersection in one of our largest cities recently when a taxi almost ran him down.

"Hey," he called out to the cabbie, a young man in his twenties, "you could have killed me!"

"So what?" the driver coolly replied.

A disturbing segment of today's young, particularly those in their late teens to early twenties, the Reagan Generation, seem to be without roots, values, or a direction beyond wanting to take care of their own needs and desires. That's not necessarily where they will be when they get older, of course. Every younger generation is described by its elders as lost and hedonistic, and still thus far the young have made a successful transition into more responsible adulthood. But if a sizable part of a generation matures without learning to think of the needs of others, we can't assume that they will feel an obligation to pay taxes to support their parents' old age.

The notion of "reciprocity"—what young and old owe to each other and under what conditions—as a factor in binding generations is a subject that has begun to attract attention in the scholarly community. We can expect this thinking to filter into the more general discussion of intergenerational ties in the next few years.

Edward A. Wynne, an authority on youth and intergenerational relationships and author of *Social Security: A Reciprocity System Under Stress,* has been concerned for some time about whether young people are being sufficiently socialized to appreciate what old and young owe to each other. He envisions a new emphasis in our schools on "such themes as loyalty, students' 'debts' to previous generations, the benefits that previous generations have won for the students by their sacrifices, and the centrality of character and honor in social life." The rights and duties that each generation has and owes to others may loom as large in the twenty-first-century curriculum as race relations have in the last half of the twentieth. Universities may create whole new departments of age studies. Courses of study would involve the history of old people in the family and in the work force; bioethics; and the relationship among politics, economics, and the varying historical experiences of generations.

A factor that should help is the high percentage of aging baby-boomer elementary and high-school teachers. Over the next several decades, they will present the young with role models of active elders. And they are likely to be especially sensitive to any negative feelings they detect among their students about intergenerational responsibilities. These older teachers could be society's front-line defense against the stirrings of Age War sentiments.

## Something We Haven't Thought Much About

That we can speak at all of age wars tells us that we have very little sense of what the relationship between young and old *should* be. That's easily understandable because when we look to the past—even the recent past—for guidelines, there are no clear lessons to learn. We may thus be on the edge of a period of social invention in which we will have to define and clarify, sometimes for the first time—philosophically, religiously, politically, legally—what the generations owe to one another.

One question that will come up involves something nobody has dealt with adequately because we all avoid it. Greg Arling of the Virginia Office on Aging stated the bare facts some years ago when he wrote:

> Childhood is the only stage in the life-cycle in which the individual can appropriately assume the dependency role; and, in that situation, the child can anticipate increasing autonomy with advancing age. The older person must anticipate a further loss of autonomy as he or she ages.

In a society that emphasizes independence, how can we deal with the issue of dependence in a way that does not demean the one who receives help? This question is as much practical as philosophical. With so many living to 85 and beyond, a lot of people are going to ask it before too long.

While the particular way the problem will be framed for baby boomers—in the context of growing old—will be new to them, the problem itself is something they've encountered before in other guises (and in that sense Greg Arling is not entirely right). Most prominently, they have faced it in their concern with the nature of romantic relationships. Boomers are a product of a time of changing values in which lovers and spouses have wrestled with issues of independence. But relationships imply a surrendering of some freedom and placing oneself in a position of dependence upon another for support of all kinds. We most often see the problems this raises in the self-help books directed at women who must deal with men who want to keep one foot out the door in their relationships.

Baby-boomer women were mostly raised by mothers who communicated to them notions about the family that they received from *their* mothers: A woman should be dependent upon a man. But women born from the mid-1940s through the mid-1960s have learned other lessons in the swiftly changing world of the past three decades. While they still may hear echoes of an older style of relationships, they have gone far toward revising the role of dependence in their lives. This suggests that they will take the lead in grappling with this issue yet again in their later years. This theme could be prominent in the increasing importance that twenty-first-century developmental psychologists are likely to give to the role of friendship in the lives of older women (which we discuss in chapter 8).

As we pass the year 2000, articles and books probing the general principles behind the ways that young and old interact will inundate us. The advance guard of seventy-five million baby boomers bearing down on age 60 all but guarantees that our social philosophers will undertake the project.

What are they likely to conclude? Is there a "natural" way for young and old to interact? Who owes what to whom, and why? Will we discover "inalienable rights" that come with a certain part of the life cycle? It would be premature to even hazard a guess at this point. But the questions will be asked, and the answers will color our lives.

# 7

# Hale and Hearty

"I predict that we will find cures for the major killers of older people—hypertension, heart disease, and many forms of cancer."

DR. T. FRANKLIN WILLIAMS, Director of the
National Institute on Aging

Man reading the *Gazette* remarks to his wife about the news: "There's been so many medical breakthroughs lately that if you aren't dead already, you probably never will be."

Cartoon in *The Gray Panther Network*

Advances in medical research in the past few years could easily tempt a person to believe he or she might live forever. Anything seems possible to the generations whose adult lives have coincided with several revolutions in the practice of medicine.

Medical progress since World War II has deeply affected today's elders at two stages in their lives. First, it made their experience of parenting different from that of any previous generation. As a young mother Esther Keller, now 67, spoke reverently of the wonder drug penicillin and the other antibiotics that became available in rapid succession in the 1940s and 1950s. She remembers sending her son, Fred, born in 1949, and her daughter, Arlene, born in 1951, back to school a week after they had contracted a strep infection that might have endangered their lives ten or fifteen years earlier.

Now, as an older woman, Esther talks about CAT scans and triple coronary bypass operations with a matter-of-factness that belies the novelty and complexity of these procedures. And she is alive today because ten years ago she had open-heart surgery to replace a faulty valve. (Her heart problem developed because she had rheumatic fever as a youth, and of course modern antibiotics prevent all such problems now.)

Many of Esther's generation will benefit further from the fruits of medical research over the next decade or two. And her children's generation, now entering middle age, will enjoy an old age even more free of disease, disability, and pain than their parents' because of new discoveries and innovative procedures.

According to a Harris poll of 225 prominent medical researchers worldwide, the next ten years will bring us many breakthroughs: better drugs to deal with heart disease and make the still-risky bypass operation obsolete; improved cancer treatments, including protective vaccines for some kinds and cures for two-thirds of all cancers; artificial bones and blood; pumps implanted in the body to deliver precise amounts of drugs automatically for conditions such as diabetes; implantable hearing aids. To get a sense of the difference such advances might make in what it's like to be old, consider this: Among the most frequent chronic conditions that now occur in almost 80 percent of people 65 and older are arthritis, heart disease, high blood pressure, and a decline in hearing. Heart disease and cancer are the greatest killers.

Medical progress affects every age group, of course, and its effects are cumulative. Old age does not suddenly begin to ravage the body at 65. By the age of 35, for example, a person's metabolism is already slowing up, the immune system is not what it used to be, and bone mass is likely to begin its gradual decline. But today's Americans in their thirties and forties are already taking their old age into their own hands. Their interest in health and nutrition will pay them dramatic dividends several decades from now, for many even into their ninth and possibly tenth decade.

As important as new cures will be for this generation, on the horizon is another possibility: increased insight into the process of aging itself.

The dementia that doctors used to ascribe to old age has been found to be a product of disease, not years. As the mysterious aging process is deciphered, researchers will be better able to design drugs and other treatments to deal with the underlying physical changes that produce the diseases and decline that are now part of getting old.

Finally, the next few decades will see basic changes in the way that elders interact with the medical profession. The transformation of this relationship is already well under way. Group practices, health maintenance organizations (HMOs), Medicare, the new emphasis on outpatient treatment, greater stress on patient self-help and a decrease in the authority of doctors, hospitals serving as the hubs of vast networks of treatment centers—all are creating a medicine for old age that is radically different from that experienced by past generations.

## THE HEART OF THE MATTER

A change in what people consider a healthy lifestyle is one of the many things that distinguish the experience of one generation from that of another in the twentieth century. Each generation has had the good fortune to know more than the previous one about what constitutes healthy living. The members of each generation have had this knowledge at an early enough age so they could alter their living habits to make a difference in the length and quality of their lives.

For example, we know that there is much that can be done through preventive medicine—the best kind—to decrease a person's chances of ever having heart disease. "Clearly, the best way to treat a heart attack is not to have it," as Dr. Eugene R. Passamani of the National Heart, Lung, and Blood Institute put it.

Baby-boomer parents have recently learned exactly what to look for: High cholesterol levels in a child are the most important predictor of elevated levels in an adult. In 1988 the American Academy of Pediatrics recommended that doctors test the cholesterol levels of all children over the age of 2 whose families have a history of high cholesterol levels or heart disease. This screening will greatly increase the chances that this generation will be able to avoid heart disease in the distant future.

The baby boomers have benefited in the same way from long-term studies done since the 1950s that have identified several risk factors for cardiovascular disease. By not smoking, keeping their weight down, and lowering their intake of saturated fats in order to control cholesterol, younger American adults are already ensuring that the declining rate of heart disease in this country will continue into the first three decades of the twenty-first century.

Their parents had the same type of experience with *their* parents when new nutritional information about vitamins and a balanced diet became widely known in the 1920s and 1930s. Their ability to act on this knowledge is one of the reasons the current old are in better shape than previous generations of old people.

At the same time, today's elders also benefit from breakthroughs in the development of new medicines and surgical procedures that have provided a second chance. Many older people whose eating habits and levels of exercise might ordinarily have made a long life unlikely will get a new lease on life through improved medical care. For example, they will have bypass surgery, which has become almost the equivalent of a Purple Heart for some elders who delight in showing off their suture marks.

Of the 1.5 million Americans hit by a heart attack each year, 300,000 never make it alive to a hospital, and upwards of 230,000 die in the hospital. At dawn on a crisp fall morning in 1986, Angelo Donato, 63, of Brooklyn, New York, became one of the survivors. Awakened by chest pains, nausea, and a cold sweat, he was about to undergo a procedure that would have been science fiction only a decade earlier. Maria, his wife, took one look at his pale face and called his doctor, who told her to get her husband to nearby Maimonides Medical Center. Their next-door neighbor all but pulled Mr. Donato into his car and sped to the hospital.

At Maimonides, the staff, alerted by Donato's doctor, called Dr. Jacob Shani, a cardiologist. Within ninety minutes of receiving the call, Dr. Shani had stopped Angelo Donato's heart attack in its tracks, possibly saving his life. The doctor's tools were deceptively simple: a wire, a balloon, and a televisionlike monitor. Angioplasty, the procedure he used, is a recent technique developed to unblock plugged arteries. Doing it while the victim is in the throes of a heart attack is newer still, and Jacob Shani is one of the pioneers in the field.

The doctor inserts the balloon into the artery through the groin, moving it along a wire until it reaches the point where a fatty substance has blocked the flow of blood, reducing the supply of oxygen to the heart and causing a heart attack. He watches the progress of the wire and balloon on the monitor. By inflating the tiny balloon at the blockage, he can push the fat against the artery wall, thus opening the passage. It's a relatively safe procedure that in many cases has replaced bypass surgery, although sometimes the artery may have to be cleared again months later.

Aggressive measures such as these to deal with coronary artery disease are barely two decades old and are still being developed. People over 65 today were already middle-aged when coronary-care units became a standard part of major hospitals. Before their advent, about 30 percent of heart attack victims died even if they lived to reach a hospital. Within five years of the development of these units, in which cardiac patients are constantly monitored and trained personnel are ready at a moment's notice to use measures such as electric shock to get a heart beating again, heart attack death rates in some hospitals were down to 12 percent.

It's only been ten years since the role of blood clots in heart attacks has been recognized. Medical researchers have come up with drugs like streptokinase and TPA—created through the biotechnology of gene splicing—to dissolve the clots. Widespread use of these drugs—and aspirin—is now becoming commonplace. By observing their effect on tens of thousands of patients, researchers will know within a few years which work best and when. Another recent discovery: Cheap, common aspirin can prevent many heart attacks and strokes from ever occurring.

When used soon enough after a heart attack begins—preferably within twenty minutes but within no more than four hours—streptokinase and TPA can reduce the chances of dying from a heart attack by as much as 50 percent. Ultimately, doctors believe, hospital death rates from heart attacks may drop to as low as 3 percent because of these drugs. By minimizing heart muscle damage, quick infusion of one of them also gives the patient a good chance of leading an active life afterward. People now in their sixties and seventies who know they have heart disease can even look forward to the possibility that by 2000 these drugs will be available for home use—but under a doctor's direction—in the event of a heart attack.

Researchers still don't know if reducing high blood pressure will decrease the chances of having a heart attack, but they do know that high blood pressure is associated with increased risk of an attack. Until now, diuretics were most commonly used to alleviate hypertension. But new kinds of drugs called beta blockers have shown promise of greater effectiveness in protecting against heart attacks, although they have some side effects and are considerably more expensive. Comparative tests to determine which should be the drug of choice are now under way, with results expected by about 1995.

Meanwhile, doctors continue to refine the more intrusive measures they use to deal with coronary artery disease. Computerized pictures that better enable cardiologists to monitor the progress of blood-vessel-clearing angioplasties have made this procedure safer. These doctors can now scan back and forth between images as easily as TV viewers reverse their VCRs, all while the patient is still on the table. Researchers are also experimenting with "hot" and "cold" lasers as tools to destroy fatty deposits in blood vessels.

Sometime in the 1990s we can look for the widespread use of a heart pump no bigger than the eraser on top of a pencil that will temporarily assist the heart of someone who has suffered a heart attack. This support will allow the heart muscle to heal better by temporarily reducing the amount of work it has to do. Surgeons have already successfully used the device, which they can implant in twenty minutes through an artery in the thigh, and it's now undergoing further tests. If it proves safe and effective, the pump, which is disposable and costs only three thousand dollars, may become standard equipment in emergency rooms and help as many as 150,000 people in this country every year. Permanent pumps, for people with chronic heart failure, could also be available before too long, replacing the heart transplant.


## CLOSER TO CONQUERING A DREADED DISEASE

The tumor under his armpit was the size of a half-grapefruit. Michael Kelly, age 64, was sure he'd never leave Memorial Sloan-Kettering Cancer Center alive. Ten or fifteen years earlier, he probably would have been right. In fact, the surgery he endured at the world-famous facility in New York City almost killed him. It took Kelly a year to recover. His wife kept him going by serving as his nurse, his cheerleader, and the part-time manager at his grocery store.

Many of today's elders still will not say the word *cancer*. For their generation, it has been an unmentionable scourge. Not so long ago this dreaded diagnosis was almost the equivalent of a death sentence. The only question: Would the victim "go quickly"?

In 1900, almost no one survived cancer. By 1950 the cure rate had reached 30 percent, and today it has risen to 50 percent. Still the second-greatest killer of old people, cancer can now be detected earlier and fought with ever more refined surgery and drug therapies. We can finally look forward to the possibility of all but vanquishing it—if not with one super vaccine then at least by winning the battles against its many manifestations, one by one. "I can foresee the day when cancer is no worse than a chronic disease," says Dr. Vincent T. DeVita, Jr., director of the National Cancer Institute.

Cancer chemotherapy over the past two decades has become a valuable weapon aimed more and more accurately with less chance of hitting innocent bystanders. The new drugs can be used in bigger doses and do less damage to nonmalignant tissues, reducing the side effects of treatments that some patients have come to fear as much as their disease.

Researchers are now in the initial stages of using computers to custom-design new cancer-fighting drugs. Instead of randomly sampling as many as five thousand substances to find the one that helps treat a particular kind of cancer, they will use computer models and various types of imaging devices to discover theoretically how human cells might interact when something in the body goes wrong, causing cancer. Then they will design a substance that will enter the field of battle and act with these molecules in such a way as to set things right. The enormously complicated process has many variables and the key to its success is improved computer speed, memory, and graphics generation. These technologies are progressing rapidly, so success on this front may not be too many years in the future.

Mobilizing the body to fight its own battle would ultimately be the best way to defeat cancer. The groundwork has been laid for intense research in this area. In 1988, for the first time, medical researchers transplanted the equivalent of the human immune system into live mice. Their fellow scientists describe this achievement as "remarkable" and "incredible." Now researchers can study more closely than before the way the immune system reacts to cancer and other diseases, such as AIDS.

A related path of inquiry involves what one scientist has termed the pursuit of the "Holy Grail" of blood research: the hunt for human stem cells, from which the immune system and all blood cells originate. Stem cells are somewhere in the bone marrow. If and when scientists can isolate them, they could use them to make much safer bone marrow transplants, an important method of treatment in some cancers. Now radiation therapy and cancer-killing chemicals destroy healthy bone marrow as well as diseased cells. If stem cells were available to replenish vital tissue, doctors could administer larger and more effective doses of radiation and chemotherapeutic agents—a potential supertreatment of the near future. Stem cells could also play a crucial role in gene therapy, enabling transplanted genes to become a lasting part of a person's blood system.

## GENE THERAPY

Perhaps nothing will change the meaning of old age in the next few decades so much as the manipulation of genetic material in the pursuit of new cures. In cancer research, "antisense DNA" is one of the most exciting examples of what biotechnology could achieve. This technique involves the manipulation of DNA, the substance in genes that contains the encoded information of heredity. It involves stopping the genes that make cancer cells grow out of control and enable them to resist some kinds of chemotherapy. Rather than attacking the cancer cells directly, antisense DNA would allow doctors to infiltrate their communications system, thus holding their growth process in check through a kind of "inside job." "It's unique among therapeutic approaches—something that's that selective," says Thomas Rogers, a scientist at the Monsanto Company. "The technology is so superb that now every molecular biologist is a potential therapist," adds Dr. Vincent DeVita. If this research can be successfully applied to human cancers, antisense DNA will be to the treatment of cancer what penicillin was to the treatment of infection in the 1940s. But we're not there yet. So far, scientists have been experimenting with slime mold and mice ears. Testing on humans is still a few years away.

Researchers at the National Institutes of Health may be about to embark on a course that will open a new chapter in the history of medicine. Scientists carried out the first successful gene splicing, transferring genes between two species of bacteria, only a little more than fifteen years ago. Now they are on the verge of transplanting cancer-fighting cells carrying a "marker" gene into humans. The marker will permit doctors to follow the progress of the cells as they reach a tumor and attack it. The beginning of the project awaits final safety clearance.

Using genetics to create new disease-fighting drugs will require a map that chemically defines and pinpoints the hundred thousand or so genes on the twenty-three pairs of human chromosomes. The mapmakers are about to get down to work. The National Institutes of Health has selected Dr. James D. Watson, Nobel Prize winner, codiscoverer in 1953 of the structure of DNA, and author of the best-selling *The Double Helix,* to head the project. Assuming timely Congressional appropriation of the billions of dollars required, the work may be done by the middle of the first decade of the twenty-first century.

What use will be made of this mapping information? Genetic tests could tell us early in a person's life if he or she is at risk for getting cancer—or heart disease or diabetes or Alzheimer's disease or any one of possibly thousands of other diseases and conditions. This information will enable people to modify their lifestyles—for example, by watching what they eat—to minimize their chances of actually developing the illness. They will also be able to take advantage of regular examinations to spot the first signs of disease so that they can deal with it in its early stages.

Within ten years people will have their own genetic profiles, according to a prediction by Michael McGinnis, director of the United States Office of Disease Prevention and Health Promotion. This profile will enable us to make mid-life corrections in the way we live. Employees of the Chesapeake & Potomac Telephone Company in the Washington, D.C., area are already undergoing a preliminary genetic screening for diseases such as cervical cancer and diabetes with the aim of having those who test positive take preventive measures. "It's one thing to tell a smoker he has a tenfold greater chance of getting lung disease based on national statistics," as McGinnis puts it, "and quite another thing to tell him he lacks the gene for a lung-protective protein and will almost certainly get emphysema."

This kind of information will have profound consequences for the future old. If the gene-mapping project works out as planned, people now in their twenties, thirties, and forties will be able to learn before they reach old age of any genetically determined health hazards in their future. By acting to head them off, they will be able to live longer and better, with the result that there will be many more older and healthier people in the population. Thus biotechnology could accentuate the graying of America.

But will people want this knowledge? That's another thing entirely. Some of the tests will turn up vulnerabilities to diseases for which there is neither a cure nor a preventive regimen. Under these conditions many people would feel better not knowing. And who will be entrusted with this very personal information? Would insurance companies, for example, have access to it? The prospects for abuse will surely raise central scientific, political, and ethical questions as early as the first decade of the next century.

Imagine a person's employer gaining access to this information, for example. The aging employee tests positive for a vulnerability to Alzheimer's disease. The firm might feel justified in trying to force the worker to retire early. But there's no guarantee that he or she will contract the disease. Who is in the right?

## BRAIN RESEARCH

By 2020, elder boomers may look at Alzheimer's disease, a debilitating condition that destroys memory and afflicts 2.5 million Americans, the way New Elders now view cancer: still dreaded but an illness that can be fought with a good chance of a cure. Research on the intricacies of the brain is one of the frontiers of medical inquiry. New computer-assisted imaging devices permit precise monitoring of neural activity in parts of the brain previously inaccessible to such study, offering the possibility of accelerating the rate at which new cures and treatments for neurological disorders may be found.

New Elders have already benefited from recent neurological research. Since the mid-1970s, the death rate from stroke has declined by 30 percent, mainly because doctors understand its multicausal character more thoroughly and can diagnose and more effectively deal with it through drugs and surgery. Contemporary medicine is also more adept at curbing high blood pressure, which causes about half of all strokes.

Some reports of medical research describe procedures that are truly fantastic—such as nerve transplants. For at least a century scientists have dreamed of such things. Now, as we enter the 1990s, some of them are coming to pass. Researcher Barry Hoffer expressed his amazement at what he was doing this way: "If I were to tell a fellow scientist back then that I took fetal brain cells and placed them near an area of a lesion and that the cells survived, grew and reversed disease symptoms, well, it would have smacked of Mary Shelley [the creator of the Frankenstein monster]."

Alzheimer's disease may eventually be treated through brain cell implants, although researchers do not expect such a breakthrough in the near future. Meanwhile, they patiently test the possibility that one or more drugs could do the job. Physostigmine, a substance known to enhance memory performance, is one such chemical now undergoing testing.

It's possible that elder baby boomers will not have to worry about getting Parkinson's disease, which attacks brain cells and causes muscle degeneration in older people. Dr. Murray Goldstein, director of the National Institute of Neurological and Communicative Disorders and Stroke, predicts that

> within a reasonable number of years we're going to see a remarkable break-through in Parkinson's disease. We now have an animal model—a way to produce the disease in animals—and that will help us to understand why the affected cells die and give us an opportunity to halt the process or even prevent it.

With improvements in neurological surgery and drug therapies over the next several decades, physicians are likely to take a much more aggressive approach to spotting any problems early, since there will be ways to deal with them. The annual physical examination that people over the age of 40 are now encouraged to have will probably include tests of short- and long-term memory, as well as a brain check by a computer-assisted imaging device.

## IMPROVING THE QUALITY OF DAILY LIFE

Besides the lifesaving miracles of modern medicine, older people bene-fit from medical advances that bring them a higher-quality, less restricted life. For example, in barely a generation, the very face of old age has been changed by advances in dentistry. A periodontal prevention program can be effective even when begun in one's fifties, and such prevention makes a toothless old age, common only a generation or two ago, no longer inevitable. For baby boomers, the prospects of keeping their teeth are even better. "Teeth for a lifetime" is the prognosis of Dr. Harold Loe, director of the National Institute of Dental Health. Prevention programs started at earlier ages, antibacte-rial rinses, and tooth implants will make visits to the dentist in the later years of life less of an emotional trauma than they have been in the past.

About 30 percent of Americans over 65 are hearing-impaired, while 10 percent have severe visual problems. But these generations—New Elders and the Old Guard—have been helped to overcome the effects of the diminution of hearing and sight to a greater extent than previous generations did. In recent years, for example, electronic miniaturization has made it possible for older people with hearing difficulties to function normally without wearing obviously visible hearing aids—witness Ronald Reagan. These devices still have to be inserted in the ear and turned on, and their batteries have to be recharged. But in the coming decades hearing aids containing long-lasting batteries are more likely to be surgically inserted, making them maintenance-free except for occasional checkups. Wearers will adjust volume and turn them on and off by remote control.

This technology will come none too soon for baby-boomer rock fans, who are likely to be especially vulnerable to hearing difficulties by the time they reach their fifties. "Their ears look very much like those of war veterans who have been exposed to artillery," says Dr. George Haspiel of teenagers who attend rock concerts. According to the United States Occupational Safety and Health Administration (OSHA), the maximum sound level to which an individual can be exposed and not suffer hearing loss is 100 decibels for two hours. The sound level at a rock concert can easily reach 105 decibels, sustained, and the shows may last longer than two hours. "Someone exposing themselves to fewer than ten rock concerts would probably develop hearing loss," according to surgeon Alvin Katz.

Cataract surgery has become routine over the past decade, with seven hundred thousand procedures done annually in this country. Before long medical research will uncover the causes of glaucoma and cataracts, two impairments that dim the old age of so many elders. Scientists have recently simulated the development of these conditions in the laboratory, allowing them to observe closely how the diseases progress under controlled conditions. There's also a good chance that macular degeneration, a disease of the retina that is the chief cause of blindness in Americans over 60, will yield to surgical cure by the year 2000. The procedure will involve a retinal transplant, with drug therapy following the operation to avoid tissue rejection.

There is no general cure for diabetes approaching breakthrough in the labs, but the disease is much more manageable and less intrusive in the lives of elders than it used to be. Oral medications have been improved, insulin pumps to supply that substance continuously are now a reality, and the genetic manufacture of insulin has made the drug safer and cheaper than it used to be. By the mid-1990s, diabetics will be able to administer insulin through a nasal spray. There are even some indications that fish-oil products, thought by many doctors to be helpful in preventing heart disease, could aid in the treatment of diabetes. Researchers are currently looking into this possibility. In the more distant future, predicts David Rollo, vice-president for medical affairs of the Humana Corporation, cells from an animal's pancreas implanted into a diabetic may supply missing insulin.

Progress has also been made with the problem of urinary incontinence, which troubles as many as 20 percent of Americans over 65. Incontinence is now recognized as a symptom of several specific medical problems rather than an inevitable result of aging. Treatments include electrical stimulation, catheterization, exercise, drugs, and surgery. As many as 90 percent of people who are incontinent can have their symptoms substantially improved, but patients tend not to bring up the subject with their doctors, and physicians are not always as informed about it as they should be. Dr. Alan J. Wein of the University of Pennsylvania Medical School decries the prevalence of ads for adult diapers and absorbent pads because "they are sending a message to people that there is nothing else to be done." Younger people, who have grown up in an age of frankness and strong consumer-rights consciousness, are not as likely to accept this limitation on their lives as they age. Should they become incontinent, they will have themselves thoroughly tested by doctors trained to spot the particular causes of this condition and to deal with them.

## IN SEARCH OF THE CAUSE OF AGING

The most comprehensive way to deal with illnesses and impairments related to the process of aging would be, of course, to slow down the process itself. In 1975, Congress established the National Institute on Aging to oversee and sponsor research about the causes of aging. The NIA funded little more than fifteen million dollars' worth of research at its beginning, but now it issues grants totaling about two hundred million dollars a year. It may yet prove to be what Alex Comfort, author of *The Joy of Sex* and *A Good Age,* predicted at its creation—"the equivalent in this field [of what] NASA is in space research."

Experts in gerontology generally agree that 115 to 120 years is about the longest life span humans can expect under ideal conditions. Despite claims of greater longevity for people in some parts of the world, the longest life for which we have documentation—in Japan—is 120 years.

Researchers have yet to come up with one general reason why people age, and increasingly it looks as if the cause will be found in several processes. Most explanations are grounded in one of two broad hypotheses: Aging is the consequence of accumulated damage done to body tissues over the years, or is somehow programmed into people from the beginning of their lives. The major theories so far, according to the National Institute on Aging, include:

• *WEAR AND TEAR.*   This approach likens a human being to a car that eventually wears out over the years, with repairs becoming less effective as the vehicle ages. Brain cells called neurons are lost as a person ages, for example. But nearby neurons enlarge and fill in the space left vacant, doing the job the missing cells did. Does this repair process itself wear down and lose effectiveness with age?

A related theory suggests that life span is directly connected to metabolic rate. Individuals in species with high metabolic rates—species that, in effect, live faster—die sooner. People live longer than mice, which metabolize their food more quickly than do humans. In an intriguing experiment, mice that were given less to eat lived longer than a control group fed normally. Having them eat less is the only way scientists have ever been able to extend the life span of laboratory animals. But no one has yet been able to make the connection between these results and the extension of human life.

• *CROSS-LINKING.*   The random interaction of proteins in human cells leaves an accumulation of molecules tied to one another in ways that, over time, cause our bodies to lose flexibility. For instance, collagen, which is needed to support tendons, cartilage, and bones, becomes more rigid as people age, decreasing their mobility. This process also causes skin to become wrinkled.

• *FREE RADICALS.*   Certain unstable molecules are produced in the body and interact with other molecules to damage them. Ordinarily, our bodies detoxify these free radicals before they can do any harm, but aging may reduce the body's ability to defend itself in this way. Species in which individuals have large quantities of one of the enzymes important to the detoxifying process, superoxide dismutase, or SOD, have been found to have long life spans. One study found that humans, the

longest lived among the species surveyed, also had the highest levels of
SOD. Aging may have something to do with the genes that regulate
SOD in the body.

But the human body does not absorb SOD taken in pill form, and
the pills do not prevent aging. Similarly, although some experimental
results suggested that vitamin E might protect against free radical
damage, long-term studies showed this dietary supplement to be inef-
fective in halting the aging process.

• *ERROR AND CATASTROPHE.* This theory says the aging process is
caused by the faulty creation of proteins in the body. Proteins themselves play a part in the body's manufacture of other proteins, so as the
defective proteins accumulate with age, the protein-building process
leads to an increasingly larger number of faulty ones. The result is
damage to the organs of which they form an important part.

• *SOMATIC MUTATIONS.* If this theory is true, cells malfunction and
deteriorate with age because of spontaneous changes in the heredity-
information-bearing material, DNA.

• *PROGRAMMED SENESCENCE.* Our life spans may be genetically
encoded in our cells. In effect, this theory says we carry a biological
clock within our bodies. Some scientists suggest that the pituitary gland
secretes hormones on schedule that cause aging—the "death hor-
mone" concept. Similarly, other researchers stress the programmed
decline of the immune system with age, which renders the body less
able to fight off foreign organisms and more likely to mistake its own
tissues for invaders and attack them.

While none of these theories has been totally proved or finally
disproved, the free radicals hypothesis has been attracting a lot of
attention. "We may be able to intervene in the aging process, not just
to prolong life, but to alter the way in which we age," according to the
NIA. A study is under way to determine whether drugs that combat
free radicals might slow down the neurological damage caused by the
progress of Parkinson's disease. Researchers also plan other projects to
investigate the relationship of free radicals to Alzheimer's disease and
to rheumatoid arthritis.

The project to map all human genes could also yield a harvest of information about how to slow the aging process and maximize longevity. As many as seven thousand genes may be involved in controlling aging, according to George M. Martin, a professor of pathology at the University of Washington. The mechanism by which genes affect aging is likely to be quite complicated, and baby boomers should not anticipate a genetic fountain of youth awaiting them in their sixties and seventies. As one scientist at a recent conference on aging put it, "Life itself may be considered a terminal disease."

## "Normal" Aging

"People practice to get old," George Burns complained in a 1988 interview. "The minute they get to be 65 or 70, they sit down slow, they get into a car with trouble. They start taking small steps."

Part of feeling old involves accepting the image of what an old person is supposed to be like. But long-term studies have shown that people manifest old age in a wide variety of ways. There is no one specific way to feel and act at a certain age. In the Baltimore Longitudinal Study of Aging, as many as one thousand people of different ages have been returning to the Gerontology Research Center in Baltimore every two years for two and a half days of physical and psychological testing that measures how aging has changed them. The study has confirmed the diversity of human aging.

"We still know very little about the difference between a healthy young person and a healthy old person," according to Dr. John W. Rowe, director of the aging division at the Harvard Medical School. But we're learning. The Baltimore study, for instance, has turned up certain chemical and biological standards for aging that permit doctors to differentiate between what's normal at a certain age and what might indicate disease. It's normal for people to need less food as they age, for example. Serum cholesterol levels tend to decline in healthy individuals after peaking in middle age (although we still need more information to determine the role of lifestyle in this measurement). More than half of people over 65 who do not have diabetes still show aberrations in their sugar metabolism. Scales are now available to judge normal kidney functioning in an older person. All these data help to ensure that older patients are not being overtreated for conditions that are normal for their age.

## TAKING MATTERS INTO OUR OWN HANDS

One important thing many of today's elders have learned from the popularization of these findings is that they have considerable control over their aging. They are the first older generation in history to have this knowledge, and they are acting on it. For example, by decreasing their consumption of saturated fats and cutting down on smoking, people are lowering their chances of contracting heart disease, emphysema, and cancer.

"A lot of what we commonly call aging comes from disuse and atrophy," according to Everett L. Smith, director of the biogerontology program at the University of Wisconsin. Exercise not only can slow down and stop the clock, it can even turn it back. Exercise is "not an unending fountain of youth. Eventually we all decline," observes Smith. "But the quality of life is so much higher for the elderly who are physically active than for people who sit in a rocking chair waiting for the Grim Reaper." Studies have confirmed that 70-year-olds can improve their physical work capacity—their ability to use oxygen—by 35 percent, increase their strength proportionately as much as younger people, lower their blood pressure, substantially improve joint flexibility, and sharpen their mental powers—all by exercising.

Newspapers delight in feature stories about great-grandmothers climbing mountains, but the real story of this new generation of elders is about how widespread regular exercising has become in their cohort. In a suburb of Birmingham, Alabama, Alf Thompson, a woman of 80, cultivates her two-acre lawn *and* exercises. "I don't want to lose weight, though," she notes. "I just want to shape up what I've got." In Flint, Michigan, 76-year-old Bill Genske, arthritic knees notwithstanding, swims three times a week before some people have sat down to breakfast. "The pool opens at 6 o'clock, and I'm usually in the water by 6:50," he boasts. Kelly McCollum, director of women's fitness at a health club in Flint, says the number of elders working out over the last few years has visibly increased.

At 8:00 A.M. on weekday mornings in the Galleria shopping center in Fort Lauderdale, Florida, there's not a rocking chair in sight. But there are plenty of people with gray hair limbering up for their daily mall walking, a form of exercise that is spreading throughout America. It's reached the Valley View Mall in Roanoke, Virginia, where three hundred elders mark off half-mile circuits around the still-empty shopping center before the business day begins. Mall walking is also popular at the Park City Mall in Lancaster, Pennsylvania. At the McKinley Mall in Hamburg, New York, two members of the YWCA mall walkers, a widow and widower, met while walking and eventually got married—at the shopping center.

The trend of older people exercising has become so pervasive that it's even reached nursing homes. At the Mystic Manor Convalescent Center in Mystic, Connecticut, patients have been on a twice-a-day walking regimen. Residents who previously had to be served their food in their rooms started eating in the dining room. People who had been mentally confused became more alert. The routine has produced social as well as physical dividends.

Physical activity has made many in the current generation of elders a different breed from yesterday's older people. What about the next generation? How fit will those now in their early adulthood and middle age be when they reach their later years? If their well-known enthusiasm for keeping fit survives with them into old age, and there's no reason it shouldn't, the baby boomers will rewrite the book on what vigorous, healthy old people are like.

Baby boomers are now realizing that even *they* are not as young as they used to be, and they're shifting their exercise routines with the long haul in mind. The sale of barbells appears to have peaked, and the upsurge in jogging may have run its course. In their place have come increased sales of gentler workout apparatus such as rowing machines and stationary bikes, a heightened interest in walking, and "soft," low-impact aerobics that put less stress on the joints.

In the next twenty years we can expect to see the graying of the health clubs. A baby boomer working out in 2010 is likely to go on a stationary bike tour of anywhere in the world he or she chooses. A laser-read disk linked electronically to his or her exercise bike will project on a screen a road on which the exerciser will have to make constant choices between turns and forks in the route. Should he or she choose an upgrade, the resistance on the pedals will automatically increase in proportion to the grade.

By 2020 the clubs will probably cater to the aging baby boomers by providing facilities and personnel that enable clients to engage in mental as well as physical workouts. The generation that made health into a national obsession is not likely to tolerate any backsliding. By the time the baby boomers begin to forget names, concern with their memory performance could reach an anxious pitch—and memory tune-up equipment might push the other apparatus into the corner at the health club.

What might this new equipment look like? The Concentration Grid, named after the old TV quiz program "Concentration," is a likely standby of the health club of the future. Exercisers will face a checkerboardlike pattern of squares on the floor, some of which, at the sound of a bell, will be lit for only about five seconds, during which time their positions will have to be memorized. A person will then run across the grid, stepping only on squares that were lit. Should the person step on a "bad" square, sensors in the floor will deduct points from his or her final score. A formula taking into account the points lost for misstepping and the person's time in crossing the entire grid will produce a memory-agility rating.

## DISTANT DOCTORS

The good health enjoyed by so many of the current generation of elders has had its price. Modern medicine, Medicare, and Medicaid have combined to give these New Elders a special relationship to the medical system. Never before have older people spent so much time having checkups, diagnostic tests, and other medical procedures. The vigilance required for effective preventive medicine at this age has its equivalent only in. the close scrutiny that babies get from their pediatricians. (In fact, *geriatrics,* the word describing the specialty concerned with the medical care of the old, was coined in 1909 by a doctor who saw the resemblance between this field and pediatrics.) And with improved anesthesia and surgical monitoring equipment, never have so many people in their seventies, eighties, and sometimes nineties spent so much time in hospitals recovering from surgery.

New Elders expect much more from the medical system than people their age have ever received in the past—and they get it. When their grandparents aged and got sick all their doctors could give them was reassurance. It's been estimated that of the 360 or so serious and relatively common diseases in 1928, doctors could treat or cure only about 5 to 10 percent. By 1975 they could effectively deal with at least 50 percent of them. That percentage has continued to increase, shrinking the number of untreatable diseases and raising patient expectations. Yet despite these dramatic improvements in general medicine, the spread of knowledge about the particular medical characteristics of older people has not kept pace. In this area, elder baby boomers will benefit more than their parents have from trends just now coming into focus.

"All practitioners except pediatricians are going to be spending a large part of their time with the problems of older people," says Dr. T. Franklin Williams, director of the National Institute on Aging. But many physicians today suffer from ignorance about the medical needs of elders and about the behavior that is normal for old age. Some doctors still misinterpret depression or toxic prescription-drug interaction as dementia, for example.

"Most physicians in practice have no formal training in the use of drugs with elderly patients," says Dr. Jerry Avorn of Harvard's Department of Social Medicine and Health Policy. They receive little help from the drug companies, which usually don't test their products on people over 60. Yet this age group accounts for 30 percent of their sales. People over 65 average 15 prescriptions a year compared with 5.5 for younger patients. The lack of knowledge can be deadly: Thirty thousand elders in this country die every year because of adverse drug reactions that might have been prevented by more comprehensive testing, according to Dr. Williams.

Geriatric medicine is a much smaller specialty than many people think. Only a few thousand of the 450,000 doctors in the United States identify themselves as geriatricians. Although 75 percent of American medical schools offer geriatrics electives, as of 1985 only 4 percent of medical students had signed up for them. The first board certification examination in geriatrics was not offered until 1988. Few geriatricians practice outside big medical centers, in the community, as primary-care physicians. "Today, community-based geriatrics is in the corner of the closet under a mouse," says geriatrician Dr. Frederick Sherman.

Since Medicare and Medicaid pay physicians more for specific procedures than for general care, the practice of geriatrics is not as lucrative as other, less time-intensive specialties. Geriatricians spend more time managing chronic conditions than dramatically curing diseases, making this a less interesting specialty for many young doctors. And the relative nearness to death of older people is a threat to many physicians, who take the death of a patient as a personal defeat.

But geriatrics will attract more doctors in the future. Coming advances in medicine will make this specialty more interesting. The availability of board certification in geriatrics shows that the medical profession is beginning to realize the significance of the graying of the population. And some hospitals are starting to develop innovative programs to cure ageism among young physicians and attract them to geriatrics. At the Mount Sinai Medical Center in New York City, for instance, fourth-year medical students participate in an intergenerational "Well Elderly Program" with the seniors division at a local Y. The program aims to "familiarize the student with the concept of old age as a normal stage of human development, and to teach him to differentiate between normal and pathological aging," according to participating doctors who reported in *The Gerontologist.*

The program seems to be working. "The group was vibrant, intelligent, concerned and involved," wrote one student of his contact with the elders. "I was very impressed with their vitality and quality of life."

The doctor surplus looks as if it will continue. The AMA estimates that there will be 24 percent more physicians by 2000 but that demand for their services will probably rise by only 15 percent. As older people make up a larger percentage of the population, they will be in a good position to pressure the medical profession to meet their needs. Baby-boomer women, who will make up a large part of geriatrics cases several decades from now, have already changed the traditional doctor-patient relationship. The generation raised on the second wave of feminism and an aggressive consumer-rights movement is not likely to put up with shoddy medical treatment. As we move into the twenty-first century, they will play a hand in reshaping medical practice.

## HOSPITALS: THE HUB OF THE NEW MEDICAL NETWORK

American hospitals are looking more and more like the big businesses they've become—hardly the institutions today's elders knew in their youth. Huge chains like the one run by Humana have bought up many institutions. Some hospitals create spin-off profits by franchising successful programs they've developed, such as alcoholism treatment centers. If they've discovered a particularly successful way to run a laundry or a billing office, they might franchise that too.

Like any successful business, hospitals do market research and try to offer their services where their customers are. Increasingly, a major part of their clientele is over 60. That's why the famed Mayo Clinic opened satellite facilities in the retirement areas of Jacksonville, Florida, and

Scottsdale, Arizona, where much of its potential business was thought to be. The two units treat a total of twenty-four hundred patients a month, "beyond our fondest expectations," says Robert W. Fleming, Mayo's chief administrator.

Advances in telecommunications have made this kind of decentralization possible. For example, an X ray taken at a satellite clinic can be sent instantly to specialists at the Mayo Clinic in Rochester, Minnesota, who can then advise doctors at the Florida or Arizona locations of their opinion. This process is a harbinger of the future, in which each giant medical center will serve mostly as the hub of a group of small hospitals, institutes, ambulatory surgery centers, clinics, hospices, and programs oriented toward specific diseases and conditions.

"The medical center of the future will be a network," says David L. Ginsberg, executive vice-president for planning and program development of the Presbyterian Hospital of the Columbia-Presbyterian Medical Center in New York City, one of the first great medical centers. Ginsberg says that this is not a new approach:

> We're actually returning to an old model of health care where physicians' offices and their related hospitals were close to their patients. Why provide routine care in a highly specialized academic medical center? Why offer ambulatory care that requires a lower level of technology in a basically high-technology center?

The hospital itself will be reserved for teaching and for the treatment of the most serious illnesses, those that require the increasingly complex and expensive technology only central institutions can effectively use. Thus modern medicine will push the high technology of curing to its outer limits and, paradoxically, also restore most medical care to the neighborhood level.

## HOME CARE

Medicare's limit on payments for hospital stays, begun in 1984, is also bringing medical care closer to home. As we noted in discussing the crisis in the Social Security programs, home health care is the wave of the future. Hospitals themselves are already in the home health care business in a big way. About two thousand institutions offer this service. The HMOs will also be stressing home care in their programs for the best reason of all: It sells. "Consumers can see themselves using home health care," writes Val Halamandaris, president of the National Association for Home Care. "They often cannot see themselves using a nursing home."

Today's technology permits home care that would have been risky or just impractical not too long ago. For example, a three-ounce device worn on the belt buckle can now replace the old forty-pound intravenous pump on a pole. Telemetry, the system that allows NASA to monitor the vital signs of astronauts, can also be used by patients to update their doctors from home. Until recently, this sort of transmission was limited to patients with pacemakers who could send electrocardiograms by phone to their physicians, but now patients with many kinds of cardiac problems can do the same thing.

"It gave me a feeling of security to know that my doctor was in touch with my readings on a constant basis," recalls a 79-year-old Chicago man, recovering from bypass surgery. An alarm on his equipment reminded him to hook himself up to the phone five times a day to relay his blood pressure and other measurements to his physician automatically. "It was almost like being in the hospital," he says.

Today's fax machines can be repaired over the telephone, with malfunctioning units relaying self-diagnostic data to a central station from which an expert then makes the needed repairs. Equipment is now available that allows doctors to perform similar services for their homebound patients, who attach sensors to themselves and to their phones and let their bodies do the talking. For example, MDphone, which is about the size of a briefcase and costs about thirty thousand dollars, can be attached to a person with heart disease. If the patient thinks he or she is having a heart attack, the machine will relay vital information over the phone to a cardiologist who can make a diagnosis. The doctor can even signal the machine by phone to administer a shock to the patient's heart to stimulate it. Some medical rescue workers and fire fighters are now equipped with automatic external defibrillators, machines that cost less than seven thousand dollars and can automatically correct abnormal heartbeats through electric shocks. Perhaps these devices will see home use someday soon.

These machines are not cheap, but heavier demand should bring the prices down in the future. Insurance companies and Medicare officials have so far not committed themselves to paying for them, but at some time in the future they will probably decide to support such technology for one simple reason: Its use in the home is cheaper than long-term care in a hospital setting. However, before its use becomes common practice, the medical profession, insurance companies, and the government will have to come to terms with the issue of long-distance malpractice. "It could be considered kind of like trying to do medicine without seeing the patient," observes one doctor.

## A SHIFTING BALANCE OF POWER

The increasing involvement of the patient in his or her own treatment has significant implications for the doctor-patient relationship. The miracle drugs and medical technology of the post–World War II era concentrated a tremendous amount of authority and power in physicians' hands. Doctors became miracle workers. But with a looming doctor surplus and a middle-aged generation that has grown up accustomed to "miracles" and disinclined to accept authority, the balance will shift. We can expect older patients to be more assertive.

In coming years patients will probably know more about their condition than they do now. In at least fifteen states people can already gain access to their medical records with their doctors' permission. The general trend toward the consumer's right to know suggests a medical freedom of information act in the near future that will demystify the practice of medicine.

The movement to install resident philosophers in hospitals has already moved the doctor-patient relationship toward a new openness. There are now one hundred to two hundred of these ethicists or "biophilosophers" on the staffs of United States hospitals. They are called in to help doctors deal with troubling moral issues, such as the right to die, which will become more important as the number of older patients grows. These philosophers have made physicians more respectful of their patients' feelings and rights. They encourage doctors to see patients less as passive subjects and more as active participants in their treatment, according to the observations of Dr. Arthur L. Caplan, director of the Center for Biomedical Ethics at the University of Minnesota.

With the expansion of the home health care system in the future, doctors will also go back to making occasional house calls. By then most physicians will probably have no memory of this venerable practice. Patients saw doctors in their offices 60 percent of the time in 1930, while house calls accounted for the other 40 percent. By 1950, however, house calls were already down to 10 percent of nonhospital doctor-patient contacts.

Dr. Lawrence Bernstein, author of *Primary Care Medicine in the Home* and vice-president of the National Association for Physicians in Home Care, offers his colleagues a glimpse of possible things to come:

> The patient is no longer a captive in the hospital; the physician is a guest in the house. . . . In the hospital, I sometimes rather brazenly sit where I wish and wash my hands in the nearest sink when the exam is finished. In the patient's home, I very politely ask where I may sit and where I may wash my hands. As it should, this gives the patient a much greater sense of control.

The doctor's black bag is likely to look different from the one many adults can remember the doctor carrying when he arrived at their homes. The portable computer in the bag, hooked to a compact-disk data-base system, will allow the physician to extract information on just about any geriatric condition. Should the malady prove too esoteric for this portable data base, the doctor will access the latest in-depth data from a central data bank by plugging the computer into the patient's phone.

The relationship among doctors and the nurses, home health aides, and other personnel under their leadership will also change. With care decentralized and patients often less physically accessible to the physician in charge of a case, the authority of medical workers other than doctors will increase. Nurses working in home health care will be less subordinate, since by being on the scene they will establish more control over the course of treatment. In greater demand—one medical personnel recruitment firm estimates the nurse shortfall at more than 250,000 by the year 2000—they will make more money. Women who had few other career options have traditionally filled the nursing ranks, but those days are ending.

Pharmacists will also play a more important role in the delivery of health services. Already they do more to monitor toxic drug interactions than they used to, through the use of computerized prescription records. When a patient comes in with a prescription that could cause a problem with other medications he or she is taking, the druggist's computer flags down the problem and the druggist can call it to the doctor's attention.

In the future, pharmacists may become more specialized, with some running the business side of the enterprise while others dispense advice about common ailments that used to be the exclusive territory of doctors. That's not so farfetched. Pharmacy is a profession that is still evolving. It was only in 1932 that pharmacists were first required to have a college degree, and boomers have seen the corner drugstore give way to the chain drugstore/emporium. Before long we may see the pharmacist-practitioner, trained in the rudiments of medicine as well as in drug preparation.

## SELF-CARE AND SELF-HELP

Self-help health groups have been playing an increasingly bigger role in doctor-patient relationships since the 1950s. These organizations, such as the Stroke Club and Mended Hearts, bring together people who have a disease or chronic condition in common. They know things that only another patient can know and understand, and thus serve a function that their doctors cannot duplicate. Often the patients' families are involved in the groups too. Patients trade information about their experiences with doctors and about treatments, and they offer one another moral support and role models in dealing with problems. The groups do not operate in opposition to traditional medical institutions. Indeed, they often meet in hospitals. They are patients acting to help one another and in that they have set an important precedent.

Perhaps the greatest change in the treatment of older people in the near future will come from an increase in their banding together to deal with common problems. Patients will take more control of their own lives and treatment. Since geriatrics is a relatively new discipline, it more than any other specialty offers the opportunity of bypassing the medical-institutional model of care. As Medicare heads toward a financial crunch there is new room for more nontraditional approaches to healing and the management of chronic conditions.

Gerontologists Tom Hickey, Kathryn Dean, and Bjorn Holstein suggest a future generation of elders who will take some of the doctoring out of the physician's hands: "The caretaking of parents and other chronically impaired family members should foster the development of at least some basic skills for expanding the lay care network." More courses in home nursing will be offered by hospitals to meet caregivers' demands for practical knowledge.

These same experts also see "more holistic health care options for the elderly," which "will gain greater acceptance, increasing the potential for a wide range of informal care." Holistic medicine could come into its own with the aging of the baby boomers in ten to twenty years. When the members of this cohort begin to feel the first aches and pains of age, they may reach for positive thoughts rather than for the phone to call their doctors. They have matured, after all, in the era when Norman Cousins, a former editor of *Saturday Review,* wrote a book about the power of laughter to heal *(Anatomy of an Illness)* and was appointed an adjunct professor at the UCLA medical school.

The baby boomers are a generation already much taken with nontraditional healing techniques such as shiatsu massage, acupuncture, biofeedback, and health food. So they will need little encouragement to move further away from the medical model in pursuing wellness in their old age. It's even conceivable that drugstores, to accommodate them, will go back to selling the herbs and exotic potions they did generations ago.

People now in their thirties and forties may also take their health care in their own hands collectively by the time they're old enough to need a good deal of it. Florida and Missouri have begun small, innovative programs designed to foster such activities. They involve volunteer service banks in which elders can help to provide home care for others and then may "withdraw" the credits they build up in the form of assistance for themselves if they ever need it.

Daughters and daughters-in-law, the traditional caregivers for elders at home, are now likely to be employed outside the home. To fill this gap, more older people will serve nonfamily members as caregivers in home settings, both as volunteers and as paramedical workers on salary. Because of their numbers, healthy baby boomers as elders will have to play a large role in caring for the less fortunate members of their cohort, since there will not be enough people of other generations around to do so. But if this may create some hardships, it will also be empowering for their generation and foster empathy and a spirit of communality among them.

## A STORY OF THE FUTURE

In the spring of 2018, 71-year-old Alice Conroy, severely disabled by arthritis, one of the few chronic conditions not yet banished by twenty-first-century medicine, realizes that she can no longer make it on her own. She's divorced, and her 36-year-old son, who lives in another state, is not able to care for her. Needing help with such basics as shopping and housework, and also feeling lonely, she calls the local Elder Skills Bank. A nurse-practitioner at the bank makes an initial evaluation of Alice's condition over the videophone and dispatches a visiting nurse to make an on-the-scene diagnosis. Once Alice is approved for service, her domestic needs are fulfilled by a combination of elder volunteers and workers paid by Medicaid, which charges her a small fee based on her ability to pay.

Marian Burgess, 67, one of the volunteers, strikes up a friendship with Alice when she realizes how much they have in common. Each owns a rare first edition of *Our Bodies, Ourselves,* the pioneering work, now in its fourteenth revised edition, which helped spark the self-help health movement among women back in the 1970s of their youth. Grateful for Marian's help, Alice begins to teach her new friend stress-reduction techniques that help Alice bring down her once-threatening high blood pressure without medication. Gradually their friendship deepens, and before long they become . . . well, just like family.

# 8

# The New Older Woman

"In those days [the 1970s] I was always asked to explain why I worked outside the home. Today the pendulum has swung, and if you're a woman you have to explain why you don't."

Divorce lawyer LYNN GOLD-BIKIN, in her forties

The phenomenon of women working outside the home has coincided with the adulthood of the baby boomers. Their lives have differed markedly from their mothers', and the contrast between the experiences of the two generations will result in elder boomer women with a wider range of lifestyle choices and a different set of problems than those faced by New Elder women.

Until recently, the media portrayed older women as self-effacing helpmates to their aging spouses, quaint grandmothers, pathetic widows, or eccentric "biddy" spinsters. With the coming of menopause in their late forties or early fifties, their most important job, bearing children, had ended. Publicly they were held sexless, no longer desirable to men.

Even the awakening of academic interest in older people at first bypassed older women. Until the 1980s, studies of retirement usually focused on the plight of the suddenly dispensable working *man*. Descriptions of the stages of adulthood were developed from samples that included mostly male subjects. Scholars and policymakers assumed that the older woman's traditional role as housewife and mother made her a mere appendage of the man of the house.

But several trends have joined to create a climate for a new image of the older woman. Since 1940, older women have increasingly outnumbered older men. As late as 1960, the ratio of older women to older men was six to five. But by 1986, there were 17.4 million women over 65 in the United States, compared with 11.8 million men, almost a three-to-two ratio. While the increase in male life expectancy has begun to narrow the gap slightly since about 1980, women will still significantly outnumber men when the baby boomers reach this age bracket (there are now about 37 million baby-boomer men and an equal number of baby-boomer women).

With the rise in divorce and an increasing demand for skilled office workers, many middle-aged and older women have entered or reentered the work force, becoming wage earners, sometimes with their own pensions. And they have lived to see television, the movies, and the press begin to project an image of the older woman who is a person in her own right.

Women now past the age of 60 have lived much of their lives in the shadow of men. But when their daughters and granddaughters reach old age, they are likely to be living in ways their mothers and grandmothers would not recognize. The women of the baby boom have grown up assuming that women work outside the home. They take for granted the economic and social equality for which feminists fought in the 1970s. They know that many marriages will not survive till death do us part. They will age with more role models of active elder women than the present generation has had, and they should prove to be a powerful force in society.

## OLDER WOMEN TODAY: AT AN ECONOMIC DISADVANTAGE

New Elder women have shared in the prosperity of their generation. But in most cases they have been economic junior partners, largely dependent upon their husbands' earnings and pensions. This has left them especially vulnerable to downward mobility resulting from widowhood or divorce. The poverty rate for women over 65 is 15.2 percent, while 8.5 percent of their male counterparts are below the poverty line. Most women over 65 today have been career homemakers. Even those who were employed—probably part-time, at low pay, or in jobs they started late in life—may have had to give up their own meager Social Security benefits in order to collect the better rates for which they were eligible as dependents of their husbands, who held "regular" jobs. (Benefits are determined by averaging earnings. New Elder women in most cases earned less than their husbands, and their years as mothers and homemakers—despite a credit of five years built into their benefits formula—pull down their average.) Even women of this present elder generation who have worked outside the home are unlikely to have earned pensions—only 20 percent do—since they probably entered the work force late and never earned substantial salaries.

Widowhood often makes matters worse, especially if the husband first ends up in a nursing home, forcing his wife to spend down most of their assets before he can qualify for Medicaid. Divorce can also impoverish an older women. About two hundred thousand couples over the age of 50 divorce each year. The men are more likely to remarry—we still expect men to marry younger women—and their former wives are left with financial difficulties they have never been taught to handle.

The precarious economic position of older women has prompted the formation of many advocacy and self-help groups, including the Older Women's League (OWL). Tish Sommers, who cofounded OWL in 1980, coined the term *displaced homemaker* to describe women "forcibly exiled from our jobs as homemakers." Divorced at 57, Sommers lost her health insurance just when she needed a mastectomy. Among her group's accomplishments are state laws that ensure the continuation of health insurance for women whose coverage is threatened by divorce or widowhood.

OWL also emphasizes the importance of self-help for older women. Today many in the current generation of elder women are getting together in support groups to cope with their problem. There are now hundreds of such groups in every part of the country, some independent, others affiliated with local colleges and universities.

## THE NEXT GENERATION

Anne Tolstoi Wallach was not typical of her generation. Her husband "allowed" her to work outside the house. "We worked in a separate wing," she recalls of her job as a copywriter for the J. Walter Thompson advertising agency in the 1950s, "and wore hats to distinguish ourselves from the secretaries outside our enclave." She eventually made it to vice-president. Wallach also raised a daughter while pursuing a career, but knew very few women who dared to be both mothers and career women.

Today her daughter, Alison, born in the early 1950s, also works for J. Walter Thompson, and she, too, is a working mother. The difference between mother and daughter is that Alison is one of the many millions of women of her generation who are both workers and mothers.

It hasn't been easy for baby-boomer women to play both roles. Many have experienced burnout trying to be "superwomen." Some have fallen back into a "sequencing" pattern, dropping out of the work force when the kids are small and then reentering the job market later, presumably to take up where they left off. Guilt from internal conflict over whether they're doing justice to their children while trying to build careers is sometimes reinforced by outside pressures stemming from the upsurge in "traditionalist" values in the 1980s. In 1988 *Good Housekeeping*, for example, gave its seal of approval in a full-page ad to the "woman who has found her identity in herself, her home, her family."

But social and cultural pressures notwithstanding, this generation of women continues to be employed. Of women with children under the age of 18, 65 percent are in the labor force (56 percent of mothers with preschoolers, 73 percent of those with older children). For many of these mothers, economics dictates their dual role. They are employed because their families can't make it on one salary or because divorce has made them the sole breadwinners for themselves and their children.

According to a Bureau of Labor Statistics projection, the percentage of women who work outside the home will rise from the current 55.9 to 62 by the year 2000, and the percentage of working mothers should increase as well. The next generation of older women will therefore have had a significantly different experience of adulthood from the one their mothers had.

When they are employed, baby-boomer women do better economically than those of their mothers' generation who were in the work force. For example, in 1987, women 25 to 34 working full-time made 74 percent of what men of their age made, while for women 55 to 64 the comparable figure was 58 percent. Today's working women will have their own pensions. They plan more for their financial future than did New Elder women, and are thus likely to be in a much better position after their years of full-time work than were earlier generations. Retirement planning companies now target women as prime customers, a far cry from when "the central characters of all the retirement booklets were men and women were pictured crocheting," according to Henry M. Wallfish of Retirement Advisors, Inc.

More and more of these boomer women are becoming self-employed entrepreneurs. By the mid-1980s women owned 25 percent of the small businesses in this country, and their ranks continue to grow. Women now make up over a third of the business travelers in the country (as opposed to 1 percent in 1970); in ten years they will represent 50 percent. When women travel on business, they stay in expensive rooms and the hotels are working hard to accommodate them, adding such features as wide counters in the bathrooms to make it easier to use cosmetics and secured club-floor lounges that require special elevator keys for access.

Baby-boomer women will thus reach old age much more financially independent than did women of the New Elder cohort. Economically, the later years of the women now moving into middle age will offer lifestyle options rather than a narrowing of choices dictated by financial need.

## LOOKS AREN'T EVERYTHING, BUT . . .

The image of older women is in flux. On the one hand, greeting cards, whose messages reflect our underlying values, have treated older people with condescension, and have given older women, particularly, the short end of the stick. On greeting cards "women are more likely than men to be the focus of messages dealing with physical appearance and age concealment," according to sociologists Vasilikie Demos and Ann Jache. Often the cards' humor evokes the image of a dirty old man, a caricature for which there is no female counterpart.

Nevertheless, women aged 50 to 65, of the Eisenhower Generation and the younger part of the New Elder generation, are beginning to benefit from changes in social attitudes. These women now seem younger than did women of similar ages in the past, partly because we all perceive the chronology of aging differently. They even have a benchmark for their place in the new chronology. Gloria Steinem, a founder of *Ms.* magazine, has become their decade marker. The media celebrated Steinem on both her fortieth and her fiftieth birthdays as a model of what women of those ages have become. When Steinem turned 40 in 1974, a reporter told her that she certainly didn't *"look"* 40. "This is what 40 looks like," she replied. "We've been lying so long, who would know?"

Ten years later, Steinem anticipated that 50 would be "serious, grown-up, and finally old: a year that would be a rite of passage, a transformation, and a proof of mortality." But scouting the edge of late middle age for her contemporaries, she reported back a more optimistic scenario. She saw longevity, women's successful adaptation to careers, the continued sex appeal of celebrities such as Shirley MacLaine and Joan Collins, and the phenomenon of older women attracting younger men as redefining this part of the life cycle for women. "Fifty is what forty used to be," she concluded.

Steinem's refreshing look at the beginning of a woman's later years has helped to correct the long-standing negative image of older women that has pervaded our media and the wider culture. Dalma Heyn, a columnist for *Mademoiselle,* former executive editor of *McCall's,* and a contributor to similar periodicals, should know something about how women's magazines view their principal subject. In an article she wrote in 1987, she said that in magazines, adulthood for women stops somewhere around 35 to 40. Editors delete quotes from older women in stories and excise age from photographs as well. Women who are 60 have no realistic image models in these magazines—"They're comparing themselves to some retouched face smiling back at them."

Yet the situation is changing even as such articles are still being published. In 1988, for example, *McCall's* began its Silver Line edition, a special supplement bound into the magazine for subscribers in the 50-to-64 age bracket. Also in that year, 62-year-old Frances Lear, tired of being "shut out of the media for so long that we have not seen ourselves in positive images anywhere," brought out the first issue of *Lear's,* a magazine for women over 40 who "weren't born yesterday."

In its first twelve months of publication, circulation increased from 200,000 to 350,000 copies a month.

Until recently, television entertainment programs were not much better than magazines in depicting older women. "Their characters tended to be powerless, befuddled, inflexible, and feeble," wrote Sally Steenland in *Prime Time Women: An Analysis of Older Women on Entertainment Television,* a 1986 study commissioned by the National Commission on Working Women. They also had no sex appeal. But the last ten years have produced changes. Twenty percent of the characters on these shows are now women over 50, up from 10 percent, and about 25 percent of these women are over 65. Just as important, many of them are "powerful, creative, appealing, and affluent." In fact, 25 percent of the women portrayed, on shows like "Dallas," "Falcon Crest," and "Dynasty," are millionaires owning their own businesses.

On most shows that have introduced more realistic older women, their behavior and interests suggest middle rather than old age. But one show, "Golden Girls," an Emmy Award winner, has introduced believable older women. These characters are attractive, and they deal with the problems of widowhood, sexuality, desertion by a man for a younger woman, their children's marriages, their grandchildren, and the trials of making do on modest incomes. They hold real-life jobs, such as substitute teacher, and talk about the real-life conditions of older women.

## ENDURING DOUBLE STANDARDS

Despite the media's "discovery" of the older woman, certain double standards of age still prevail. Gloria Steinem noticed that "an over-50 Dan Rather is regarded as the young replacement for Walter Cronkite," while "Barbara Walters is treated as a miracle of longevity." A film casting Katharine Hepburn and Richard Dreyfuss as lovers would never make it, gerontologist Elizabeth Markson points out, while audiences easily accepted a sexual relationship between Burt Lancaster and Susan Sarandon in *Atlantic City.* An older man can be glamorous, powerful, certainly sexy—but an older woman?

Attitudes on this subject may not be changing as quickly as some observers suggest. Why is it always Elizabeth Taylor, now entering her late fifties, who is dragged out to show that older women can be glamorous? Is she the only glamorous woman her age? The attention given to Taylor's romance with Malcolm Forbes may demonstrate our fascination with wealthy celebrities rather than our acceptance of love at a later age.

However, mature sirens such as Joan Collins certainly give women viewers past the age of 50 the chance to identify with glamorous and powerful women close to their own age. It is no surprise that, according to a 1984 poll, 58 percent of "Dynasty's" audience and 61 percent of those who watched "Hotel" were women—and nearly 50 percent of these female viewers were over 50. If they can see themselves as powerful and glamorous, maybe others eventually will too. The brisk sales of books on beauty care by older stars such as Joan Collins, Linda Evans, Jane Fonda, and Victoria Principal confirm that these celebrities are providing role (or at least fantasy) models for today's New Elder and Eisenhower Generation women.

On the other hand, exactly what *is* the image with which they are identifying? When 50-year-old Joan Collins, 52-year-old Vicki LaMotta, and 55-year-old Terry Moore pose nude for *Playboy*, what does it mean? Katha Pollitt, a poet and a former editor of *The Nation* magazine, now in her late thirties, expressed her skepticism in a column in *The New York Times:*

> It's true that in recent years there's been a certain vogue for older women as sex symbols. But what does that vogue really mean? Joan Collins and Linda Evans may be goddesses after 40, but what makes them "beautiful" is precisely that they don't look middle-aged, they look embalmed. These actresses' popularity is no tribute to mature femininity, but to the dubious arts of the makeup man and, I suspect, the plastic surgeon.

## SNAP, CRACKLE, AND POP

Some things will change slowly. The baby-boomer generation, whose youth was so celebrated, does not figure to let the bloom go too easily—especially the women, since the double standard of aging against which they are measured hasn't died yet, Gloria Steinem notwithstanding. Many boomer men, it seems, also prefer sweet young things.

Anna Quindlen, whose "Life in the 30's" column for *The New York Times* was one of that newspaper's enticements to baby-boomer women readers, got the first real intimations of what old age could mean to a woman, paradoxically, when she was pregnant. The men she passed on the street looked at her differently. Something was gone from their eyes. She feared

> it was a precursor, not of a temporary loss but of a permanent one. Will the chemistry be there 20 years from now when I walk down a city street, edging toward 60 years old? I don't know. I never thought about it before the other night. I like the snap, crackle and pop of those momentary encounters. I wouldn't want them to become extinct.

It didn't help that her husband, younger than she is by five weeks, "looks like he serves 8 o'clock Mass every morning at Our Lady of Perpetual Youth." Nor did she feel comforted by reports of increases in marriages between older women and younger men. Quindlen thinks "that trend has more to do with Cher than with reality."

## THE NEW LATE-LIFE COURTING STYLES

Robert Ragaini will never forget that mid-1950s weekend in Connecticut. Then in his early twenties, he and his girlfriend had arrived at his parents' house to spend a few days. Although his mother and father knew he was living with his lover, they made it clear to the young couple on their arrival that they would sleep in separate bedrooms. Ragaini was "taken aback," but his protests got him nowhere.

Now, at age 52, divorced, Ragaini is again living with a woman. He still likes to take his lover to Connecticut for weekends at his mother's house. But these days Ragaini and his woman friend do share a bedroom, and why not? His mother has a live-in lover too. "Times change and people change with them," he observes. "Some of us simply change sooner than others."

Because of improved health, greater longevity, and more divorce, many more older singles are "available" and "looking." The social etiquette that lends structure to romantic involvement is still evolving for this new age group of consenting adults; uneasiness abounds among older people in the dating pool. "Widows and divorcées who start dating after long marriages frequently suffer from culture shock because during their married years the sexual revolution took place," the magazine *50 Plus* advises readers in its guidebook for elders living alone.

What is the relationship of sex to romance after the age of 50? Noel

Perrin, a professor of English at Dartmouth who is in his fifties, says he's barely been able to finish dialing the number when he's called women for dates. "Dear God, how I dread it," he confesses. "There is not going to be that instant and spontaneous attraction that leads to second and third dates when you're young. For the young, sexual attraction serves as a kind of handy glue, keeping a couple together until other and more durable bonds take hold," Perrin theorizes.

There is bound to be awkwardness in the dating situation for people who were raised in an earlier era, but not all older people become unglued in romantic settings. Sociologists Kris Bulcroft and Margaret O'Conner-Roden studied forty-five midwestern elders who had been widowed or divorced and were dating. It was true, they found, that older people had some problems knowing when sex outside of marriage was "appropriate," and how much they could publicly acknowledge their own sexual activity. A 61-year-old woman in one couple was very much concerned with discretion. "I have a tendency to hide his shoes when my grandchildren are coming over," she confessed.

But these elders were clear that they *were* sexual beings. Their palms got just as sweaty as teenagers' do when they felt the rush of attraction for another person. And romance for them was more than roses and dancing. "You can talk about candlelight dinners and sitting in front of the fireplace," said one 71-year-old widower about his girlfriend, "but I still think the most romantic thing I've ever done is to go to bed with her."

## THE JOY OF ELDER SEX

Consumers Union shone a spotlight on elder sexuality with its widely quoted 1984 book, *Love, Sex, and Aging.* The organization that publishes *Consumer Reports* presented all the facts about the sexuality of older Americans, as far as it could ascertain them from 4,296 responses from readers over 50 to a sex survey questionnaire. It was "the largest geriatric sample ever assembled for a sexuality study," according to Consumers Union.

Most of the participants agreed with the statement, "Society thinks of older people as nonsexual." Then they went on to disprove it. The majority said they had happy marriages, even the women and men who admitted to being adulterous. Of the women, 75 percent said that marital sex was important to them, along with 87 percent of the men.

The men tended to initiate sex. About 75 percent of married women and men said they had sex once a week or less, and a great majority of both sexes declared themselves happy with the frequency of relations. Oral sex was popular: 43 percent of the women and 56 percent of the men engaged in it. A smaller sample used hard-core pornography for stimulation, and a still smaller group had fetishistic fantasies.

By about four to one, people in the survey thought masturbation was a good thing. The practice was common within all segments of the sample, particularly among the unmarried. "I was brought up by my mother to believe masturbation would drive me crazy," wrote a 68-year-old man. "It hasn't yet." A 66-year-old widow found it "pleasurable and do so without any feeling of guilt."

The elders surveyed thought it was OK for unmarried people to have sex—57 percent of the women and 72 percent of the men. A "surprising number" of unmarried women, 29 percent, were involved with men at least five years younger than themselves. Being in scarcer supply gave unmarried men more lifestyle options, from casual sex to marriage. But "being unmarried and female is fully compatible with leading a rich, busy, happy, and—for some—sexually rewarding life during the later years," the study concluded.

An insignificant number of respondents described themselves as homosexuals, but 13 percent of the men and 8 percent of the women said that they had had at least one homosexual experience, the majority of them when they were much younger. Most people in the survey professed toleration for homosexuality.

On the downside, the survey showed that increasing age tended to bring a decline in sexual activity. Ninety-three percent of the women were sexually active in their fifties, 81 percent in their sixties, and 65 percent after age 70. Fully 98 percent of the men were sexually active in their fifties, 91 percent in their sixties, and 79 percent of those over 70.

"Grandma, Grandpa, you couldn't, you don't . . . ," *Psychology Today*'s Morton Hunt wrote when the study was published. "Maybe they don't," he suggested, noting that this was hardly a scientific survey. But Hunt concluded that on the whole, "one is hearing the truth about sex and aging," and when he reviewed the book in *Reader's Digest* three months later, the magazine's headline called it a "landmark survey."

Buttressed by the imprimatur of our most important consumer magazine and by favorable notice from two of the most influential periodicals in the country on a subject like this one, the findings of the Consumers Union report have become the new wisdom for many people. Powerful social support and approval now shore up the self-esteem of those older people who remain sexually active and who talk openly about it. By the same token, elders who feel that they don't measure up to the new sexy "norm" need to be reassured that they're OK too, lest they suffer from elder performance anxiety. In other words, the situation that prevailed for younger Americans' reactions to publications ranging from the Kinsey reports to *The Hite Report* now colors old age.

## SEXUAL REVOLUTIONARIES

Could baby boomers, the generation that made cohabitation before marriage a new and acceptable part of the life cycle, be anything but secure about their own sexual lives with the coming of their first gray hairs? Ah, yes. In 1985, Myrna Lewis and Robert Butler revised their book, *Love and Sex after 60*, retitling it *Love and Sex after 40* (there is already a newsletter on the same theme). They and their publishers knew that the baby boomers, closing in on middle age, would have something important on their minds.

The members of the postwar generation figure to do much more public agonizing than their parents did about the changes in sexuality that come with age: first, because they are likely to look upon such self-examination as both respectable and "therapeutic"; and second, because they will feel that more is expected of them in the way of activity and performance than was ever expected of *their* elders. Women as well as men may seek through a celebration of their continued sexual vitality the comforting thought that their youth has never really left them.

Baby-boomer women will be in their ascendancy and in the majority within the ranks of their cohort as they age. These older women will be much more likely to define the terms and the agenda of sexual encounters. Taking advantage of the longer arousal times required for both sexes in later life, they may well steer their mates toward long, slow sexual experiences that fill whole evenings, in which the only thing premature would be the phone ringing. One could even imagine the evolution of new rituals, perhaps languid intercourse with stylized music—something almost resembling a Japanese tea ceremony.

The preponderance of older women living alone also suggests more openness about other avenues of sexual expression. Lesbian relationships could finally emerge as an acceptable and respectable lifestyle for older women—a trend just barely under way now. This would further serve to validate women who did not conceal their same-sex preference in the first place.

Solitary sex could also grow in importance for this future generation of older women. Ever since Masters and Johnson people have been assured that masturbation can be fun. Since elder baby boomers matured in a society in which the pleasures of sex have been widely proclaimed as well as practiced, they will not feel the need to be circumspect. We can anticipate tasteful sexual boutiques in mainstream stores such as Bloomingdale's and Macy's to accommodate these needs. These shops will carry the latest in intimate apparel and also sexual aids such as computerized vibrators, in which sensors read levels of genital lubrication and automatically adjust the machines' action to maximize orgasmic pleasure.

## TILL DEATH DO US PART

New Elder married couples who stay together face unprecedented adjustments. Few couples in the past anticipated such long lives together. "Never in history have the lives of husbands and wives remained interwoven in intact marriages so long as to encounter the constellation of life-changing events that the last stages of the marital career now bring," according to sociologist Rosalie Gilford. Or as one wife in a less formal inquiry put it: "What is retirement? Twice as much husband and half as much pay."

For the present generation of elders, for whom the wife's primary career has been full-time mother and homemaker, a husband's retirement can mean a stranger invading her sphere. Postretirement adjustments for this generation often involve territorial disputes. Edna Stengel is said to have remarked about her retired baseball manager/banker husband, Casey: "I married him for better or worse, not for lunch."

All of a sudden, the former breadwinner is home during the day in this new stage of the traditional marriage. His wife may feel that she should schedule his activities *and* make his lunch. And her husband will often be unaware of how he's disrupted her life or how much she has to do to accommodate the new state of affairs.

The husband may have made most of his social contacts at work and they are now gone with his job, whereas the wife is more likely to have a network of friends who are still there. If he's a man who's having trouble adjusting to life away from the office, he could be especially difficult to be with. June P. Wilson, a 69-year-old writer who has seen this phenomenon up close, describes this kind of husband as "a caged and wounded beast who wants cosseting."

Aside from agreeing to new ground rules to promote peaceful coexistence, a couple may also have to contend with significant differences between them that the man's new idleness and the departure of now-adult childen have uncovered. Gerontologist Ruth Harriet Jacobs describes marriages that were organized around child rearing as "pediatric marriages." With the kids gone, aging husbands and wives have more time to speak to each other, but many couples find they have little or nothing to say. Kathryn, a 68-year-old California woman, would like to be more active, but her husband, Ralston, just wants to read and watch television. "There is conversation," she says, "but it is mainly surface."

When a wife is employed and continues working after her husband retires, problems can also arise. For example, the man may have his heart set on retiring to a warmer climate, but that would mean his wife would have to quit her job, with no guarantee she could find something similar near her new home. "We're used to having our own money and doing our own thing," one New Elder woman remarked about herself and other women her age she knew. A career woman in her thirties would understand that perfectly.

One adaptation that enables older couples in traditional marriages to enjoy retirement is a gradual change in their gender roles. If their adjustment is successful, they move toward a common denominator of androgyny. The woman makes more decisions for the two of them and becomes more dominant in the relationship. The man starts to share household tasks; his personality softens.

## FRIENDS, LOVERS, AND HUSBANDS

"Being a wife doesn't say what you are or who you are," a 25-year-old unmarried woman said in a 1983 *New York Times* poll of women's attitudes toward family and work. Women "realize that they can't depend on one man because when that man walks out, their whole lives are pulled out from under their feet and they don't know how to pick up the pieces. It happened to my mother."

The members of this young woman's generation will come to their later years determined to be different from their mothers. They will surely have different expectations about their relationships with men. On the one hand, their outlook will have been influenced by the prevalence of divorce in their cohort throughout their adult lives—they will know better than to depend on one man for identity or security. These women will aspire to lives beyond the home and to financial independence from their husbands.

On the other hand, theirs will be the first generation of women who may anticipate, from the beginning of their marriages, a span of four, five, or six decades of living with the same man. Not defining themselves solely as wives and mothers will help their marriages because these relationships will not have to shoulder all the burden of providing satisfaction in their lives. Their retirement is unlikely to get bogged down in territorial clashes or in the tending of psychic wounds. Instead, they will be creating a new elder lifestyle in a spirit of equality with their mates.

Women baby boomers will have chosen their lifestyles from a wide variety of options open to them. For the present generation of older women, a single life track of motherhood and helpmate led straight from youth to old age—with relatively few women having an opportunity to branch off for careers or happy and respected lives as single women. Compared with these women, their daughters and granddaughters have evolved a world of choices: traditional marriage, a two-career family with or without children, divorce, serial marriage, remaining single, or an openly lesbian lifestyle.

Among the baby-boomer women, relationships with the opposite sex in or outside of marriage have been less rigidly defined than in their mothers' time. Platonic friendships with men are fairly unusual among today's older women. They assume that friendship with a man means romance. "Little has been written about cross-sex friendships during old age," according to sociologist Rebecca G. Adams, "perhaps because such relationships are relatively rare." In an early 1980s survey of 70 women over 65 living in a Chicago suburb, Adams found that 90 percent of their friends were women. "The women reached old age without being exposed to real models for non-courting, cross-sex friendships."

This is hardly the case for their daughters and granddaughters. Cross-sex friendships are often part of their lives. In big cities, single men and women share apartments as friends, without romantic or sexual involvement, sometimes just for convenience. These women work with men, confide in them, drink with them, and participate in sports with them—all without necessarily sharing a bed. They may even be friends with their ex-husbands. There's every reason to believe this will continue into their old age.

## A POWER IN THE WORLD

As elders, women of the 1946 to 1964 generation will be movers and shakers in areas their mothers viewed mostly as spectators. Women are gaining strongholds in traditionally male enclaves, including industries and professions that influence the way all of us see women. For instance, before the 1990s are over, women will hold more than half the chief executive positions in advertising agencies, with increased influence over media images of women. In an even more significant realm, there are now more than sixteen thousand women clergy. Their presence in a growing number of denominations and faiths represents a dramatic challenge to the image of God as an old man with a white beard.

The financial, psychic, and social rewards working women now in their twenties, thirties, and forties will attain from their careers will give them a different outlook on themselves when they age. They are likely to be much more self-confident and independent than the present cohort of older women and less willing to defer to their husbands and lovers on decisions ranging from when to retire to where to live.

Besides their increasing influence in business and religion, women are also gaining power through politics and government. From 1974 to 1988, the number of women holding elective office in this country increased by 300 percent to eighteen thousand. While constituents over the age of 60 now tend not to vote for women, this will certainly change by the early twenty-first century. Current elders were raised to think of politics as a man's world. Among the baby boomers, men as well as women have grown up with many fewer divisions of labor by gender. As the generation of 1946 to 1964 ages and fills the ranks of America's elders, it will bring different assumptions into the voting booth.

Candidates for major office are often chosen from among the ranks of lawyers, a profession that has attracted many boomer women. (Between 1967 and 1980, the period during which most Early Boomer women lawyers attended law school, the percentage of law degrees earned by women rose from 4 to 26.) Geraldine Ferraro, who broke the ice with her run for the vice-presidency in 1984, came up through this route. And women are also playing a leadership role in running political campaigns. Susan Estrich, director of the Dukakis campaign in 1988, was the first woman to direct a presidential candidate's campaign for a major political party.

By the second decade of the twenty-first century, virtually the entire electorate of this country will have come to maturity assuming that women are entitled to equal rights and are competent to do just about any job. Thus women will be poised to secure the one position that would most symbolize their political ascendancy: the presidency of the United States. It could happen as early as the year 2008. A substantial number of women who will then be in their fifties will have had the political careers and the experience people expect of a presidential candidate. We may have had a woman vice-president by then. The succession of generations will produce an electorate who can see a woman in the White House as a natural choice.

An older woman president, particularly the first one, is likely to have an agenda that includes matters of special interest to other older women, an important part of her constituency. Among them could be gender-based adjustments in the Social Security retirement system that will reduce the greater poverty rate that will still probably characterize older women. ("By the year 2020, poverty among elderly Americans will be confined primarily to women living alone" if nothing is done to improve the situation, according to a 1987 report by the Commonwealth Fund Commission.) Social Security credit for those who remained homemakers, mothers, and full-time caregivers for older relatives should help. In Great Britain's retirement benefits system, such people can earn credit for as much as twenty years of work. Alterations in Medicare to cover procedures that affect only women could also be high on an older woman president's priorities list. Now, for example, the system does not pay for tests for breast and cervical cancer or osteoporosis.

## THE NEW MATURITY

Choice has been a persistent theme in the lives of women now in their twenties, thirties, and forties. Compared with their mothers and grandmothers, they have had many more options in choosing a career, motherhood, or both, and in selecting the types of relationships they will have with men and other women. As they approach middle and old age, baby-boomer women will experience an even greater and more profound freedom. They are likely to have more leeway in defining the "self" that they grapple with in trying to achieve self-fulfillment, rather than have the defining done for them by the precepts of an outdated developmental psychology. And they will also probably have more to say, as they age, about what it means to act one's age.

There is a strong likelihood that adult developmental psychology will undergo a major overhaul in the next decades because of the influence and ascendancy of baby-boomer women, who just don't fit well in the current models. Most of this new work will probably be undertaken by women researchers and theorists. As we mentioned in chapter 1, the very notion that adults are supposed to develop psychologically in a series of well-defined stages tied to their chronological age has recently come into question. It now appears that categories such as "the mid-life crisis" are not as universal as previously thought. Many of the stages seem particularly inappropriate when applied to the development of women.

Erik Erikson, the central figure in developmental psychology, the "ages-and-stages" approach to growth and maturity, adapted Freud's work to describe maturation after childhood. Erikson suggested that there were eight stages of growth, from childhood to old age. In the first seven stages, a person had a "job" to do in order to negotiate the challenges of that stage successfully and move on to the next part of life. Failure to deal adequately with this task could leave a person stuck at an inappropriate stage, unhappy, and insufficiently prepared emotionally for the future. A classic example is the identity crisis that adolescents are supposed to pass through.

Erikson's thought was a powerful corrective to earlier and more rigid views of growth, and his insights are still important. But his writings are no more holy writ than were Freud's. Erikson carried out his clinical research, on which he based his theories, in the 1940s and 1950s, as gerontologist Matilda White Riley has pointed out. He saw people dealing with these life stages at a particular point in history, when the nuclear family, men's single-track careers with one company, and women's single-track careers as homemakers and mothers were the norm. Old age as a major stage of life, as we are now coming to know it, didn't exist. In fact, as he himself has reached his mid-eighties,

Erikson, with his wife, Joan, his lifelong collaborator, has been revising his ideas about old age, focusing on the struggle to maintain one's psychological integrity and avoid despair in the face of physical decline.

Gail Sheehy's *Passages*, a 1976 best-seller—five million copies sold to date—is the most prominent popularization of the ages-and-stages approach to psychology, particularly on the subject of the mid-life crisis. But she based her book primarily on the research of three male psychologists who studied mostly men, universalizing their subjects' career and family problems. Much of the appeal of this book rested on its almost formulaic approach to the stages of life, offering the comfort of certainty in the midst of life's chaos. Such neat packages are "a little like horoscopes," according to sociologist Orville Brim, Jr. "They are vague enough so that everyone can see something of themselves in them."

One of the psychologists from whom Sheehy drew her material, Roger Gould of UCLA, has since rejected the idea that there is a structure of successive, well-defined stages of life that must be successfully resolved before passing on to the next stage. Now he calls it "hogwash." Dr. Paul Costa, a psychologist at the National Institute on Aging, reached similar conclusions based on interviews with thousands of people in the 1970s and 1980s. Sharply defined stages are just not necessarily the way everyone's life works. Nancy Schlossberg, who teaches counseling at the University of Maryland, agrees. "Give me a room full of 40-year-old women," she says, "and you have told me nothing."

Where does that leave us? With less than we thought we knew about adult development and also with a wider span of growth possibilities. The historical experience of each generation, not a fixed chronological age, may be the starting point for talking about norms of growth. In other words, what was "right" for women now past 60 may not prove a helpful guide for their daughters, who grew up under different social, economic, and cultural conditions.

While it is impossible to suggest precisely what it might mean for baby-boomer women to act their age twenty or thirty years from now, it's worth noting that in other cultures, in which different historical, economic, and cultural forces have shaped human development, behavioral expectations for older women differ substantially from ours. In the Kikuyu tribe in Kenya at the end of the nineteenth century, for example, a woman reaching menopause was "not expected to behave with the decorum expected of women in their childbearing years and was free to make ribald jokes and ostensibly flirt with younger men," according to anthropologist John M. W. Whiting. Among the Comanche Indians, the wife of a medicine man could learn his job but could not exercise the healing powers he could until she had passed menopause. Life thus seems to offer a world of possibilities.

## Generativity

While the chronology of adult development may be less certain, some of the challenges of adulthood on which psychologists have focused are still likely to remain. For example, Erikson posed *generativity* as a task of the adult years. To fully realize himself or herself as a mature adult, Erikson believes, every person must resolve the conflict between self-absorption and the need to be of help to others—through parenting, mentoring, creating useful work, contributing to the solution of social problems, and so on. Generativity "is primarily the concern in establishing and guiding the next generation," he wrote. Most psychologists agree that some similar quality is a necessary part of growth in adulthood.

For baby-boomer women, these matters are likely to prove more complex than they were for their mothers, for whom parenting arrived like clockwork in the developmental scheme. Their daughters, so far, have found themselves caught in the cross-demands and strains of marriage, divorce, careers, and motherhood on no particular schedule. The encounter with generativity could come early, in motherhood, or even in their sixties, as executive mentors to younger women on the corporate career ladder.

For the baby-boomer generation, the cultural cues are less clear than they were for their mothers. Pressured by the forces of tradition to feel guilty if they give too little time to their children—or have no children at all—they are also expected to achieve in the outside world of work. Their mothers were raised as nurturers and taught to identify with and meet the needs of others. The line between themselves and those close to them was supposed to be a thin one. Their daughters, on the other hand, matured into a world of autonomy and independence for women. Generativity could thus pose more of a challenge for them, since the poles of "self" and "other" they may feel a need to bridge seem to be farther apart than those confronted by previous generations of women.

### Individuation

*Individuation* is another process that could pose new challenges to younger women. This widely used concept, when applied to adults, involves a person's coming to terms with the facets of his or her personality that have been suppressed during earlier years. This reorganization generally occurs after age 50. For example, a woman now in her sixties who was raised to be supportive and passive, traditional female behavior traits, would have to confront the natural aggressiveness she has always denied in herself. Thus she would have to deal with the side of herself traditionally associated with males, as older men must come to terms with the part of themselves formerly regarded as "female."

This process helps to make the older person "whole," a quality found at the root of the wisdom attributed to the old. They encompass within themselves more of the world's possibilities than a younger person would be likely to understand.

Women of the New Elder and Eisenhower generations have sometimes had trouble with this process. Therapists Roberta G. Sands and Virginia Richardson have observed about them that

> the women who refuse to accept their aggressive impulses experience the most conflict at this time. These women believe on some level that achievement negates their femininity. They recognize that men do not seem to like aggressive women, that the traits of passivity and compliance are more socially acceptable. The men with whom this is most likely to cause conflict are their husbands, who may object to their wives working or seeking some other outlet such as returning to college.

But how will individuation work for baby-boomer women? Many of their generation have had to "go for it" since their early twenties, playing hardball in what had been a man's world only a generation earlier. Also, as we have noted, they were getting mixed signals from the culture about what was appropriate for a woman to do and be. This could complicate the sorting-out process of individuation when they reach their fifties.

Where their mothers (and older sisters) had to come to terms with their own unexpressed aggressiveness, boomer women may come up against the passive traits they spent much of their adulthood fighting and denying. These were characteristics they could not have safely expressed even to themselves while trying to make it in what had only recently been (and in many ways still is) a man's world.

One result of all these swirling psychological currents could be some very interesting conversations between mothers and daughters in the first decade of the twenty-first century as boomer women move into their fifties. Their New Elder mothers will have had to cope not only with their own latent aggressiveness but also with their feelings about seeing the wife/mother role so central to their lives and identities implicitly disparaged by the new women—their daughters—for most of whom fulfillment had to involve more than domesticity. Therapists with boomer women patients at this time will be getting an earful about this interaction.

## The Importance of Friendship

While the nuclear family has been the stage on which much of the psychic drama of development has been enacted, members of this generation of women have found new sources of wisdom, support, solace, and nurturing in *friendship*. As choice instead of tradition determines more of their life paths, relationships freely chosen rather than those into which women were born can become more important. And when the experience of preceding generations is so sharply different, intimates whose lives parallel their own can offer the best guidelines for living and the strongest lifelines in crisis. This is the generation of women whose older members helped to develop the consciousness-raising group into a tool of survival in the 1970s when all the rules about how to live one's life were rapidly changing.

Women entering their sixties two decades from now are likely to find a "haven in a heartless world" in friendship, not traditional families. It is likely to be women supporting each other through self-help and mutual aid, creating *ad hoc* communities of assistance, who will get them over the rough spots. They will come to each other's aid in a world in which their roles—who they are supposed to be and how they are supposed to act—have been in flux since they were adolescents. These relationships could become more ritualized, with formal obligations and rights, as we pointed out earlier when discussing the new families. Here older women will pioneer and men will follow, since psychologists still agree that women have a greater capacity for close friendships than men do.

## BABY-BOOMER MEN

Where are men in this scheme of things? They, too, grew up in families in which their mothers were likely to remain at home while their fathers went to work. The new order of work-family commitments and role changes has been stressful for boomer men, as it sometimes has been for women of their generation. In fact, a survey of sixteen hundred public-utility employees by researchers at Boston University showed that as many working fathers felt "a lot of stress" trying to juggle family and employment as did working mothers. But for men, the new family lifestyle has meant *accepting* new roles; for women in their cohort the emphasis has been more on taking the initiative and *doing* what their mothers never did. Women of their generation can leave their husbands, choose single motherhood, stay single and childless, or be working mothers. For men of their age, adulthood has often meant responding to the lifestyle of the new woman, unlearning expectations of family dominance represented by their fathers.

While employee benefits are increasingly being expanded to make life easier for mothers and fathers, the changes are really aimed at women. Although some companies now offer leave time to men for child care, a man may be stigmatized for taking it. In a survey of 384 large corporations conducted by Catalyst, a research firm, more than a third offered paternity leave, but men used it in only 9 of them. As a human resources manager at a large company put it, "If a man requested a leave for this purpose, his career would take a dive."

Individuation for baby-boomer men could be even more complicated than for their women age mates. These men have had to display just as much aggressiveness in the world of work as their fathers did. But at the same time the men of the generation of 1946 to 1964 have been expected to be both more nurturing than their fathers were and supportive of newly assertive women. The demands on these men have been great and the rewards—what with divorce and career uncertainties—somewhat mixed. They, too, might make therapy a thriving profession as we begin the twenty-first century.

## OLDER WOMEN

Few if any aspects of old age will change as much by the second decade of the twenty-first century as the status and behavior of elder women.

These women will experience family and working lives almost entirely different from those of their mothers, who occupy this part of life now. Their marriages not only differ from those experienced by New Elders, the institution of marriage itself plays a less central role in their lives. Unlike their mothers, boomer women will reach their later years financially independent and politically powerful. Their aging will even cause a reassessment of what we thought we knew about human development. These women will thus have been on the cutting edge of virtually every major social change in our society in the latter part of the twentieth century. As elders, the men of the baby boom are likely to accept women as the social innovators and trendsetters of their cohort.

And what of baby-boomer women's final years? Old women have not always been powerless in the past, but their strength was often based on a subconscious fear of their sex. "Contemporary fairy tales and myths are filled with fairy godmothers and wicked witches but relatively few male counterparts," writes Boston University gerontologist Elizabeth W. Markson, describing the ambivalence toward old women in Western culture. "In *The Wizard of Oz,* for example, the Wizard is a benign, bumbling, older man, but the Wicked Witch of the West is a warty old hag, feared for her ugliness and powerful evil."

It will be a long time before even the oldest women of the baby boom reach and pass their eighties. It would be going far out on a limb to say what they will be like and how society will regard them that far in the future. But it's reasonably safe to conjecture that the second half of their lives will differ so much from that of any previous generation of older women that even our fantasies of old women will have changed. It's likely that children of the future will have to go to the dictionary when they encounter *hag* in literature. What they will find is that the word is *"obsolete."*

# 9

# The Last Mass Market in America?

"If somebody handed me a magazine that was clearly labeled for the elderly, I would have to read it inside of *Playboy* or *Esquire*."
A 56-year-old executive

"Talk to a person, not a birth date."
From an advertisement directed at potential advertisers by *Modern Maturity*, the magazine of the American Association of Retired Persons

B aby boomers are finally getting too big for their britches. An increasing number of those born in the late 1940s and in the 1950s have found that blue jeans, the uniform of their generation, are getting a little too tight where they used to be body-hugging right. As they shift to sweatpants and casual slacks, blue jeans sales have fallen from 560 million pairs in 1981 to about 450 million pairs a year these days. Levi Strauss & Company, once virtually the outfitter for the baby boom, has taken notice. Now it features looser-fitting clothing, and it's replaced the teenagers in some of its commercials with adults, such as a father showing his child how to fish.

This is just one example of what will be happening throughout the American economy over the next decade as the youth market finally begins to lose its dominant role. The tide officially turned on July 20, 1988, when United States Census Bureau figures showed that the number of Americans in the 35-to-59-year-old age bracket outnumbered those 18 to 34 for the first time. After steadily losing influence since the early 1970s, the young have now surrendered the source of their most important power—the purse. In no time in the foreseeable future will they again be the most important consumer group in America. As *Prevention*, the health magazine, put it, "the money in the middle" will now call the tune.

Social critic Ben Wattenberg has suggested in his book *The Birth Dearth* that the smaller baby-bust generation replacing the baby boom in what we have come to think of as the prime consumption years will cut consumer demand, thus endangering the economy. It seems more likely that the new needs of older consumers will ultimately fuel a continuation of the dynamic growth of consumption that has been a vital part of the American economy since World War II (after a possible economic dip in the early 1990s).

The changes that are coming in American product development, merchandising, and marketing will touch everyone's life. At the supermarket the aging of America will bring less packaged snack and junk food and more health food. Individual-serving-sized food packages will replace large economy-sized packages. Package labels will have larger type and fewer colors. Manufacturers will design all products for easy use by people with minor physical impairments. And advertising will feature fewer slogans and more reasoned arguments for buying a product. Virtually everything we see, touch, and hear in our daily lives will be different.

## FITS AND STARTS

The emergence of the New Elders as a force to be reckoned with has offered American business its first opportunities to sell to this previously invisible age group. No business can afford to ignore them now. Their customer credentials are impressive: 25 percent of Americans now over the age of 50 own 75 percent of the country's assets and do about half of our discretionary spending. There are at least four times more people in households headed by a person over age 50 who can afford an above-average lifestyle than there are yuppies. Older Americans watch television and read newspapers and magazines like everyone else.

Advertisers are already paying to reach these elders—but do they have a message for them? Many businesses are loath to part with old marketing strategies that have helped them prosper in a society dominated by the young. Their inability to adapt is a classic example of what social scientists term "cultural lag": Conditions have changed, but ideas and perceptions about them lag behind.

Marketing to older people is a new challenge. There is little precedent for successfully conveying the message about a product to this audience. And corporate America has sometimes tripped over its own misconceptions and stereotypes about older people in its sudden rush to sell to these active consumers whose existence it has just noticed. Like travelers arriving in a country for the first time, some companies just don't know how to dress appropriately for the climate. They often cloak their products and services in unsuitable ways when they try to appeal to the "mature market." They set up generational barriers against sales to elders when they mean to be building generational bridges.

When Johnson & Johnson first advertised its Affinity shampoo, a product developed specifically to improve the look of older hair, the company almost scuttled it. In the original television commercial for the shampoo, a man perhaps in his fifties eyes a woman also middle-aged. "Beautiful hair," he muses. "I wonder how old she is." She faces the camera and confides to the audience, "Over forty—and proud of it." An announcer's voice-over underlines the message: "Now there's no age limit to looking good. Now there's new Affinity Shampoo, the first shampoo created for hair over forty . . ."

Unimpressed, older people did not buy the product in anywhere near the numbers Johnson & Johnson had anticipated. Only when the revised commercial delivered the same message but with a much more subtle tone did the shampoo catch on. This time an attractive woman of late middle age said, "When my hair looks good, I feel great," with the announcer suggesting discreetly that the product would do wonders for "hair that time has changed."

"Increasingly, businesses will encounter elderly people who act much younger in the marketplace than past marketing experiences and their chronological age would suggest," business scholar William Lazer warned a few years ago. Companies are discovering that there's no point in trying to get older people to identify with a product presented as *for* the "old" because they will not recognize themselves in the description or imagery chosen. One survey found that 72 percent of people ages 60 to 64 thought of themselves as young or middle-aged, and even 28 percent of those over 70 would answer to the same description (although they would be likely to regard as old anyone else of their age). According to a study done by the advertising firm of Cadwell Davis Partners, Americans past 50 usually feel anywhere from five to fifteen years younger than their chronological age. *Reader's Digest* caught the spirit of this new wisdom when it purchased the magazine *50 Plus* and renamed it *New Choices*.

Elders like advertisements that feature people of varying ages with the main models only a bit younger than the age of the targeted group. Such images minimize the isolation of older people as individuals needing special treatment or products. Successful ads also focus on the need that the product fulfills, not the age of the person who will buy it. A hair product is good because it will get rid of the gray or restore body, for example, not because it's just the thing for somebody who is approaching 60.

Those who design ad campaigns aimed at older people may need to pay special attention to the motivation behind some of their purchases. Older people make up a large segment of the travel industry's customers, for example. But while younger people travel for "escape and adventure," as David B. Wolfe, founder of National Senior Living Industries, points out, elders seek "gateways to personal growth and development." They want activities promising choice, action, and social opportunities. Contrary to what many people assume, most do not want to travel with a group made up exclusively of elders.

Inaccurate assumptions about personal priorities can also undercut a marketing campaign in which elders are at least one of the targeted groups. Everyone wants products that save time—right? Not necessarily. A recent study by the Yankelovich Group turned up a surprising reaction to time saving as a product convenience. While it did appeal to younger people pressed for time, older people did not need this feature. In fact, if the advertising emphasized saving time, elders would turn away from the product. Why? Because time is something many of them have in abundance. They don't want to save it, they want to fill it.

Publications directed at elders walk a thin line between carrying ads for products whose appeal is obviously to people with the minor infirmities that come with age and helping those same readers maintain a positive view of themselves. For instance, the editor of *Modern Maturity* once suggested that the appearance of his periodical should say, "This could be any magazine." Since 1980 the magazine has carried no ads for dentures, hemorrhoid treatments, products dealing with incontinence, or wheelchairs (although it does accept ads for three-wheeled scooters). Ads for products in some other categories, such as painkillers, are kept to a minimum, and the headline may not contain the word *pain*. Above all, the tone must be upbeat. An ad agency submitting copy to a mature-market publication to advertise a product that helped fight periodontal disease was asked to change its headline from "Without healthy gums, your teeth are worthless . . ." to something like "Healthy gums are priceless."

Corporations wishing to increase their share of the mature market for products they also sell to younger consumers must show sensitivity to both age groups. Their task is to find a way to appeal to older people without identifying the products as *for* elders, since today old age can still have many negative connotations. For example, people over age 50 buy about 40 percent of new cars in this country. They are the mainstay of the market for large luxury cars, which are advertised to appeal to them directly. But for most other automobile models, identifying the products as attractive to older people would chase away younger as well as older buyers. The industry's strategy has been largely to target the young and middle-aged in its ads for these models, on the assumption that it will keep its customers through brand loyalty as they age.

On the other hand, there's also money to be made adapting existing products to the needs of older people. For example, Bristol-Myers recently brought to market a "senior" version of its Naldecon cough medicine, the first over-the-counter cold product thus promoted. Naldecon omits the familiar antihistamines, which may aggravate glaucoma, asthma, and enlarged prostates.

## DINKS AND GRUMPIES

Older consumers "could be called the last mass market in America," according to Franchellie Cadwell of the Cadwell Davis Partners advertising firm. "But it is a very splintered market. There are black and white differences in terms of attitudes and life styles." The youth market is already broken down by sophisticated marketers, sometimes into year-by-year segments, but the same companies that recognize these distinctions may still treat people over 50 as if they were all the same. To be successful in this market you need to see more than just grown-up mature people (grumpies); perhaps the product or service you want to sell is specifically designed for older couples with a double income and no kids (dinks).

Generational differences are as important between elder cohorts as they are between older and younger Americans. For example, the current 70- and 80-year-olds knew the economic fears engendered by the Depression. When they were in their fifties and sixties they were careful with their money because of their history. "They worked hard, got very little in return, and feared for their security," observes Stephen Hittner, publisher of the Florida-based magazine *Golden Years.* "They're stingy. They may have money, but they're not where the money is."

Those whose ages now range from their early fifties to their late sixties were, for the most part, a comparatively privileged generation. They are the bull's-eye in the "elder market" that many companies are beginning to target. Too young to have felt the full brunt of the Depression and just the right age to have begun their careers during a period of almost constant economic expansion, these people in their fifties and sixties have benefited fully from increased Social Security benefits, substantial pensions, and remarkable increases in the values of their homes and other assets. They are the principal actors in the drama of early retirement. What's more, they have no compunctions about going after the good life for themselves.

Their values and attitudes set them a world apart from the people who populated this age bracket in the early 1970s. What's a parent's obligation to adult children, for example? Twenty years ago, 80 percent of parents then in their fifties and sixties said in one survey that they felt obligated to leave as much money as possible to help their children get a better start in life. That same survey reports that today's fifties-to-sixties cohort believes almost the opposite: 73 percent of them say that their obligations to their children end when the kids leave home. New Elders have more money to spend than people of this age did twenty years ago, and they have a different attitude about how to spend it. The culture in which they live has given them the expectation that good living is possible in old age, as well as "permission" to live it up.

Some members of this generation are the proud owners of those luxury cars with bumper stickers that read, "We're Driving Our Children's Inheritance." In fact, they share many tastes and values with their children; both groups prefer natural to synthetic fabrics, for example, and see wellness as a lifestyle that will keep the medical industry away from their door. Their spending helped fuel the long Reagan economic recovery, and nowadays they are being courted by those who sell travel, automobiles, furniture, clothing, and dinner at fine restaurants. Florence R. Skelly of Yankelovich, Skelly and White called them "affluent consumers unafraid to consume."

## PSYCHOGRAPHICS

Marketing professionals are using ever more refined techniques to distinguish and classify differences among segments of the population, even in groups already defined by a narrow age range. One approach that has gained favor in recent years is "psychographics," which concentrates on values and lifestyles. Among those in their fifties and sixties, according to one classification, there are some who are "socially centered," others who are "self-absorbed," and so on. In another scheme, "ailing outgoers," although poor in health, are socially active, while "healthy hermits," although physically sound, are socially withdrawn. Market researchers match these characteristics with tendencies to buy certain kinds of cars, eat out in restaurants, purchase imported goods, be willing to go or fear going into debt, and so on.

At the moment this sort of groping toward a sense of where people are is as much art as science. The findings of market researchers in this area often conflict, and the researchers need to refine their techniques further. As marketing expert William Lazer wryly observed,

> it has been noted that mature consumers are both more cautious in their purchases and shrewder as comparison shoppers, and also more set in their purchase patterns and more brand loyal. They are more susceptible to social influences but also are described as being more likely to be individualistic and to express themselves without caring what their neighbors think. They are more likely to buy nationally advertised brands, yet at the same time they are seen as being more likely to seek the best deal.

# ADVERTISING AND THE IMAGE OF OLD AGE

For the most part, advertising does not create new social values. For example, feminism had already made its mark and women who worked outside the home were well on their way to becoming the norm before women began to show up in ads and commercials as employees on a par with men. "By the time you see it in an ad," says Joseph Smith, president of a market research firm, "it has already happened."

But while corporate marketing departments and ad agencies are out to sell products, not cause a revolution in age consciousness, their efforts have consequences beyond their original intent. The black models who began to appear in advertisements during the 1960s have helped to confirm the worth and potential of black Americans as well as to sell products to black consumers. In the same way, ads that depict elders as people "just like us" will help to confirm a more positive image of older people as active, contributing members of society. And that *is* a revolution.

The process has been under way since the mid-1980s. "Less than a decade ago, the only work I could find was in the area of what I call pharmaceuticals—hemorrhoid and arthritis remedies," celebrated elder model Kaylan Pickford said in 1985, when she was 54. Now she's a hot property when companies want to advertise more attractive and varied products. Claudia Black, the director of older models at a major modeling agency, said that their assignments, previously confined to ads for diuretics and products related to menopause, have expanded to include ads for cosmetics and credit cards. "Women can have wrinkles now," she says. "They just have to look good in them."

Jockey, the underwear company, started paying attention to demographics and suddenly there were 55-year-olds in its ads. The management of Great Factory Stores of Reading, Pennsylvania, observed that Great Factory's customers were looking older and changed the makeup on the model featured in the stores' ads and also gave her a "more mature" haircut. Mannequins, too, are beginning to age; some even sport gray hair.

Major corporations that sponsor television shows with older characters no longer hesitate to have their products associated with older people. This phenomenon, too, grew in the mid-1980s. In 1985, Gray Panther media consultant Lydia Bragger commended television executives for finally acknowledging that elders "can walk and talk and think and be attractive." That year, women such as Angela Lansbury and Bea

Arthur were helping the audience of older women see themselves as valued, and leading shows also featured older men, such as 64-year-old Brian Keith ("Hardcastle & McCormack"), 65-year-old Jack Warden ("Crazy Like a Fox"), 67-year-old John Forsythe ("Dynasty"), and 55-year-old Edward Woodward ("The Equalizer").

Television programming is designed for entertainment, not social engineering. As CBS programming executive Kim LeMasters noted, "It's not a conscious effort to gray television with the graying of America; it's a conscious effort to manufacture a hit." Nevertheless, elders have been validated by increased attention to their age group on the tube. George Gerbner, dean of the Annenberg School of Communications at the University of Pennsylvania, thinks that television's portrayal of elders still isn't serious enough, but he acknowledges that the new and more powerful picture of older people will have vast repercussions in society. Young people will get a positive cultural lesson as they are prepared to see aging as a natural stage in their own life cycle. "The time to learn how to grow old is when you're young," says Gerbner.

Of course, progress is never linear: There's always some backsliding. In 1988, for instance, CBS, which attracts more viewers over 50 than the other networks, came up with a show called "Coming of Age" that provided Americans with regressive elder role models. Set in a retirement community, the show joked about old people being "toothless." A child assigned a composition in school wrote about his grandparents who "became retarded and moved to Arizona."

## HERE THEY COME

The age-based changes we are now seeing in marketing and merchandising merely introduce what is to come. By the year 2000 the leading edge of baby-boomer consumers will be over 50 and forcing the gradual pace of change in American business to quicken. Their purchasing power will become a major force in the marketplace, and marketers will have to get it right.

The advance guard of the baby boom has already started to cause a few ripples in the marketing of products to older people; before long it will be making waves. Clothing manufacturers and retailers have felt it first. The sale of women's apparel, for example, fell off sharply in the late 1980s, leaving the clothing industry wondering what happened.

Goldman, Sachs & Company partner Joseph H. Ellis can tell them. "The number of 14- to 24-year-old females *declined* 12.8 percent between 1980 and 1988, while those in the 35-to-44 age bracket increased 35.8 percent!" He says that too many retailers regard these demographics as mere "background music," doing little to alter the emphasis on teenage clothes in effect since the early 1970s. Baby-boomer women no longer want what's hot, says Ellis; instead they want "something that is stylish and flattering, and that fits."

That's only the beginning. While automobiles, home furnishings, and consumer electronics fuel today's economy, health-related products and services will be in the forefront in the future. With increased possibilities of living longer and better, we can expect today's young adults and the middle-aged to pursue a vital old age at every turn when they become elders. The result will be an even larger pharmaceutical industry than we have now, more drugstore-item-related advertising, and a food and beverage industry much more health-related than it is at present.

Merchandising will change as much as the product mix. For example, the graying of the population will alter the way supermarkets look. New stores have been getting progressively bigger over the past decade. By the mid-1980s, they were averaging about forty-four thousand square feet—at least one megamarket, in Ohio, covers two hundred thousand square feet—and stocking about twenty thousand items. Yet according to a survey of two thousand households each of which contained at least one person over 60, older people put a high value on personal interaction as well as convenience when they shop. There is no evidence to suggest that today's young and middle-aged adults will expect anything less in their later years. To meet this service demand, some supermarkets will divide their huge spaces into boutiquelike sections in which customers can get more service from store personnel, thus personalizing the shopping experience.

Vertical shelving that's more accessible to people whose joints aren't quite as supple as they used to be is already replacing deep frozen-food compartments that require people to reach over and in for packages. Shoppers will be able to push a button in any aisle to page the nearest clerk for information or help. Or they may have the option of calling up the information they need from computer terminals strategically placed in each aisle. Powered shopping carts may come into vogue. Retailers will also manage to create space for benches throughout these huge stores, as has the Publix chain of super-markets in Florida. To attract more affluent elder boomers, upscale supermarkets may feature in-store spas. Aside from the money they will make, such services will enhance the mundane image of grocery shopping with a little sensuality.

The products stores sell will also reflect increased health conscious-ness. Salt- and sugar-free foods, low-fat delicacies, and fiber-laden ce-reals and baked goods will monopolize even more shelf space than they do now. Even off-diet treats are likely to make their contribution to health: Look for vitamin-enriched Coca-Cola. Sales of single-portion packages, which have proliferated because of busy young professionals and two-career couples, will get a further boost from older adults living alone.

Warnings about overconsumption of fatty foods and salt have become commonplace and Americans have responded by changing their diets—witness television advertisements from the meat industry trying to convince consumers to return to beef, "real food." Now the effects of new eating patterns are beginning to show up on the farm, in the stores, and at the table. As this trend continues, we can antici-pate a flood of entirely new products, particularly ingenious substitutes for salt and fat to flavor foods. These are especially important for older people, whose taste buds and sense of smell diminish with the passing years (a 75-year-old has only half the taste buds of a 20-year-old).

Procter & Gamble's olestra (sucrose polyester, or SPE), a "no-fat fat" that contains neither calories nor cholesterol and that, in fact, seems to reduce blood cholesterol levels, will probably be the first such prod-uct to reach the market, sometime in the 1990s. "When you think of what it does, it sounds like more of a miracle than penicillin," says Gail Levey of the American Dietetic Association. "But you have to be careful when any food is introduced into the diet to the degree which SPE will probably be." If it has damaging side effects, it could be years before we know about them.

We will also see more manipulation of the food sources throughout nature, a continuation of efforts such as those to breed chickens that produce eggs with less cholesterol and cattle that produce beef with less fat. Genetic engineering, now in its infancy, will affect American farming as much as corporate ownership of farms has influenced Ameri-can agriculture in the last two decades.

Another area to watch is the developing interaction between the food and pharmaceutical industries and the medical profession. As products are developed to meet specific health needs, these industries will have to persuade both health-care professionals and the general public that the need is real. Consider the way that the American public has been educated by advertising about the virtues of lower cholesterol levels in blood. The head of marketing at Merck, which sells a drug that reduces cholesterol, acknowledged that having created a pill, it has also had to inspire people to become concerned about their cholesterol level. "We've had to develop a market as well as develop a drug," he said, referring to the "public service" ads the company had been running on the subject. The Quaker Oats Company ran the same kinds of ads focusing on the cholesterol-reducing properties of high-fiber foods such as oatmeal.

In both these examples the health warnings were appropriate, but consumers will have to become more vigilant in the future, as enormous amounts of money and the existence of entire companies could be riding on public acceptance of new medications and food products. The temptation to exaggerate or falsify will be great—as in cereal commercials that all but guarantee that eating a certain brand will keep you from getting cancer.

## A CONTINUED BOOM IN SERVICES

People over 50 are now responsible for more than 75 percent of tickets sold for vacation travel on United States carriers. Baby boomers were born into a society in which frequent travel by the middle class had already become an accepted way of life—in fact, their childhood coincided with the beginning of commercial jet air service in 1957. As they grew up, the travel industry had to cater to them. When they reached college age they caused a boom in charter flights to Europe. Now that they're raising families, Club Med has begun to feature family vacations.

One thing is virtually certain about elders vacationing in the twenty-first century. They will not be spending nearly as much time in the sun as they do now. Skin damage from excessive exposure to the sun is *cumulative* over a person's lifetime. Warnings about the relationship between a terrific tan and skin cancer have been sounding for several years, with public recognition of the seriousness of overexposure to the sun increasing gradually. The boomers are already old enough to have absorbed a substantial amount of the harmful rays, and more of them will be motivated to control the risk. So warm-weather spots such as the Caribbean will give way to more temperate locations for trips, such as Toronto and Montreal in the summer and the Pacific Northwest in the winter. The greenhouse warming effect, should it prove to be as potent as many scientists now suggest, will further this trend. When they do travel to sunny climates, today's 30- and 40-year-olds are likely to wear little sensor patches that will turn color when they have absorbed a specific amount of sunlight.

The availability of fuel will also place some constraints on their travel. While we came out of the oil crisis of the 1970s with our taste for traveling intact, it's likely that reduced yields from mines and wells in the early twenty-first century will change traveling styles.

*Trends to watch for:* (1) The return of the sailing ship. Windjammer cruises off the New England coast, now just an interesting change of pace for jaded vacationers, may be the model not only for recreational travel but also for basic transportation along the east and west coasts. (2) The expansion of bicycle touring, including rail-biking, which we discuss in the next chapter. (3) First-class camping. Campgrounds will offer amenities such as gourmet barbecues, live entertainment, and individual enclosed bathrooms next to each campsite.

## SHOP TILL YOU DROP?

Shopping should continue to be an important activity, but it's likely to take much less time than it does now. Many goods will be purchased through interactive television, possibly even some groceries. From the comfort of his or her home, the shopper of the future will select specific packages of food from choices on the screen by touching a pad on the television set. The complete grocery order will then be delivered to the door. A similar procedure will make it just as easy to order a complete dinner from a restaurant.

Both dining out and ordering full meals in will keep the restaurant and catering businesses busy. Elders are likely to remain the anchor of the upscale part of the industry—people over 65 are now more likely to eat at an expensive restaurant than those who are younger. Places for middle-class elders to eat and socialize will also be needed.

Perhaps cafeterias will become a familiar institution. If they do, they will probably offer many more international dishes than today's cafeterias, since boomers have matured in an age in which no cuisine is foreign to American tastes. Customers are likely to take their selections from microwave ovens—possibly coin-operated—instead of from steam tables.

The boomers will grow old in the midst of the information and service age. In the current part of their life cycle, businesses such as Mom's Amazing have created entirely new industries to fulfill their needs. This company caters to busy working mothers who don't have the time to find tutors for their children, information about camps, reliable people who give music lessons, and the like. Mom's Amazing provides the parents with referrals to whatever businesses, experts, and institutions they need.

Elders in the twenty-first century will need services and information relating to being old. United Seniors Health Cooperative of Washington, D.C., has already designed software that enables older people to determine the government benefits and services to which they are entitled. In the year 2020, 60-year-olds with parents in their late eighties will need information about reputable home-care personnel. They might also want up-to-date information about natural cures for whatever ails them. Perhaps they'll want to find a tenant for part of their large house but won't know which of the hundreds of matching services have been highly rated by users.

Baby boomers, especially the well-off professionals among them, have a reputation for going about things methodically, getting all the information they need about the important things in their life so they can do them well. "I'm used to being competent in the world and knowing what I'm doing," said one 33-year-old woman who was going to have a baby. "I wanted to get a handle on pregnancy. I took childbirth classes and special exercise classes, and I had no coffee, alcohol or aspirin. I wanted a perfect baby." When she is 60, this woman could be looking for the perfect retirement home for her elderly parents—and she is likely to seek it in the same methodical, thorough way.

Imagine a company called All Things to All People that, for a fee, would find the answers to *all* these information needs and perhaps help make any necessary arrangements—for assistance, for classes, for whatever might be needed. Providing this sort of service and information could develop into a very big industry.

One product for which these elders will spend less time shopping is loans from banks. If nothing else does it, the aging of their generation will begin to reduce the amount of private debt in the United States. As they reach their forties and their advance guard enters their fifties, boomers will be settled in houses, surfeited with consumer goods, and beginning to think seriously about their children's college education. They will have moved out of their prime borrowing years and into a period in which they are likely to be saving money (except for those who married early and had several kids—they may now have to borrow to finance their now-college-age children's school expenses). While that might somewhat reduce consumer demand, it should also help lower both the trade deficit and interest rates.

## FEWER SENIOR DISCOUNTS

Businesses will direct future product and store promotions to older consumers more often than they do now. Early-bird specials will become the norm in all but the most expensive restaurants. In fact, off-hour sales and special discounts will probably spread from restaurants and movie theaters to just about every kind of business. Free blood pressure tests and instant diabetes screening will become everyday features in large discount drugstores. If these establishments take their cue from a recent Johnson & Johnson survey of what elders want, they will institute "frequent filler" discount programs to encourage elders to take all their prescriptions to the same store.

At the same time, the "senior-citizen discount" may become less widespread. Reduced rates for elders at hotels, in restaurants, on airlines, and for a myriad of other goods and services are an accepted practice in America. But economics and demographics are gradually undermining the basis for this special treatment. With more older people well off, they don't necessarily need these discounts. And with a new generation of elders who think and act and buy as younger people do, discounts should prove increasingly unnecessary as a promotional tool to bring in the elders' business. If that isn't reason enough, the cost of giving a discount to so many customers could end the practice. So these privileges are not likely to last much longer than early retirement will, and baby boomers will probably never get to take advantage of most of them.

## A WORLD ADAPTED TO THEIR NEEDS

Catered to in their youth and middle years by business, the baby boomers will find their material world altered to suit them as much as possible when they grow old. For instance, since people over 50 use many of the same products as those of other ages, their level of vision—normally, some trouble with small print and a need for more contrast—will become the common denominator as their numbers grow and business begins to pay more attention to their buying power. By the time people now moving into middle age start retiring, one of our great department stores will no longer print its Christmas catalog in minute white type against a red background, which older people need a magnifier to read.

Look for large black lettering on white backgrounds on most product labels, which will be easier to read because of the contrast. Similarly, there will be more white space between numbers and letters in cookbooks, clocks, and just about every other kind of product. Restaurant menus will contain larger print. Software that magnifies a small area of personal computer screens will come installed in the machines. And more of the common machinery of daily life will be able to "talk," making reading less necessary.

There will be less color-coding as a means of distinguishing one item from another, since older people sometimes have difficulty telling some colors from others. When it's convenient to label by color, we are more likely to see orange, red, and yellow than green, blue, and violet, which give elders more trouble.

The circulation of *Reader's Digest*'s large-type edition increased from 189,000 in 1980 to 504,000 in 1988, only a hint of the explosive growth to come in this segment of publishing. Once special library items, large-print books are now a growth product among volumes sold in regular bookstores and through the mail. The breakthrough came in 1983 when G. K. Hall & Company made a concerted and successful effort to market its line of large-print books to the general public. Now it publishes two hundred such titles a year and derives 30 percent of its revenue from this line. We can also expect the publishing of books on audiocassettes to take off. Some libraries for visually impaired people have already experienced a surge in demand for these products and fewer requests for braille as more of their patrons are older people.

A glance at the office of the future or a look through a living-room window is likely to present an image of people moving a dark gray, rectangular piece of cardboard with an opening cut into it over printed matter. This inexpensive, simple, but ingenious device is a typoscope, which helps eliminate the glare that also poses problems for older eyes. It will be a common sight in America just a few decades from now.

## TECHNOLOGY AND ERGONOMICS

Baby boomers have become accustomed to finding scientific and technological wonders waiting for them at each stage of their life cycle—as if these innovations were put there just in time to make their lives better. The appearance of penicillin made their childhood healthy. Television entered the mainstream of consumer products just in time to be their baby-sitter. Jet travel made them the first generation of Americans to go abroad in large numbers while still in their youth. Computers opened new jobs in areas such as financial services, where a substantial number of them have made a good deal of money. And in their future are technological products to make their old age by far the most comfortable that any generation has ever experienced.

Ronald Mace, an architect, 46 and disabled since age 9, knows how important control over the material world can be when one's body is not functioning at full tilt. "There are two things in this country people don't want to be," he says: "One is disabled. The other is old." These days as many as 45 percent of people over age 65 have some disability. That figure may well decline in the future with improved health technology, but because people will be living longer, we can still assume that the percentage of disabled older Americans will remain high. However, both age and the disabilities that accompany it will be easier for baby boomers than they have been for the present generation or any other generation.

The personal robot industry, which put in a brief but premature appearance a few years ago, will be flourishing by 2020 with inexpensive machines that do a lot more than just open the front door and fetch drinks from the bar. The technology is already in place; we lack only sufficient consumer demand. As large numbers of people approach old age it will become worthwhile for business to do what it takes to sell "smart" machines to this market. Through the application of artificial-intelligence techniques to their computer programs, these personal robots will probably be able to do at least some of the cooking, housekeeping, and repairs around the house. When bending over becomes a task and reaching for an object begins to become a major operation, the future generation of elders will summon their robots and thank their lucky stars they aged when they did.

Ergonomics, the science of adapting the man-made physical environment—such as furniture—to fit human needs best, will become central to industrial design. Because of their numbers and their buying power, older baby boomers will force business to make and build most products to fit the common denominator of age. Emphasis will be on the ease of use, simplicity, and safety that become more important to people when some of their powers start to wane.

That's not the way it's done now. Whether it's a seat on the fifty-yard line, the tub in the bathroom, or the front seat of your car, industrial designers work under the assumption that the average American is as likely to be male as female and probably five feet eight inches tall with good joint flexibility. But in tomorrow's America, products and structures are likely to be designed with smaller and less mobile older women in mind, since they will be the most significant segment of the most important age group.

A company called Advanced Living Systems in Oxford, Mississippi, is already laying the groundwork for this phenomenon. It's designed a mannequin called E-Mann that industrial designers can program to simulate the physical characteristics and movement of either sex at any age. E-Mann could become a major factor in the development of transgenerational products that all adults can use.

### . . . Including the Kitchen Sink

When Ted Pappas became president of the American Institute of Architects for 1988, he declared: "Builders must design living quarters specifically for older adults. They require wider halls, grab bars, lower fixtures, cabinets that pull down from the wall, and controlled exposure to the sun."

Virtually everything in a typical house, including the kitchen sink, is likely to be redesigned to make it more accessible for elders. Designers will plan for people with a wide range of needs: those with a touch of arthritis or other minor physical impairments, and those with major disabilities. That kitchen sink, for example, could have a swing-out seat to make dishwashing less tiresome. The height of kitchen countertops could be adjustable. Easy-grip levers might replace doorknobs. We may see more refrigerators placed off the floor and redesigned to be wider than they are high to minimize bending and reaching. For similar reasons, shelves will be shallower. Stoves will probably be located closer to the sink to make it easier to carry heavy pans between them.

Sliding fiberglass inserts on the side of bathtubs to permit entry without having to step over the rim will be common. The switches on table lamps will be on the lamp base rather than near the bulb, which is harder for some people to reach. Builders will put nonslip floor coverings in all new houses as a matter of course—in fact, by then federal law may require it.

Public places will also be made more accessible to elders and others with physical impairments. In theaters, for example, rows of seats may have occasional gaps to provide room for wheelchairs, allowing people with disabilities and their nondisabled friends to sit together. Recreational equipment will reflect the new design criteria, keeping baby boomers who become disabled in old age almost as active as they were when younger. Lightweight sport wheelchairs are already available, some built of the kind of aluminum found in airplanes. There are even skis for people who can't stand up, not to mention walk. With sufficient demand this kind of special gear could become commonplace wherever Americans play.

Besides working well, these artifacts especially designed for an older America are likely to look good. In 1988 the Museum of Modern Art in New York City staged a show of objects designed to foster independent living for those with physical impairments, confirming that these products had "arrived."

Adapting the material world to those who may need just a bit of assistance helps everyone. Designing for those with special needs is teaching us more about designing for people in general. Curb cuts in sidewalks, for example, initially created to ease the way for people with disabilities, also help those pushing strollers and shopping carts. When Whirlpool introduced washers and dryers with oversize dials and buttons for people who had trouble seeing, the response from every group of consumers was so positive that the company added the feature across its entire product line.

In the mid-1980s, discerning consumers might have noticed that it had become easier to unscrew the top from a jar of Tang, the orange drink product, and that it required less effort than it used to to pry open a box of Grape-Nuts cereal. About 70 percent of older Americans have trouble opening containers, according to a recent nationwide survey of one thousand older people conducted by the Georgia State University's Center for Mature Consumer Studies. Obviously some companies have already become sensitive to their needs, and this kind of response from business will become the rule in the coming decades. One can even hope that this new attention to user-friendly packaging will finally produce a childproof medication container that doesn't break the fingernails of people of all ages.

Older people will favor certain options in automobile design. Automatic headlight shutoff, for example, allows an elder to negotiate a dark garage or unlit path more comfortably. (Not to mention all the batteries it saves for those who just can't remember to turn off the lights.) It's the kind of feature that's useful for anybody, and before long it may come with every car. Similarly, when the automobile industry, prompted by demand from older customers, finally provides pivoting seats as standard equipment to ease getting in and out of cars, the many Americans of all ages who have back problems such as sciatica will also be served.

All these predictions may seem a bit fanciful, but consider some common supermarket products: decaffeinated coffee, sugar-free foods, and skim milk. They got their start as specialty items for people—primarily elders—with particular needs. Look at them now.

It could be that in coming years the needs of older people will serve the function that the needs of Californians have performed during the reign of the youth culture: a laboratory for discovering the direction social and economic trends will take in America.


## WHITHER "YOUTH"?

"She's 70 *and* she still plays tennis. She's a college graduate, drives a sports car, eats the right foods and takes the right supplements. She represents a future we can all look forward to," read the opening lines of the advertisement for *Longevity, Omni*'s entry in the mature magazine market. The model was remarkably well preserved for her age—almost too good to be true. And that turned out to be the case, as anyone observant enough and with perfect vision could have seen by reading the disclaimer—"Featured profile is a dramatization"—printed upside down in tiny type at the bottom of the ad.

The ad was a clever attention-getter, but it also made a point about imagery, reality, and our consciousness about aging. Is it desirable for a 70-year-old to look as if she's 35? Should advertisers assume that's how older people want to see themselves? Or can we expect a greater acceptance of the appearance of physical aging as our population grows older? Billions of dollars in sales will soon be riding on the right guess as marketers decide how to shade their product appeal.

Over the next twenty years the baby boomers will begin to give their answer. Never has a generation been so identified with youth. Will they cling to their youthful image no matter what they see in the mirror? Whatever image they choose, it will certainly influence what a large segment of our population looks like at the beginning of the twenty-first century.

There's little doubt about how those just chronologically ahead of the baby boom feel about aging and their appearance. "I've always thought that it's more important for people to feel good about themselves inside," said a 53-year-old woman after her face-lift. "But the world judges you from the outside. It's unfair, especially for an older woman. But this is the culture we're living in. What are we supposed to do?"

The feminist movement and the growth of more positive feelings about elders notwithstanding, it would seem that most older people still prefer to look younger. The enormous demand that greeted the news about the wrinkle-removing properties of Retin-A, the acne medication, proves the point. (The same cream that baby boomers used to improve their appearance in their teens could turn out to be the way some of them also cheat the weathering of age.)

If anything, the trend toward looking younger is now spreading—to men. According to one study of one thousand men ages 35 to 64, they are more concerned about the effects of aging than are women. Grecian Formula, the product that hides the gray in men's hair, has been successful because, as the ad says, "millions of men quietly demand it." Perhaps the experience of the 58-year-old magazine editor who had *his* face lifted will become common. He "didn't want to take the age thing lying down." After consulting his psychiatrist, he went ahead and did it. Now he has nothing but "positive" feelings about plastic surgery.

One thing is certain: We will see less baldness in older men in the future than we do now. Federal approval of the prescription product minoxidil for stemming hair loss will see to that. Minoxidil's appearance on the market couldn't have been timelier for baby boomers, since it is most effective when hair loss begins. No doubt the drug companies will give us improved products in the next few years that do the job even better than this alleviator of male-pattern baldness.

But will their obsession with looking young carry over into this generation's old age? That's harder to predict. The attitude won't necessarily prevail in the future just because that's the way it is now. The present desire for youthful appearance is at least partly a product of the youth-based culture that was built around the boomers and their cultural clout and consumer dollars. By force of numbers they made America think young. But what happens to the ideal of youth when this powerful generation is no longer young? A different picture of what it means to look good could emerge.

Bill Strauss, a Sears executive put in charge of that retailing company's Mature Outlet, Inc., a division set up to market to elders, is sure he knows what's coming. By the time they start reaching their fiftieth birthdays, baby boomers are "gonna make everybody want to be 50. Just as they made everybody want to be 20 and listen to rock n' roll when they were in their 20s and 30s . . ."

With many more consumer dollars and much more cultural influence and political power concentrated in the ranks of America's elders than there is now, looking good could mean looking more like these social leaders. "Maturity" could be *in* as much as youth has been since the 1960s. It would thus not be hard to imagine a worker in his early thirties buying a product that might add a little fashionable gray to his hair—just a bit on the side, perhaps, to suggest distinction. We might even see a product that adds *just* a little crinkle or two around the eyes to suggest wisdom, experience, solidity.

## THE FUTURE OF ADVERTISING: THE MEDIUM AND THE MESSAGE

Until the coming of radio, all commercial messages were carried in print, an information-intensive medium. But broadcasting, by its nature, encouraged the use of brief, punchy messages backed by music, and broadcast advertising was built out of the slogan and the jingle. Television added the memorable image to the mix. The result is the modern advertising industry, one of the economic and cultural forces that has created prosperity in twentieth-century America.

Advertising is possibly on the verge of another basic transformation that could change the very tone of life in this country in the next two or three decades. Many effective copywriters who have created memorable slogans in their careers now believe the value of a powerfully worded theme has lessened.

Advertising has turned more subtle since the 1960s, implying more than telling, according to J. Walter Thompson chairman Burt Manning. Jackson Lears, a historian and an authority on American culture, sees a "self-conscious, satirical, self-deprecating" element coming to the fore, a rejection of the more sentimental view of life. It can hardly be a coincidence that this shift in consciousness coincides with the entry of baby boomers into full adulthood, not to mention their presence as copywriters in advertising itself.

What does this suggest for the future? Paradoxically, the graying of America is likely to combine with advances in computers and communication technology to turn advertising back to what it was before the revolution in modern communications: an institution conveying *information*, mostly through print.

Here's why: Studies of current elders consistently find that they are harder to impress than other age groups when it comes to selling them things. They have more "smarts" about the merits of product claims and counterclaims and they insist that advertising messages contain good, convincing arguments for the purchase of a product or service. They are "the scientists of purchasing," as Richard J. Balkite of Donnelley Marketing puts it.

If anything, the baby boomers will be an even more skeptical lot in their old age. They will be substantially more educated than most present elders. The experience of their generation—Vietnam and Watergate, for starters—has been to be wary of messages of all kinds. Their penchant is for the satirical. As elders, they will want even more of the good life than their parents—the economy permitting. But they will be a hard sell; slogans won't do it.

While sociologists still talk of America as a mass society with a mass culture, the splitting up of the mass audience undermines the meaning of these terms, and advertising will be significantly affected by this splintering. Cable television is a prominent example. Once Americans were united by the television programs they watched on the same networks, simultaneously. "In the 1950s, an advertiser could reach half of the households in America just by sponsoring *Lassie*," notes demographer Brad Edmondson. "Those days are gone forever." Viewing options are increasing every year as cable reaches into every corner of the country. Even when people watch network programs, it's often on their VCRs, at times of their convenience. And they fast-forward through the commercials.

To cope, business will be turning more and more to newspaper and magazine advertising. Notwithstanding all that's been written about the image replacing the word, baby boomers are as much readers as watchers and will be reachable in this way. However, the print medium will have undergone a revolution of its own. New technology will make it possible to customize ads for virtually every individual who reads a publication.

The theory, "micromarketing," in which a company's customers are broken down into as small a segment as can be reasonably defined and marketed to, has been around for a while. An automobile company, for example, will try to reach specific age and regional groups by designing its advertising and distribution patterns to take into account variations in customer preferences for vehicle models and styles—sedans to one group, pickup trucks to another.

A new technology that dovetails perfectly with micromarketing is selective binding, which allows a publisher to customize magazine ads to fit individual customer profiles based on whatever information about each customer the publisher has in a computerized data base. It's the same kind of data that allows direct-mail advertisers to focus on certain groups of likely customers. *Newsweek* and *Time* are testing selective binding for groups of customers now. "There could be a day when each subscriber's copy is different," according to Reginald K. Brack, chief executive officer of Time, Inc.'s magazine group, "when literally you would have four million different editions of *Time*, all with different ads aimed at the particular subscriber."

It sounds like a dream from the marketing point of view, but how will the baby boomers react? As young people many of them protested against the mass society that was making them feel like small cogs in a gigantic wheel, or like the ubiquitous IBM card that they were not supposed to "fold, spindle, or mutilate."

The "personalized" approaches to human interaction that are made possible by computers produce an atomized society. Common points of reference—such as those provided by the mass culture through television and advertising—are lacking. If the baby boomers are dissatisfied with the spirit of their society when they are old, it might be because they have traded their mass society for one that is atomized. They may complain that people have become too much separated from one another rather than that they are lumped together as if they were one faceless mass. They may even find themselves missing the slogans and jingles that at least provided an element of commonality in the mass culture of their youth.

Old age tends to be a more communal stage in life than the middle years, as we've already noted. In the future, this wish for community may be even stronger. Should micromarketing be pushed to its limits, speaking to each consumer separately, the gap between the needs, desires, and fantasies of the most important consumer group in the economy and the techniques marketers use to try to reach them could become unbridgeable. The result could be a further upheaval in advertising—perhaps sometime around 2010—producing an industry whose outlook and methods differ substantially from those of the one we know now and even from those that evolve in the early 1990s to deal with the *non*mass media. In yet another way the aging baby boomers will continue to cause ripples through society, changing everybody's life.

# 10

# Elderculture

"Once a young man asked me, 'What was it like in your day?'
'My day?' I said. 'This *is* my day.' "
Rosina Tucker, age 104.

"**R**oll over Beethoven," said Chuck Berry. "All you need is
love," said the Beatles. But Sgt. Pepper's Lonely Hearts
Club Band has been silent for two decades. And the generation that
created the youth culture of the 1960s is busy pursuing careers and
raising families.

They came to consciousness as rapid technological and social change
made it impossible for the young to accept their parents' version of the
world. Unprecedented affluence gave the young people in this huge
birth cohort the time and space to experiment, working out their own
answers about what was important and how one should live. In the face
of alienation they tried to create community; they saw the environment
ravaged and made respect for nature one of their central concerns;
appalled by what they considered political hypocrisy, they saw them-

selves as a new nation within society. Surrounded by what they viewed as formality, rigidity, and sexual repression, Early Boomers improvised new clothing styles, let their hair grow long, and reformulated sexual codes of behavior. They even tried to refurbish religion with forays into new spiritual realms.

An undercurrent survives—in New Age consciousness, for example. This conglomeration of interests and activities ranges from Zen Buddhism to mythology to the healing power of crystals. Florence Graves, associate publisher of the *New Age Journal*, defines New Age this way: "It is a loose philosophy with no dogma that stems in part from the modern transcendental movement, perennial philosophy, and a belief that the scientific view has dominated our consciousness and the spiritual view has been left behind."

Given the right conditions, could a more substantial manifestation of the spirit and even some of the lifestyle of the baby-boomer generation in its youth blossom once again? Is there still a seed of the youth culture waiting to regerminate? Such a birth would require some of the same elements that spawned the youth culture of the 1960s: a sense of group cohesiveness, enough leisure and freedom from the pressures of daily life to follow where their instincts might lead, and at least a vague discontent with the direction of their present lives. That's what characterized their youth. In fact, the boomers are now headed for a rendezvous with such a period: their old age.

## COMING TOGETHER AGAIN

"All of us in the '60's generation, having been part of a community that talked a lot about tribes and communality of experience, are now living very disparate lives," says Ed Zwick, one of the creators of the television show "thirtysomething." The members of this cohort feel cut off from one another because, more than previous generations, they have lived different adult lives. Some are single; some are coupled—living together, married or unmarried, straight or gay. Some are parents, with or without mates. Many have divorced, becoming part of large and complex family groups. Their interests and energies have diverged. No single vision unites them now.

But age will eventually even out their differences, as it has for the elders of their parents' and grandparents' generations. Sharon Kaufman, an anthropologist specializing in gerontology, has found that the health, psychological, and religious concerns of the later years make for more commonality among older people. In her interviews of Americans ranging in age from 70 to 97, she noted that whether or not they had raised a family had become a less distinctive factor in their lives than it might have been when they were younger. "Women in particular would discuss their child-rearing years if asked about them," she says, "but being a parent never emerged as a significant feature of their present identity." And, as Kaufman observes, "not having to worry about the future frees the elderly from many of the inhibitions and responsibilities carried by younger people."

Given their experience as adults, the baby boomers may reach their later years feeling unfulfilled, alienated from social norms as they were once before. Noted psychologist Martin E. P. Seligman, a baby boomer himself, writes of the promises of their adulthood:

> Our soaring expectations went beyond consumer goods into nonmaterial matters. We came to expect our jobs to be more than a way to make a living. Work now needs to be ecologically innocent, comforting to our dignity, a call to growth and excitement, a meaningful contribution to society—and deliver a large paycheck. Married partners once settled for duty, but today's mates expect to be ecstatic lovers, intellectual colleagues and partners in tennis and water sports.

Such expectations are by definition impossible to fulfill.

We are not suggesting that in their old age baby boomers will recreate the 1960s, a unique time gone forever. But people do retain their generational experiences into their later years. This sense of identity with others of the same age cohort encourages familiar patterns of thought and behavior from earlier years in response to the changing environment. As baby boomers age, their reactions to changes in such areas as the family, housing, work, and the interaction between men and women are likely to echo their past.

The creation of community, concern for nature, the affirmation of life in the face of alienation—this is the unfinished business of the sixties. But old age is not youth; time and experience will color this elderculture. Where the youth culture looked for what was new, an elderculture is likely to focus more on preserving endangered values and traditions and resurrecting ones that have been lost.

## THE BEGINNINGS OF AN ELDERCULTURE

Where are current elders in this scheme of things? The New Elders who have emerged as a social force in America over the past decade share an experience that somewhat resembles that of the youngsters of the 1960s and early 1970s. Economically the New Elders are relatively secure, and they have free time. In their case, modern medicine as well as the thriving postwar economy, Social Security, and adequate pensions have created a social group that has never before existed in the West.

Culturally, however, the New Elders are much more tentative than their assertive children were. When their kids met a life stage for which they had not been prepared, they improvised new ways of living and thinking about life. Today's elders still seem to be feeling their way carefully through this strange new land of extended old age. They haven't created a whole new elderculture, although they are active and continue to do many of the things that only younger people did in the past. Today's elders have established one new characteristic of the later years on which the baby boomers will build: intellectual *growth*.

At the International Center for Integrative Studies, a think tank in New York City that seeks to bridge the gap between the ever more specialized disciplines of the academic world, a group of elders are trying to make sense of this new stage in their lives. In their Quality of Later Life Project, they meet periodically to come to terms with their feelings about age, probing their perceptions and experiences for clues about what they might do to make the later years more satisfying. Milton, Pat, Phyllis, and Barbara, ranging in age from 59 to 80, sit around a table on a warm September evening, talking informally:

PAT: I talked to some people about this group and they said, "Well, what can you do but endure aging with dignity?" [She laughs sarcastically.] I believe we are developing and evolving and changing right up to our last day on Earth.

MILTON: My idea when I was growing up was that old people just faded into the woodwork. But I don't see that happening to the people that I know who are getting old. They're active, thinking people. Old people need what any person needs—warmth, connectiveness, security . . .

PHYLLIS AND BARBARA: . . . and growth . . . and challenge.

Growth is a new cultural value for the late stages of life. It is increasingly a preoccupation of today's elders, particularly in the area of education. Jane Porcino is a living example of the phenomenon that she often writes about: older people going back to school, expanding their horizons. When her seven children were old enough not to need their mother's close attention, she began to study for a master's degree in gerontology at age 50. Porcino was a Ph.D. candidate at 57, and made a book party of her sixtieth birthday celebration, which coincided with the publication of her *Growing Older, Getting Better: A Handbook for Women in the Second Half of Life.*

## BACK TO SCHOOL

There are more than two million people over 50 who have returned to school, as Jane Porcino did. Many receive life experience credit, exempting them from otherwise required courses—a formal recognition of the value of their age. Often they sit next to teenagers in classrooms, enriching discussions with the perspective of their experience in living.

While at least thirty-five thousand of these elders are studying for degrees, often to pursue second (or first) careers, an even more significant trend in adult education may be informal study opportunities for older people, which are often combined with the chance to socialize. The most prominent of these, Elderhostel, has been a smashing success and could eventually become a major institution in our society.

In 1975, 225 elders took part in a new nonprofit adult education program held on five college and university campuses in New Hampshire—the first Elderhostel. Its founders, Martin P. Knowlton, a teacher and backpacker, and David Bianco, a university administrator, originally intended to produce an American variation of European youth hostels. The program for older learners was almost an afterthought. Elderhostel has been growing at a rate of about 20 percent a year. In 1987, 142,000 people participated in Elderhostel programs at more than a thousand campuses in the United States and in thirty-seven other countries. Each participant is required to be at least 60 years old or the companion of someone that age. For about $235 (excluding transportation) elders spend a week in college dorms, eat in dining halls, attend campus cultural events, and use facilities such as swimming pools and tennis courts. They meet and socialize with like-minded people—a boon for older singles—and take noncredit courses on subjects ranging from politics to philosophy, forestry to folk dancing, quilt making to quasars. Their educational backgrounds vary from high-school dropout to Ph.D.

By scanning the Elderhostel catalog for courses and locations, many older couples are able to combine travel with study at reasonable rates. Francis and Jack Thornwood, for example, drove across country from east to west, taking courses as they went, eventually ending up in San Francisco for a visit with their grandchildren. They started at Hampshire College in Massachusetts with a course in "Language, Culture and Society," spent another week considering "The Recorder as a Renaissance Instrument" at Slippery Rock University in Pennsylvania, dallied for a while with Shakespeare at Illinois State University, and took a course in "Interpreting Dreams" at the University of Nevada. They had a lot to talk about by the time they reached their family in California.

Baby boomers have had more schooling than the current generation of elders and are likely to be very much open to a program such as this, which will be larger by the time they are ready for it and will almost certainly allow elder boomers to participate in designing courses themselves. A glance at some of the current course offerings suggests that they would already feel at home:

The Long Shadow: Human Activity and Earth's Environment
Lifestyling
The Road to Wholeness: Mind and Body Workshop
Wellness
Native American Culture
The Role of Civil Disobedience in the Shaping of Society
Transcendental Meditation

A small but growing segment of the older adult education movement offers an even more familiar echo for the baby boomers who will seek intellectual growth as they age. Older people are taking their learning into their own hands. The Institution of Retired Professionals at the New School for Social Research in New York City has served as a model for several campus-based programs in which elders plan and conduct their own programs, teaching each other what they know. These self-governing academic communities recall the "free schools" that sprang up near large campuses in the late 1960s and early 1970s. More informal but also serving a large audience are the OASIS programs that have spread from St. Louis to many other cities. This Older Adult Service and Information System, sponsored by the May Company Department Stores, provides lectures, cultural events, and courses taught by older people to other elders at centrally located department stores. The intergenerational environment at these stores is one of the elements that seems to attract older people.

## THE SEARCH FOR COMMUNITY

Several years ago, Louise Bernikow interviewed three hundred people all across the country for her book on the phenomenon of loneliness in our society, *Alone in America: The Search for Companionship.* Many of those whose consciousness had been formed by the 1960s told Bernikow that at one time they "had a feeling of belonging to something larger than themselves, whether the antiwar, women's or civil rights movement or the youth culture." The feeling was gone, and in its wake, for many, came a sense of loneliness and disconnection.

She also found a group who had learned how to overcome loneliness. Some of the old people she met "recognize that loneliness can kill you, so they try to create companionship through collective housing or by building their own institutions," such as the senior citizens' orchestra in Miami Beach. Bernikow concluded that "not a boyfriend or a girlfriend or even making peace with being alone, but creating community" was the practical answer that elders had devised to deal with loneliness.

The problem of feeling alone in the world also came up in the Quality of Later Life Project:

MILTON: I've been in a lot of discussion groups, many of them with younger people, like in singles groups where there was a lot of talk about loneliness. But I can't remember the idea of community ever coming out of those discussions. Yet now it would automatically come to me.

PAT: Yes, when you're younger you find one person who will cure you, make it right.

BARBARA: When I was little I had my family. The first experience I had of a community was a club I belonged to at the Y. Going to camp also had that feeling . . .

MILTON:   When we were talking about loneliness, it was about making a connection, getting a husband or wife; but here what I think about is getting friends, that's crucial. That means community to me.

The need to create a new community is likely to become a permanent characteristic of this later stage in the life cycle. Loneliness in old age is nothing new, but now that people are surviving into their later years healthier, less dependent, and in greater numbers than they used to, the possibilities of forging this spirit of community are becoming more realistic. Developmental psychologists in the future will reformulate the tasks of later life to include it. In fact, as Erik Erikson reworks his description of the later years he is giving a more important place to this phenomenon, stressing the critical importance of interdependence.

Current elders are laying the groundwork for a more communal old age, and of course the baby boomers are likely to be the elder community-builders par excellence. Their formative years were spent reaching out to their peers to cope with life changes through group strength. And even in their adult, career- and family-centered years, they have never quite lost the knack for collectively solving problems. Boomer mothers, for example, have perfected the play group, adding it to the repository of child-rearing wisdom. As the boomers age and begin to encounter the problems of the later years, they will reach out instinctively to one another for mutual aid. "Networking" will become a deeper, more encompassing concept than it is now in the world of work. The networks boomers form in the year 2020 will be psychological and sometimes actual lifelines.

In their youth, baby boomers were brought together by various institutions. School was by far the most important. But there are no institutions where older people are required to gather. Senior citizens' centers serve as meeting places for many of today's elders, as do ethnic clubs in big cities. But these places will be too tame for a generation that is better educated and more active than today's elders.

Where will older baby boomers "hang out"? Barring major changes in our economic system, many of them may very well pass their time in the same places where today's teenagers (and increasing numbers of older people) congregate: shopping malls. It's symbolically appropriate that there are now more shopping centers in the United States than there are secondary schools. Marketing expert Jagdish N. Sheth goes so far as to suggest that "most shopping centers will eventually phase out much of the merchandise and become more of a community gathering place." One can imagine malls coming to resemble the ancient Greek agoras, the shopping and meeting centers of that time where the public life was conducted.

The shopping mall is already turning into a campus as well. Since 1979, Indiana University- Purdue University at Indianapolis has been offering a Learn and Shop educational outreach program at malls in that midwestern city. Declining enrollments at the university had been the original impetus to offering people courses where they shop, and soon the program, in which thousands have enrolled, took on its own momentum.

Another common gathering place for elders today is the public library (including those in the malls). About 57 percent of the adult population used a library in 1987, up from 51 percent in 1978, according to the American Library Association. As the educational level of the adult population rises, they spend more time at the library. And the activities available in these multiuse, multimedia facilities make yesterday's hushed and bookish libraries seem very staid and old-fashioned.

Many library programs are especially appealing to older people: films, lectures, book discussion groups, and concerts, for example. The library may provide a New Elder's first encounter with computers, through an on-line book catalog or instruction in personal computer use. Libraries already lend everything from compact disks to videotapes. It's not hard to imagine them serving the extraordinary number of older educated patrons who will be headed their way.

Stereotypes notwithstanding, baby boomers are already heavy readers. *Book Industry Trends, 1988,* a study sponsored by the nonprofit Book Industry Study Group, found that Americans are reading more these days, with baby boomers in the forefront, despite their upbringing in the television age. If they continue to take pleasure in the printed page, the report states that "their support could sustain consumer book sales well into the next century." The same pleasure will send them to the library. In the future we are likely to see branches become even more like intergenerational social centers, providing meeting rooms for elder self-help groups and also space that older people will use to meet with youngsters who need tutoring. Older people will also take and teach courses there, possibly as part of the expanded Elderhostel system of two or three decades from now.

While probably fewer than 10 percent of older boomers are likely to retire to elder housing affiliated with colleges, these schools will draw a substantially greater number of retirees back to the campus to use their cultural and recreational facilities on a per-day or per-semester basis. With declining enrollments of younger students, classrooms are likely to have a mix of old and young not seen since the GI Bill filled the classrooms with large numbers of adults in the late 1940s.

## ON THE PHONE AGAIN

Members of the generation of 1946 to 1964 were bound by the strands of the culture they created—everything from communes to a common language inaccessible to adults—and their elderculture is likely to reflect that same innovative spirit, if not an actual restoration of some old familiar practices. In forging these renewed connections, elder baby boomers will probably use modern electronic technology, for example, the same technology that, paradoxically, is so often blamed for the isolation and loneliness found in modern society. The widespread popularity of radio talk shows among our current older population provides a hint of what is to come. Only a minority of people actually call in, but even those who just listen seem to get a sense of participation and, at the very least, a feeling that they've got company in the house.

We should expect the telephone, celebrated in so many cartoons and television shows as the effective lifeline of their adolescence, to serve again as a route of contact between the baby boomers in their later years. But it will not be the telephone of their youth. Conference calls and picturevision will encourage a full airing of troubles with friends and enhance the search for creative, collective solutions to problems. These features will also enable those with mobility impairments to stay in touch.

People will also be meeting through telephone contact. The recent fad involving calling into commercially operated party lines—mostly for young people—is likely to take on a more serious cast, with such telephone networks run by older people for others like themselves who would like to make new friends or meet new partners or just chase the blues when they're feeling lonely. Special-interest groups could form on these networks, as they now do on computer bulletin boards, a technology that should also burgeon as we eventually get a generation of elders more comfortable with computers.

Another adaptation of current technology to watch for is more widespread use of ham radio. The development of microchips has made this equipment smaller, more effective, and easier to use. The CB radio fad of a few years back suggests a widespread fascination with the informal use of this kind of apparatus. With telecommunications networks shrinking the world and English becoming a common worldwide tongue, older people will be able to broaden the horizons of their acquaintances across international boundaries.

All it will take to include ham radio in our common household array of communications technology is sufficient acceptance and demand. The largest generation of elders in history, eager to connect with other people and to share their thoughts and experiences, may well supply the impetus.

## BACK TO NATURE

Baby boomers at mid-life are widely portrayed as snuggled down and plugged in at home. From the expressions the media has coined to characterize their leisure lifestyle, one would get the impression that people born in the period 1946 to 1964 have not seen the sun since their college graduation—they are all "couch potatoes" "cocooning." Yet this is the generation that popularized the backpack, gave us the ecology movement, and inspired Earth Day in the early 1970s. Are they destined to live out their later years curled up in front of the boob tube?

Although older people in general spend more time indoors than do the young, New Elders, especially those who are more affluent and educated, are beginning to pursue recreation outside more than people their age used to. The Census Bureau conducted surveys of elders' preferences in this area in 1965 and 1982 and found that people 45 and older had become more active outdoors while younger Americans, especially those under 24, had become more sedentary.

There's no guarantee that this trend will continue into the baby boomers' old age. But given their generational experiences and concern with health, they are no more likely to spend their later years with their feet up on the couch than they are to pass them in a rocking chair.

In fact, there are already some indications that they are getting a little tired of the cloistered world of indoor entertainment, supposedly their element. Camping, for example, is on the upswing—upscale camping, at that. Baby boomers are willing to rough it if the way is softened a bit, preferring cabins to tents, for instance. Operators of campgrounds such as those in the successful franchise chain Kampgrounds of America (KOA) have noted that vacationing families seem to find the communal aspect of camping preferable to the more atomized experience of stopping at motels with the kids.

As they age, baby boomers are likely to find more and more outdoor facilities and activities geared to their needs and interests. Whatever physical infirmities they may develop will be less likely to preclude traveling and even roughing it because recreational facilities have been made more accessible. For instance, people with disabilities can now reach camping areas deep in the woods in Everglades National Park and Rocky Mountain National Park that would have been inaccessible to them only five years ago.

One recreational activity that could become popular among older baby boomers in some areas is rail-biking. The 1902 Sears Roebuck catalog advertised attachments for bikes that allowed cyclists to ride on railroad tracks. The tires are removed from the bikes and heavy-duty rims are installed. The cyclist rides on one of the rails while a metal arm extends outward from the bike attached to a small wheel that rolls along the other rail, providing balance. The practice of riding the rails in this way never entirely died out, although the railroads almost have. With so much track now abandoned or hardly used, this activity, now found on a very small scale in the Pacific Northwest and in New England, could spread. It's an ideal sport for people of all ages, but especially adaptable for those with a variety of physical impairments, including poor eyesight, since riders just follow the track and do not have to steer.

With a generational history that includes a deep concern for the Earth, baby boomers as elders figure to be even more avid gardeners than old people today. That's saying a good deal, since by the mid-1980s Americans over 50 accounted for about 27 million of the 75 million or so gardeners in this country. Indeed, the more well-off among the boomers may become absolutely obsessed with gardening, taking to the cultivation of flowers and vegetables—and sparking healthy increases in the sale of gardening tools—as they have to the acquisition of knowledge about good wines.

Cultivating the land could turn out to be one of the prime avenues through which they express their creativity and derive satisfaction and self-fulfillment. With things Japanese becoming increasingly fashionable, it would not be surprising to see these gardeners influenced by Japanese notions of garden landscaping and plant cultivation as fine arts.

The reverence for nature and the environment so characteristic of the youthful baby boomers—and still present in their strong environmental consciousness—is likely to become even stronger as they age and have more time to spend in the outdoors. The increasingly popular activity of bird-watching should become even more widespread, as will nature photography. Books about the natural world will probably be consistent best-sellers by the second decade of the twenty-first century.

As the baby boomers age, the cumulative effects of decades of Earth abuse will result in unprecedented environmental degradation. This damage could enhance their special feeling and concern for nature. We have already pointed out that the threat to medicinal plants alone is likely to energize their ecological activism. They may also become involved in implementing various conservation practices. If by then our communities haven't adopted recycling as a normal part of our interaction with the material world, for example, they may well lead the fight for it.

But successful recycling policies could depend on a healthy economy, the continued availability of wood and natural fibers, and possible scientific and technical breakthroughs in the development of new biodegradable substances. Conserving our resources will also require the boomers to transcend their own upbringing. While environmentally conscious, they *are* the first generation raised in the "plastic age"—for though introduced in the nineteenth century, this material didn't become widely used until after World War II. Will the children of the sixties be willing to abandon their disposable society? It's by no means certain. As one 31-year-old accountant candidly acknowledged a few years ago:

> Our parents had more respect for what they bought. There used to be something called a fix-it man or repair shop. I had no idea what to do when my toaster-oven broke. I bought a new one. I didn't even bother getting it fixed; I don't even know where to go to get it fixed. But our parents' generation, if something broke, if something was torn, they mended it, they fixed it. We're disposable. We throw things away.

## EMOTIONAL GROWTH

Today's young and middle-aged adults are likely to be as attuned to self as to nature when they age. "Probably at no other time in life is there as potent a force toward self-awareness operating as in old age," according to Robert Butler, former head of the National Institute on Aging. "Yet, the capacity to change, according to prevailing stereotype, decreases with age." If current elders have established intellectual growth as a new task for the later years, baby boomers are likely to do the same for late-life emotional development.

Psychologists used to view older people's talking about their past as yet another sign of age-related decline, somewhat akin to short-term memory loss. It was seen as a rather sad preoccupation with their past, not a healthy reexamination of their lives. But in 1963, Robert Butler published in the journal *Psychiatry* an article titled "The Life Review: An Interpretation of Reminiscence in the Aged" that has become a landmark revision of previous attitudes. Butler suggested that the raising to consciousness of past events and conflicts is brought on by two factors: the end of the person's absorption in full-time work, which serves as a distraction from these thoughts in the young, and his or her awareness that life is coming to a close. He suggested that this could easily be a positive process, aiming toward a kind of "reorganization" and reintegration of personality, at its best producing not pathology but wisdom. As one elder woman put it in the Quality of Later Life Project, her reminiscence is "not a life history, it's a life story, an ongoing story."

That older people might profit from therapy is a surprisingly novel idea. Freud thought psychoanalysis was wasted on people over 50. Although elders over 65 make up more than 12 percent of the population, they represent fewer than 5 percent of the people seen at mental-health centers and fewer still among those who see therapists in private practice. As late as 1981, 70 percent of American clinical psychologists had no patients over 65. Mary Erlanger, an Atlanta family therapist, has suggested another reason for their underrepresentation in therapy. "Part of the ageism older people experience among mental health professionals is that it's hard to find counselors their own age," she says. "They're all retired." And the members of the present generation of elders were raised to see psychotherapy as a treatment reserved for the weak and the sick. Their sense of propriety may also prevent them from taking advantage of counseling—one 73-year-old who wanted some help felt she couldn't "talk about private matters to perfect strangers."

The baby boomers are the first generation to grow up accepting psychotherapy as a natural and appropriate technique for dealing with the rough spots in life and for achieving self-discovery, understanding, and catharsis. They should not lack for therapists their own age—if that's what they want—when they get old. Their generation has gone into the helping professions in large numbers, and potential patients will be able to find somebody to see who is working at least part-time.

## IN THE SPIRIT

And what of religion? The First Methodist Church in a quiet middle-class neighborhood in a large city offers a vivid picture of the implications of the aging of the population for many communities. From the late 1950s through the early 1970s its Sunday school and youth groups were overflowing, as was the playground across the street from the church on mild Saturday afternoons, when kids usually had to wait an hour for a basketball court. Now the youth groups have been consolidated and children in the Sunday school get much more individual attention than they ever did. The congregation's baby boomers are raising their own families, mostly in places scattered across the country—wherever their careers have taken them. But the church continues to play an important social role in the community: Its senior citizens' programs can barely handle the demand for activities.

More than institutions has changed. Those now young or in early middle age have grown up knowing a different God from the one their elders knew. Monsignor Charles Fahey, of the Third Age Center of Fordham University in New York City, in his mid-fifties, says that for his generation and for earlier ones "the dominant image of God was of a law-giver and judge—the one who handed out punishment and was appeased by people who seek God's will in every moment. Surely there's been a shift to a God who is much more personal."

By the mid-1980s, observers had noted a resurgence of religious observance among baby boomers, but its long-term significance is by no means clear. For example, a study conducted by the Hartford Seminary Center for Social and Religious Research showed that church attendance three or more times a month by people born in the period 1945 to 1954 had increased from 34 percent in the early 1970s to 43 percent in the mid-1980s. That's a significant but hardly earthshaking change. David Roozen, the Hartford Seminary Center's associate director, attributes the shift to increased political conservatism and the desire of boomer parents to give their children a religious background.

These factors could reflect just the needs and attitudes of a particular life stage and may tell us no more about the boomers' future than they do about their past.

Perhaps more significant, when baby boomers have swelled the numbers of a congregation, they've tended to leave their generational imprint on it. Congregations report that these new members insist on "participatory democracy," according to David Roozen. They want a hand in running things and are less likely than previous generations to accept authority without question.

One thing is for certain: Among the boomers who set the trends for their generation and who are likely to be in the forefront of creating the new elderculture, fundamentalism has not made major inroads. Bob Dylan, the poet of their generation, who previously had always sensed before others did what was blowing in the wind, suffered a major drop in record sales when his songs reflected his born-again preoccupations.

*If* religion is to be a significant factor in elderculture by 2020 and after, it's likely to be different—possibly much different—from the way it is now. In their youth, many Early Boomers experimented with new forms of spirituality—adaptations of Eastern religions such as Buddhism, for example. Others found sustenance in the spiritual aspects of the culture of the American Indians, while still others communed with nature in the style of the transcendentalists.

As elders these spiritual pioneers may search for similarly creative answers to the ultimate concerns that, toward the end of their lives, will have great significance. Today's elders probably never thought they would live to see weddings celebrated barefoot on the beach, or church services held with a background of guitar music, or women clergy. The future old will bring to religion a lifetime of changing traditional ways.

The demystification of ritual given impetus by Vatican II and the "secular city" of the 1960s should continue. Pared-down rituals and more worldly religious institutions seem to be part of the modern temperament. However, look also for a strengthened parallel and competing strain of mysticism fostered by a vague feeling that in the face of eternity, plain talk, common sense, and churchly social concerns don't always deliver the goods. This emphasis will evoke the individual introspection and religious experience that were part of spiritual quests of the 1960s. It's even conceivable that we could see a return of psychedelic drugs. They would be used not so much experimentally or recreationally, but as sacramental aids to achieving spiritual discovery.

## DEATH, A CELEBRATION OF LIFE

At every stage in their lives, whatever has concerned baby boomers and their families has become a national concern. Because of their sheer size alone, their problems became everybody's business: from over-crowded elementary schools to ferment on college campuses, the remaking of the family in the face of two-career marriages, and the problems involved in adapting to an economy that does not necessarily offer the career prospects promised them in their youth. The sexual revolution, for example, in which boomers played a leading role, af-fected everybody's values and conduct.

Inevitably, death will loom large for their generation someday, and society as a whole will begin to hear a good deal more about this important subject. Again, we deal with a new phenomenon. It wasn't until this century that death became almost exclusively associated with old age. In the past, disease and warfare killed off so many younger people that death was not seen as the almost exclusive prov-ince of old age. (Throughout most of history, only about half of all children have survived to the age of 10.) When life really *was* short, death could come at any time. That's why it was treated more mat-ter-of-factly.

In recent times death had become almost a taboo subject. But the widespread interest in Elisabeth Kübler-Ross's *On Death and Dying,* published in 1969, began death's emergence from the shadows. Whether we are truly dealing with death as a society now or have simply found a higher level of defense is debatable. Perhaps the fascina-tion with thanatology is merely a way of further abstracting a painful subject. Personal computer software called Will Maker now allows anybody to prepare a will without a lawyer in less than thirty minutes, but does this necessarily show that we have become more comfortable about death?

People once had to deal with death throughout life. But now it's usually not until at least middle age that one starts to lose those who are close. By the third decade of the twenty-first century, baby boom-ers are bound to be turning their attention to the approaching end of their own lives. With people tending to die in a more narrow age range than they used to—in later old age—the newspapers will be filled with the obituaries of boomers' contemporaries. Death will be a subject very much "with them," with important psychological and philosophical implications for American culture.

What are the baby boomers likely to make of *this* part of their lives? As much as they can, probably something positive. Concern with mortality can awaken vital thoughts and feelings repressed through much of life, encouraging people to sharpen their sense of priorities and live life to the fullest. It might break down inhibitions among many in the baby-boomer generation and make the formalities of social conventions seem trivial, leading to more free-spirited lifestyles.

Anthropologist Sharon Kaufman observed of the old people she interviewed that not one was preoccupied by a fear of death. "What they *do* fear is infirmity," she reports. "They value independence very highly." Philosopher Sidney Hook wrote a brief article for a major newspaper on the subject of euthanasia which, he recently reported, brought a greater response from readers than anything else he had ever written. The elders of 2030 are likely to make autonomy and control in the face of physical decline a central theme of late old age, and thus a dominant topic in their society.

On the one hand, as we noted in an earlier chapter, philosophers and social critics will be pondering the theme of dependence. On the other, issues such as the right to die and the moral dimensions of suicide committed by those terminally ill, which are just now pushing into our consciousness, will also come more to the forefront in the boomers' old age. Americans "must make dying a part of living," Alexander Capron, a law professor and a noted authority on medicine and public policy, noted recently. In that spirit, he thinks the question should be posed not in terms of "the right to die" but rather in terms of "the right to decide." That's likely to be high on the elder agenda in a few decades.

Unfortunately, this issue may become entwined in the twenty-first century with the more familiar problem of elder suicide. Those currently over the age of 65 have the highest suicide rate among all age groups; they make up not quite 12 percent of the population but account for 17 percent of all suicides. Baby boomers have a higher incidence of depression than people of other ages, according to psychiatrist Dan G. Blazer. He thinks that their suicide rate as elders will top those of the New Elder and Old Guard generations.

By the time the baby boomers age, the meaning of "a good death" will emerge as a central concern of society. It may even appear in the school curriculum, considered just as important for young people to deal with as subjects like business ethics or the importance of voting. Dying an appropriate death—dying as one would wish—will have become part of living a good life.

## SPEAK, MEMORY

"I am constantly impressed by the durability of memories," writes James E. Birren, director of the Institute for Advanced Study at the Andrus Gerontology Center, University of Southern California, referring to long-term recall. "The clarity with which many 80-year-olds describe early life events can be awesome." The art form most characteristic of old age, then, is an ancient and venerable one: storytelling.

It is characteristic of our time that we seem to have lost our sense of history. What happened yesterday is ancient history, and the events of the day before yesterday are already lost to memory. By the second decade of the twenty-first century our collective cultural amnesia may present a crisis of continuity. Values, rituals, and old practical solutions to problems could be lost to society if they are not perpetuated. All the computerized data bases in the world will not avail without the will and awareness needed to mine the past. Almost a century ago, in *The Time Machine*, H. G. Wells foresaw this danger.

The curators of a mid-1980s Smithsonian exhibition of the art, stories, and skills of our nation's elders, called "The Grand Generation: Memory, Mastery, Legacy," put it this way:

> What one generation wants to forget, the next may wish to remember. The old are a vital resource of cultural information and understanding—living evidence of the rich variety of human cultural possibilities available to us in the world. Their knowledge is an antidote against the threat of homogeneity. By learning what the old have to teach us, we bear a diversity of options into the future, keeping fully supplied a reservoir of possible solutions to inescapable human problems.

Elderhostel recently began an experimental program that suggests one avenue for preserving elders' wisdom. On three campuses it has invited participants to bring their grandchildren along. These youngsters and other young people from surrounding communities also live in the dorms and participate in courses such as storytelling and folk crafts.

Could the first generation raised on consumer electronics also be the one to resurrect the oral tradition (greatly diminished by the pervasiveness of television) fully in their old age—the storytelling function associated with elders in the past? At first glance that might seem to be a rash prediction. The fiction boomers read now, for example, hardly suggests such a future. Literary critic Cecilia Tichi describes as "video fiction" the work of authors such as Ann Beattie, Tama Janowitz, and Bobbie Ann Mason. These "postmodernists," according to sociologist (and onetime 1960s activist) Todd Gitlin, "recreate the experience of watching television. . . . They write in the present tense because that is television's only tense: everything is always happening right now, in the middle; there are no beginnings or ends." It's the artistic and intellectual equivalent of couch-potatoism.

Such a style seems far from the pleasures of storytelling. Yet there is a less dramatic cultural trend that has persisted since the baby boom's youth and suggests a different direction. The folk music many boomers listened to and sang with such fervor in their youth is one manifestation of their generation's narrative tradition. It's no accident that one of their cultural heroes is Garrison Keillor, who probably has more fans than all the aforementioned fiction writers combined. Keillor gained prominence mainly for his ability to spin tales on public radio about the people of the mythical Lake Wobegon, Minnesota. He was following in the tradition of Jean Shepherd, who beguiled high-school and college students on late-night radio in the 1960s with his fertile narrative imagination. Another example is Pacifica Radio Network's Mike Feder, who tells stories on the radio, on stage, and in print.

James Howard, a storyteller from Denton, Texas, recites at regional storytelling festivals. "Young and old, yuppies and hippies, all side by side," is his description of the audience at the National Storytelling Festival in Jonesboro, Tennessee. "But in spite of the diversity," he adds, "there's a wonderful cohesiveness." The intergenerational appeal of storytelling could provide an important social glue in the twenty-first century if tensions between the generations do develop. And having grandparents who tell stories will be especially important to the current generation of younger people if they continue their enchantment with the visual and abandon the written word.

# THE BEAT GOES ON

The youth culture of the sixties defined itself as the antithesis of the culture of everyone over thirty. And nothing more fully expressed the differences between young and old than rock and roll music.

Young people have been staking a claim on their own music as a source of identity for several generations. Until the development of modern popular music, young and old played, sang, and listened to the same tunes. Musical preference began to reflect generational tastes in the 1920s. It was jazz, the new popular music of that decade, that first captured the spirit of a rebellious younger generation. For the first time the energy of black culture broke directly through to whites, scandalizing older whites, who thought jazz was sinful and lascivious. They associated it with the worst excesses of flappers and "flaming youth."

For the members of each successive adult generation still alive today, music has marked the times of their lives. By the early 1940s, when people who are today in their late fifties and in their sixties were adolescents, bobby-soxers were swooning over young Frank Sinatra, the featured singer with the Tommy Dorsey band. And they were jitterbugging in the aisles of New York's Paramount Theater to performances of music by the big bands and their singers, giving older people a sense that something was happening that excluded them.

In the 1950s and 1960s, as in the 1920s, young whites again tapped into black culture, this time hearing something in the blues that spoke to them—first through Elvis Presley and other early white stars and directly from black rhythm and blues, then via the British sounds of the Beatles and the Rolling Stones. By the early 1960s the black experience had generated the civil-rights movement, a political, social, and cultural explosion, which energized white American teenagers to create their own upheaval.

For the first baby-boomer adolescents, rock and roll was a musical declaration of independence. It not only entertained them but also served as intergenerational social criticism. It confirmed their feelings that being "a teenager in love" really *could* be painful, their parents really *were* a "pain," and much of what they were subjected to in school was nonsense. Their music expressed an often inchoate teenage *angst* and provided some catharsis. The erotic undercurrent—*rock and roll* came from black slang for sexual intercourse—foreshadowed the sexual revolution of the 1960s.

The popular music of the 1920s, 1930s, 1940s, and early 1950s passed into middle age with the generations that had clai·ned it in their youth. The young of succeeding generations took up with other styles and rhythms. Today the pages of *Modern Maturity* often carry ads for collections of the music of Frank Sinatra, Louis Armstrong, Bing Crosby, the big bands, Perry Como, Eddie Fisher, Patti Paige, and similar stars of the past. Only Sinatra has managed to retain some intergenerational appeal.

Rock and roll, through its evolution into rock and through all its variations, from disco to punk to new wave, has retained its attraction for successive generations of the young. The appeal of rock has lasted longer than any other generation's music has since the 1920s—about thirty-five years now. At present, essentially the same musical style serves several generations, something that hadn't happened since the early years of this century. "Why shouldn't it still be appealing today?" asks Greg Geller, vice-president for artists and repertoire at RCA Records, about the music of the sixties. "It's not as if music has evolved that much in the past 20 years. The Beatles still sound pretty contemporary." In fact, "Twist and Shout," an early Beatles hit, rode high on the charts again in 1986. In at least one case today's youth literally listen to the second generation of 1960s rock—witness the career of Julian Lennon, son of the Beatles' John Lennon.

More than previous generations, baby boomers continue to buy recordings and attend concerts. And what they like now is to a great extent what they liked back in the 1960s and early 1970s. *Newsweek* recently commented on the resurgence of old stars such as Paul McCartney, Aretha Franklin, Steve Winwood, the Moody Blues, Paul Simon, and Tina Turner. Will their music speak for baby-boomer elders too?

Holding on to the past may be fine for listeners but it can be agonizing for recording artists. Should the work of rock musicians age with the generation that nurtured them, or would it be better for them to hitch their fortunes to the energy of the young? The travails of one band, in particular, reflect the current state of generational drift in rock. The self-proclaimed—and by many acknowledged—"greatest rock and roll band ever," the Rolling Stones, has been pulled in two directions. Its lead guitarist, Keith Richards, has pushed for a more mature image for the group, allowing it to grow with its increasingly middle-aged fans. On the other hand, Mick Jagger, in his mid-forties, wants to play to the young. In the words of critic Stephen Holden,

Jagger "still refuses to give up the voluptuous, adolescent Jumping Jack Flash persona he has flaunted for more than two decades."

What does the future hold? An elderculture could only differentiate itself from the young. How will that show up on the pop charts? Is rock and roll here to stay? We may not know until we hear the lyrics to Bruce Springsteen's *Getting Old* album, due out about the year 2015.

# Selected Bibliography

Anyone investigating the subject of aging is indebted to the pioneering work of gerontologists such as Robert H. Binstock, Elaine Brody, Gunhild O. Hagestad, Robert Hunter, Bernice Neugarten, Matilda W. Riley, and Ethel Shanas. The best guide to the basic work in the field is Robert H. Binstock and Ethel Shanas, eds., *Handbook of Aging and the Social Sciences,* second edition (New York: Van Nostrand Reinhold, 1985).

The basic work on the baby boomers is Landon Y. Jones, *Great Expectations: America and the Baby Boom Generation* (New York: Ballantine, 1980). Cheryl Russell's *100 Predictions about the Baby Boomers* (New York: Plenum, 1987), also has useful information. *Our Aging Society: Paradox and Promise* (New York: W. W. Norton, 1986), edited by Alan Pifer and Lydia Bronte, is an excellent introduction to the issues raised by the transformation of old age. *The New York Times, The Wall Street Journal,* and *Advertising Age* are invaluable sources of facts on and analysis of trends in aging. *Newsweek, Time, USA Today,* and *U.S. News & World Report* also carry useful material. The reports of the United States Senate Special Committee on the Aging are helpful, as is its *Aging America: Trends and Projections,* 1987–88 edition (Washington: 1987). *American Demographics* is important to anyone working in this field, as are the *AARP News Bulletin, Aging, Generations, The Gray Panther Network, Modern Maturity, New Choices* (formerly *50 Plus*) and *The*

*Older Worker. Psychology Today* is a good source for information about changing views of human development; *Ms.* reports on women and aging. *Selling to Seniors* and *Mature Market Report* monitor the business side of the increase in the number of older people and changes in their lifestyle.

A chapter-by-chapter breakdown of other important sources follows:

## Chapter 1

Carter, Paul. *Another Part of the Fifties.* New York: Columbia University Press, 1983.

Howe, Neil. "America in the Year 2007." *The American Spectator,* December 1987, 27–31.

Linden, Fabian. *Baby Boomers in Midpassage.* New York: The Conference Board, 1987.

Neugarten, Bernice. "Age Groups in American Society and the Rise of the Young-Old." *Annals of the American Academy of Political Science* 415 (1974): 187–198.

*Recent Social Trends in the United States: Report of the President's Research Committee on Social Trends.* New York: McGraw Hill, 1933.

Riley, Matilda White. "Aging and Cohort Succession: Interpretations and Misinterpretations." *Public Opinion Quarterly,* Spring 1973, 35–49.

Ryder, N. B. "The Cohort as a Concept in the Study of Social Change." *American Sociological Review* 30 (1965): 834–861.

## Chapter 2

Blieszner, Rosemary. "Trends in Family Gerontology Research," *Family Relations* 35 (1986): 555–562.

Brody, Elaine M. " 'Women in the Middle' and Family Help to Older People." *The Gerontologist* 21 (1981): 471–480.

Hagestad, Gunhild O. "Able Elderly in the Family Context: Changes, Chances, and Challenges." *The Gerontologist* 27 (1987): 417–422.

———. "Problems and Promises in the Social Psychology of Intergenerational Relations." In *Aging: Stability and Change in the Family,* R. W. Fogel, E. Hatfield, B. Keisler, and E. Shanas, eds. New York: Academic Press, 1981, 11–46.

Johnson, Colleen L., and Barbara Barer. "Marital Instability and the Changing Kinship Networks of Grandparents." *The Gerontologist* 27 (1987): 330–335.

Kornhaber, Arthur, and Kenneth L. Woodward. *Grandparents/Grandchildren: The Vital Connection.* Garden City, N.Y.: Doubleday, 1981.

Shanas, Ethel. "Family Kin-Networks and Aging in Cross-Cultural Perspective." *Journal of Marriage and the Family* 35 (1973): 505–511.

Watkins, Susan C., Jane A. Menken, and John Bongaarts. "Demographic Foundations of Family Change." *American Sociological Review,* June 1987, 346–358.

Wentkowski, Gloria J. "Older Women's Perceptions of Great-Grandmotherhood: A Research Note." *The Gerontologist* 25 (1985): 593–596.

## Chapter 3

Adams, Rebecca G. "Emotional Closeness and Physical Distance between Friends: Implications for Elderly Women Living in Age-Segregated and Age-Integrated Housing." *International Journal of Aging and Human Development* 22 (1985–86): 55–76.

"Australia's 'Granny Flats' Capture U.S. Interest." *Aging International* 8 (1981): 11–12.

Calhoun, Richard B. *In Search of the New Old: Redefining Old Age in America, 1945–1970.* New York: Elsevier, 1978.

FitzGerald, Frances. "Interlude." *The New Yorker,* April 25, 1983, 54–109.

Fitzpatrick, Kevin M., and John R. Logan. "The Aging of the Suburbs, 1960–1980." *American Sociological Review* 50 (1985): 106–117.

Furnas, J. C. *The Americans: A Social History of the United States, 1587–1914.* New York: G. P. Putnam's Sons, 1969.

Gersuny, Carl. "The Rhetoric of the Retirement Home Industry." *The Gerontologist* 10 (1970): 282–286.

Hareven, Tamara K. "Family Time and Historical Time." *Daedalus,* Spring 1977, 57–70.

Jackson, Kenneth T. *Crabgrass Frontier: The Suburbanization of the United States.* New York: Oxford University Press, 1985.

Jones, Rochelle. *The Other Generation.* Englewood Cliffs, N.J.: Prentice-Hall, 1977.

Muller, Charlotte. "Homesharing and Congregate Housing: State Initiatives." *Research on Aging,* June 1987, 163–181.

Reinharz, Shulamit. "Creating Utopia for the Elderly." *Society,* January–February 1988, 52–58.

Schreter, Carol A., and Lloyd A. Turner. "Sharing and Subdividing Private Market Housing." *The Gerontologist* 26 (1986): 181–186.

## Chapter 4

Atchley, Robert C. "Retirement as a Social Institution." *Annual Review of Sociology* 8 (1982): 263–287.

Best, Fred, and Barry Stern. "Education, Work, and Leisure: Must They Come in That Order?" *Monthly Labor Review.* July 1977, 3–10.

Bove, Robert. "Retraining the Older Worker." *Training and Development Journal,* March 1987, 77–78.

Copperman, Lois F., and Frederick D. Keast. *Adjusting to an Older Work Force.* New York: Van Nostrand Reinhold, 1983.

Dillingham, Alan E. "Age and Workplace Injuries." *Aging and Work,* Winter 1981, 1–9.

McFarland, Ross A. "The Need for Functional Age Measurements in Industrial Gerontology." *Industrial Gerontology,* Fall 1973, 1–17.

Meier, Elizabeth L., and Elizabeth A. Kerr. "Capabilities of Middle-aged and Older Workers." *Industrial Gerontology,* Summer 1976, 147–156.

Pogrebin, Letty Cottin. *Among Friends: Who We Like, Why We Like Them, and What We Do with Them.* New York: McGraw-Hill, 1987.

Sonnenfeld, Jeffrey. "Dealing with the Aging Work Force." *Harvard Business Review,* November–December 1978, 81–92.

"To Retire or Not to Retire, That Is the Question." *Science,* February 19, 1988, 845.


## Chapter 5


Binstock, Robert H. "The Aged as Scapegoat." *The Gerontologist* 23 (1983): 136–143.

Chen, Yung-Ping. "Making Assets out of Tomorrow's Elderly." *The Gerontologist* 27 (1987): 410–416.

Churchill, Larry R. "Should We Ration Health Care by Age?" *Journal of the American Geriatric Society* 36 (1988): 644–647.

Etzioni, Amitai. "Spare the Old, Save the Young." *The Nation,* June 11, 1988, 818–822.

Graebner, William. *A History of Retirement: The Meaning of an American Institution, 1885–1978.* New Haven, Connecticut: Yale University Press, 1980.

Martin, Linda G. "The Aging of Asia." *Journal of Gerontology* 43 (1988): S99–S113.

Matusow, Allen J. *The Unravelling of America: A History of Liberalism in the 1960s.* New York: Harper & Row, 1984.


## Chapter 6


Arling, Greg. "The Elderly Widow and Her Family, Neighbors and Friends." *Journal of Marriage and the Family* 38 (1976): 757–768.

Binstock, Robert. "The Aged as Scapegoat." *The Gerontologist* 23 (1983): 136–143.

Campbell, John C., and John Strate. "Are Old People Conservative?" *The Gerontologist* 21 (1981): 580–591.

Fairlie, Henry. "Talkin' 'bout My Generation." *The New Republic,* March 28, 1988, 19–22.

Erikson, Erik H., Joan M. Erikson, and Helen Q. Kivnick. *Vital Involvement in Old Age.* New York: W. W. Norton, 1986.

Hoskins, Irene. "Intergenerational Equity: An Overview of a Policy Debate in the United States." *Aging International,* Spring 1987, 5–8, 13.

Hudson, Robert B. "Tomorrow's Able Elders: Implications for the State." *The Gerontologist* 27 (1987): 405–409.

Jennings, Jeanette. "Elderly Parents as Caregivers for Their Adult Dependent Children." *Social Work,* September–October 1987, 430–433.

Jennings, M. Kent, and Gregory B. Marcus. "Political Involvement in Later Years: A Longitudinal Survey." *American Journal of Political Science,* May 1988, 302–316.

Johnson, Mary. "Overcoming the Social Barriers." *The Nation,* April 9, 1988, pp. 489–491.

Lubomudrov, Slava. "Congressional Perceptions of the Elderly: The Use of Stereotypes in the Legislative Process." *The Gerontologist* 27 (1987): 77–81.

Minkler, Meredith. "The Politics of Generational Equity." *Social Policy*, Winter 1987, 48–52.

Neugarten, Bernice. "The Old and the Young in Modern Societies." *American Behavioral Scientist* 14 (1970): 13–24.

Preston, Samuel. "Children and the Elderly in the U.S." *Scientific American*, December 1984, 44–49.

Weeks, John R. *Aging: Concepts and Social Issues.* Belmont, California: Wadsworth, 1984.

Williamson, John B., Linda Evans, and Lawrence A. Powell. *The Politics of Aging: Power and Policy.* Springfield, Ill.: C. C. Thomas, 1980.

## Chapter 7

Adelman, R. et al. "A Well Elderly Program: An Intergenerational Model in Medical Education." *The Gerontologist* 28 (1988): 409–413.

Andres, Rubin. *The Normality of Aging: The Baltimore Longitudinal Study.* Bethesda, Maryland: United States Department of Health, Education, and Welfare, Public Health Service, National Institutes of Health.

Barsky, Arthur J. "The Paradox of Health." *The New England Journal of Medicine*, February 18, 1988, 414–418.

Hickey, Tom, Kathryn Dean, and Bjorn Holstein. "Emerging Trends in Gerontology and Geriatrics: Implications for the Self-Care of the Elderly." *Social Science and Medicine* 23 (1986): 1363–1369.

National Institute on Aging. *Answers about Aging: New Pieces to an Old Puzzle.* Washington, D.C.: U.S. Department of Health and Human Services, n.d.

Starr, Paul. *The Social Transformation of American Medicine.* New York: Harper & Row, 1982.

Tracy, George S., and Zachary Gussow. "Self-Help Groups: A Grass-Roots Response to a Need for Services." *Journal of Applied Behavioral Science* 12 (1976): 381–396.

## Chapter 8

Adams, Rebecca G. "People Would Talk: Normative Barriers to Cross-Sex Friendships for Elderly Women." *The Gerontologist* 25 (1985): 605–611.

Beeson, Diane. "Women in Studies of Aging: A Critique and Suggestion." *Social Problems* 23 (1975): 52–59.

Blieszner, Rosemary. "Trends in Family Gerontology Research." *Family Relations*, October 1986, pp. 555–562.

Brecher, Edward M., and the editors of Consumer Reports Books. *Love, Sex, and Aging: A Consumers Union Report.* Boston: Little, Brown, 1984.

Cool, Linda Evans, and McCabe, Justine. "The 'Scheming Hag' and the 'Dear Old Thing': The Anthropology of Aging Women," in Beth B. Hess and Elizabeth W. Markson, eds., *Growing Old in America* (New Brunswick, N.J.: Transaction, 1986), p. 97.

Davis, Kingsley, and Pietronella van den Oever. "Demographic Foundations of New Sex Roles." *Population and Development Review* 8 (1982): 495–511.

Demos, Vasilikie, and Ann Jache. "When You Care Enough: An Analysis of Attitudes toward Aging in Humorous Birthday Cards." *The Gerontologist* 21 (1981): 209–215.

Erikson, Erik. *Childhood and Society.* 2d ed. New York: W. W. Norton, 1963.

Keating, Norah C., and Priscilla Cole. "What Do I Do with Him 24 Hours a Day? Changes in the Housewife Role after Retirement." *The Gerontologist* 20 (1980): 84–89.

Markson, Elizabeth, ed. *Older Women: Issues and Prospects.* Lexington, Massachusetts: Lexington Books, 1983.

Riley, Matilda White. "Aging, Social Change, and the Power of Ideas." *Daedalus* 107 (1978); 39–52.

Rodeheaver, Dean. "When Old Age Became a Social Problem, Women Were Left Behind." *The Gerontologist* 27 (1987): 741–746.

Sands, Roberta G., and Virginia Richardson. "Clinical Practice with Women in Their Middle Years." *Social Work,* January–February 1986, pp. 36–43.

## Chapter 9

The most useful sources for the rapidly changing field of marketing to older Americans are *American Demographics, Mature Market Report,* and *Selling to Seniors,* as well as *The New York Times* and *The Wall Street Journal.*

Wattenberg, Ben J., *The Birth Dearth.* New York: Pharos Books, 1987.

## Chapter 10

Butler, Robert N. "The Life Review: An Interpretation of Reminiscence in the Aged." *Psychiatry* 76 (1963): 65–76.

Hufford, Mary, Marjorie Hunt, and Steven Zeitlin. *The Grand Generation: Memory, Mastery, Legacy.* Seattle, Washington: University of Washington Press, 1987.

Sheth, Jagdish N. "Search for Tomorrow." *Public Relations Journal,* December 1987, 22–30, 51.

# Index